NEUROPSYCHOLOGY OF HUMAN EMOTION

ADVANCES IN NEUROPSYCHOLOGY AND
BEHAVIORAL NEUROLOGY
Kenneth M. Heilman and Paul Satz, Editors

Volume 1. NEUROPSYCHOLOGY OF HUMAN EMOTION

IN PREPARATION
Volume 2. DEVELOPMENT

NEUROPSYCHOLOGY OF HUMAN EMOTION

Edited by

KENNETH M. HEILMAN
University of Florida and Veterans Administration Medical Center, Gainesville

and

PAUL SATZ
Neuropsychiatric Institute, University of California, Los Angeles

THE GUILFORD PRESS

New York, London

© 1983 The Guilford Press
A Division of Guilford Publications, Inc.
200 Park Avenue South, New York, N.Y. 10003

Printed in the United States of America

LIBRARY OF CONGRESS CATALOGING IN PUBLICATION DATA
Main entry under title:
Neuropsychology of human emotion.
  (Advances in neuropsychology and behavioral neurology)
  Bibliography: p.
  Includes index.
    1. Emotions—Physiological aspects. 2. Neuropsychology. I. Satz, Paul. II. Heilman, Kenneth M., 1938–   . III. Series. [DNLM: 1. Emotions. 2 Psychophysiology. 3. Neurophysiology. W1 AD684J v.1 /WL 103 N4936]
QP401.N385 1983   612'.8   82-15615
ISBN 0-89862-200-X

CONTRIBUTORS

D. Frank Benson, MD, Department of Neurology, UCLA School of Medicine, Los Angeles, California

Dawn Bowers, PhD, College of Medicine, University of Florida, and Veterans Administration Medical Center, Gainesville, Florida

M. P. Bryden, PhD, Department of Psychology, University of Waterloo, Waterloo, Ontario, Canada

Antonio R. Damasio, MD, PhD, Department of Neurology, Division of Behavioral Neurology, University of Iowa College of Medicine, Iowa City, Iowa

Victor H. Denenberg, PhD, Departments of Biobehavioral Sciences and Psychology, University of Connecticut, Storrs, Connecticut

Pierre Flor-Henry, MB, ChB, MD, Admission Services, Alberta Hospital, Edmonton, and Department of Psychiatry, University of Alberta, Edmonton, Alberta, Canada

Kenneth M. Heilman, MD, College of Medicine, University of Florida, and Veterans Administration Medical Center, Gainesville, Florida

R. G. Ley, PhD, Department of Psychology, University of Waterloo, Waterloo, Ontario, Canada. Present address: Department of Psychology, Simon Fraser University, Burnaby, British Columbia, Canada

Richard Mayeux, MD, Department of Neurology, Columbia University College of Physicians and Surgeons, The Neurological Institute of New York, New York, New York

Paul B. Pritchard, III, MD, Neurology Service, Veterans Administration Medical Center, Charleston, and Department of Neurology, Medical University of South Carolina, Charleston, South Carolina

Donald T. Stuss, PhD, Schools of Medicine (Neurology) and Psychology, University of Ottawa, Ottawa General Hospital, Ottawa, Ontario, Canada

G. W. Van Hoesen, PhD, Departments of Anatomy and Neurology, University of Iowa College of Medicine, Iowa City, Iowa

Robert T. Watson, MD, College of Medicine, University of Florida, and Veterans Administration Medical Center, Gainesville, Florida

PREFACE

In the past three decades there has been a tremendous growth of interest in brain–behavior relationships (neuropsychology). Initially much of this interest related to language and the role of the left hemisphere in mediating linguistic activities in both healthy and brain-impaired subjects. Although in the 19th century Hughlings Jackson postulated that the right hemisphere had a special role in mediating emotions, it is only in the last decade that there has been a substantial growth of research. The publications that have resulted from this research have appeared in a variety of neurological, psychological, neuropsychological, and psychiatric journals. In spite of the enormous growth of research articles that deal with the neuropsychology of human emotion, there have been few attempts to bring much of this information together in one volume. The purpose of this volume, therefore, is to consolidate this information. Unfortunately, however, this field is already so large and dynamic that we thought we could not cover every aspect of the neuropsychology of emotion. For this reason, we chose topics that covered some of the most recent and exciting advances as well as topics that were most pertinent to understanding human emotions in both health and disease.

KENNETH M. HEILMAN
PAUL SATZ

CONTENTS

NEUROPSYCHOLOGY OF HUMAN EMOTION

INTRODUCTION

Kenneth M. Heilman

Neuropsychology is the study of relationships between the brain and behavior. One of the basic assumptions underlying neuropsychology is that all behavior, including emotional behavior, is mediated by physical processes. A corollary of this assumption is that the brain of an organism capable of displaying a certain emotional behavior must have the necessary neuronal systems to mediate that behavior. Although learning and experience may be important factors, without the critical neuronal systems, a given emotion or emotions could not occur.

In general, psychodynamic and other behavioral explanations of emotion that do not address the physical state of the brain are not directly relevant to neurospychology and, therefore, are not discussed in this book.

Emotion, like other widely accepted constructs, is difficult to define; consequently, it is difficult to measure, and measurement is critical for neuropsychological research. In spite of this problem, one does have subjective feelings of emotion as well as physiological and behavioral changes associated with emotion. Subjective feeling can be expressed, and behavioral and physiological changes can be measured. These are the variables on which neuropsychological research on emotion is based.

Investigators in neuropsychology use several methods in attempting to understand relationships between the brain and behavior. One of the oldest methods is the brain ablation paradigm. Discrete brain lesions may alter behavior, and studies that correlate behavioral changes with lesion loci provide important neuropsychological data, which may not only aid in learning

Kenneth M. Heilman. College of Medicine, University of Florida, and Veterans Administration Medical Center, Gainesville, Florida.

about pathological states but also give us insight into how the normal brain works. Several chapters in this book discuss brain-injured and impaired subjects. The brain ablation paradigm, however, has several limitations. In regard to human neuropsychology, natural lesions do not always occur in the exact anatomic distribution that one wants to study. Lesions also cause non-specific effects such as diaschisis. And, as noted by Hughlings Jackson, the behavior after a brain lesion is not a result of the missing or damaged tissue but rather of how the remainder of the brain acts in the absence of that tissue. Lesions may change behavior because they not only interrupt a critical system but also affect other areas, which under physiologic conditions may be either inhibited or facilitated by the area in which the lesion lies. Although a given area may be responsible for mediating a certain behavior, other areas may be able to compensate for the locus in which the lesion lies.

To circumvent the difficulties with anatomic distribution of loci of lesions that occur naturally in humans, investigators have used experimental animals. Because animal brains and human brains may be organized differently, it is often difficult to generalize from animals to humans. However, some neuronal systems may not be species-specific, and in these instances animal studies become valuable. Although this book primarily addresses the neuropsychology of human emotions, Denenberg's chapter illustrates how animal research may provide us with important neuropsychological information.

If we want to know how the normal brain works, the best subjects may be normal human beings. Until two or three decades ago we did not know how to study normal subjects neuropsychologically; since then, however, several paradigms have been used successfully. By selectively delivering stimuli or by having the subjects make a selective response, neuropsychologists can determine which hemispheres may be processing a class of stimuli or mediating a response. Bryden and Ley illustrate in their chapter how much can be learned using these paradigms with normal subjects. Unfortunately, however, these laterality paradigms (e.g., visual half-field, dichotic listening) do not help us understand intrahemispheric neurological mechanisms. Recent advances in evoked potential have shown it to be a promising paradigm with which normal subjects can be studied. Additionally, when a portion of the brain is active, it may increase its energy requirements, and thus blood flow may be increased. Use of glucose may also be increased. Radioisotope studies can measure cerebral blood flow and glucose uptake. Unfortunately, the knowledge that an anatomic area is activated during a task does not always tell us what this area is doing.

In summary, there appear to be multiple methods with which brain–behavior relationships can be studied. Because each method has its attributes and weaknesses, we have included chapters concerning different methodologies.

In Chapter 1 Bryden and Ley provide the reader with an extensive and detailed review of the neuropsychological research in normal humans. The authors note that the two hemispheres are known to have different cognitive capacities (i.e., left verbal, right visuospatial). Until about 8 to 10 years ago it was unclear whether there was hemispheric dominance for mediating emotions. Bryden and Ley review the extensive laterality research performed using the visual half-field and dichotic listening paradigms at the University of Waterloo. They also review the research at other institutions where similar paradigms have been used. In general, these authors have found that emotional stimuli are perceived more accurately when presented so that the stimuli gain access to the right hemisphere. Similarly, in studies examining emotional display (e.g., emotional faces), the display is more evident on the left side, which suggests right-hemisphere mediation. In summary, their findings suggest that in normal subjects the right hemisphere has a special and dominant influence on the reception and expression of emotions.

For more than three decades it has been observed that patients with left-hemisphere damage appear depressed and patients with right-hemisphere lesions appear indifferent or emotionally flattened. In Chapter 2 Heilman, Watson, and Bowers provide evidence that patients with right-hemisphere brain damage cannot understand emotional prosody or comprehend emotional faces. Similarly, these patients with right-hemisphere disease may have difficulty expressing emotional prosody or making emotional faces. In addition, patients with right-hemisphere disease have decreased arousal as determined by psychophysiological measurements. The findings are compatible with the studies of normal subjects and give further support to the hypotheses of right-hemisphere emotional dominance.

In Chapter 3 Denenberg provides evidence that experimental animals may also have laterality or dominance. Not only is brain laterality not a uniquely human attribute, but Dr. Denenberg's data suggest that in the rat, strong emotional responses may also be mediated by the right hemisphere.

Since the writing of Egas Moniz (1936) on prefrontal leukotomy, the frontal lobe has been known to be prominently involved in mediating emotion. In Chapter 4 Damasio and Van Hoesen, after discussing the structure and function of the limbic system, describe the nature of behavioral disorders that follow focal lesions (bilateral and unilateral) of the limbic frontal cortex (e.g., cingulate gyrus, orbitofrontal cortex, supplementary motor area).

In Chapter 5 Stuss and Benson discuss the emotional behavior of 16 patients who had undergone prefrontal leukotomy to treat schizophrenia. These authors noted many emotional alterations, but the most specific changes were a lack of inhibition and a dissociation between patients' verbal behavior and other overt emotional responses.

Basal ganglia disorders are usually thought to be motor disorders; however, most patients with basal ganglia disorders also have emotional changes. With the recent neuropharmacological revolution, it has been recognized that many of these basal ganglia disorders are related to specific neurotransmitter and neuromodulator disturbances. Although many of the emotional changes that accompany these diseases may be a psychological reaction to the motor disability, neurochemical defects may also be responsible for the behavioral (emotional) changes in these patients.

In Chapter 6 Mayeux discusses five diseases of the basal ganglia—Parkinson disease, Huntington disease, Wilson disease, progressive supranuclear palsy, and Sydenham chorea. He describes the emotional changes that accompany these diseases and how the treatment may affect the emotional response.

Although interictal personality and emotional disorders have been attributed to epileptic patients for more than a century, in the past 20 years interest has been renewed with the development of improved sampling and assessment techniques. In Chapter 7 Pritchard addresses many of these controversial issues. In addition to reviewing the personality changes in epileptic patients, he discusses the sexual dysfunction and psychoses that may also occur, as well as affective symptoms that may be associated with seizures.

In Chapter 8 Flor-Henry provides evidence that neuropsychological measures can be sensitive indicators of cerebral dysfunction, including lateralizing (right hemisphere vs. left hemisphere) and localizing dysfunction. Many schizophrenic patients show abnormal patterns on batteries of neuropsychological tests, and the pattern of deficit in schizophrenia is similar to that seen in some patients with left-hemisphere lesions. The neuropsychological profile of patients with affective psychoses seem to be a mirror image of that of schizophrenics. Scores of affective psychotics are more like those of patients with right-hemisphere dysfunction. Flor-Henry discusses the findings that in psychopathy the verbal IQ is higher than the performance IQ, whereas in depression the opposite is true. He also addresses the neuropsychological dysfunction associated with the obsessive–compulsive syndrome and hysteria. Although the mechanisms underlying these changes in the neuropsychological profile remain unknown, they may provide additional clues to the pathophysiology of these psychiatric disorders.

We attempted to be comprehensive, but there is much about the neuropsychology of human emotions that we do not know. For example, it is well known from animal research that the septal areas have an important influence in mediating certain emotions. Although there have been case reports of recording from and ablations of the septal area, the role of this and similar limbic areas remains unclear. The limiting factor in the past was the absence of safe noninvasive experimental paradigms. It is hoped that in the future the newer isotope and evoked potential studies will overcome many of these earlier limitations and that the neurological bases of human emotion will be better understood.

RIGHT-HEMISPHERIC INVOLVEMENT IN THE PERCEPTION AND EXPRESSION OF EMOTION IN NORMAL HUMANS

M. P. Bryden
R. G. Ley

It is now quite clearly established that the differing cognitive capacities of the two cerebral hemispheres lead to behavioral asymmetries even in the normal individual. Thus, for example, words or strings of letters flashed briefly to the left or right visual field are reported faster and more accurately when they appear in the right visual field, whereas visuospatial tasks, such as those involving face recognition or discrimination of line orientation, are performed better when the stimuli appear in the left visual field (Bradshaw & Nettleton, 1981; Kimura, 1967; Moscovitch, 1979; White, 1972). Similarly, in the auditory modality, verbal material presented dichotically is better identified when it arrives at the right ear, while music and environmental sounds show a left-ear advantage (Kimura, 1966; Springer, 1979). These asymmetries of performance are related to the fact that, at least in the majority of right-handers, the left hemisphere is specialized for speech and language functions, while the right hemisphere is

M. P. Bryden and R. G. Ley. Department of Psychology, University of Waterloo, Waterloo, Ontario, Canada. Present address for R. G. Ley: Department of Psychology, Simon Fraser University, Burnaby, British Columbia, Canada.

more specialized for visuospatial and other nonverbal processes. Although a variety of extraneous factors may affect the asymmetries observed with a specific procedure (Bryden, 1978), the general approach of lateralized stimulus presentation has proven to be a fruitful one for investigating the capacities of the two cerebral hemispheres in the intact brain (Bryden, 1982).

Until recently, relatively little attention was paid to the affective character of the stimuli and tasks employed in asymmetry experiments. However, reports of hemispheric asymmetries in psychopathological groups (see Gruzelier & Flor-Henry, 1979) and in emotional processing (see Ley, 1979; Tucker, 1981) have stimulated research on the cerebral representation of affect and emotion. The objective of the present chapter is to review the current state of research on the lateralization of emotion in normal individuals, that is, in people without brain damage or psychopathology. The chapter is divided into three major sections: In the first, we present our own work on the lateralization of emotions; in the second, we review other research on the topic; and in the third, we provide a general conceptual overview.

WATERLOO RESEARCH ON HEMISPHERIC SPECIALIZATION FOR EMOTION

VISUALLY COMMUNICATED AFFECT

In this research program, our initial objective was to establish that the affective character of complex stimuli could produce a reliable laterality effect in normal subjects. In our first study (Ley, 1978), we chose to use a lateralized tachistoscopic presentation procedure, employing cartoon drawings of human faces depicting different emotions. In this study, as in all our subsequent work, we employed only right-handed subjects, to increase the probability that language functions would be represented in the left hemisphere and nonverbal visuospatial functions in the right hemisphere.

We prepared a set of cartoon drawings of human faces, representing three different characters and showing three different emotions: very positive, neutral, and very negative emotional expressions. Subjects were shown a single target face very briefly in either the left or right visual field. This was followed by a comparison face, appearing for a greater duration in central vision. Subjects were tested under two different conditions: In one they were to indicate whether or not the comparison face represented the same *character* as the target face; in the other, they were to indicate whether or not the two faces showed the same emotional expression. In both tasks, subjects were more accurate in the left visual field than in the right. The visual-field difference in character matching presumably is another manifestation of the usual left-field superiority reported for face recognition (Sergent & Bindra, 1981), while the asymmetry in expression matching suggests that emotional expressions, as well as faces, are more readily identified in the left visual field. It is particularly noteworthy that the left-visual-field effect for expression matching was attributable primarily to the faces showing extreme emotions, and not to the neutral faces (see Figure 1).

These positive findings encouraged us to attempt a replication and extension of the study. In this second study (Ley & Bryden, 1979a), we again employed the lateralized tachistoscopic presentation of cartoon faces. However, the number of different stimuli was increased from 9 to 25 by employing five different expressions with each of five different characters (see Figure 2). The expressions ranged from very positive through mildly positive, neutral, and mildly negative, to very negative. In this experiment, subjects were asked to make both expression and character judgments on every trial. Subjects saw a single target stimulus presented laterally for a very brief period, followed by a comparison stimulus in central vision. They were then asked to indicate whether the comparison stimulus represented the same character as the target, and whether it presented the same expression of emotion as the target. Half the subjects were tested by asking for the character judgment first, and half by asking for the expression judgment first; the order of these responses did not affect the performance.

Initial analyses revealed a left-visual-field superiority for both the character recognition and emotional expression judgments (see Figure 3). The emotion judgments also varied systematically with the degree of affect shown, with the largest left-visual-field effect being found with the very negative and very positive stimuli.

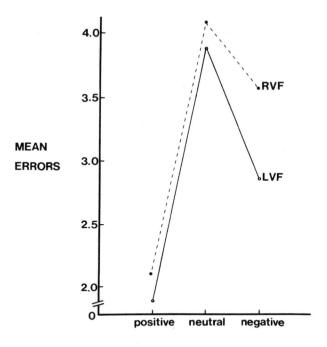

EMOTIONAL   EXPRESSIONS

FIGURE 1. *Left-visual-field (LVF) superiority for matching emotional facial expressions. RVF, right visual field. Data from Ley and Bryden (1978).*

Because this experiment involved face recognition, we were concerned that the left-visual-field effect found for matching emotional expression might be simply another manifestation of a general right-hemispheric superiority for face recognition. We tried two different statistical approaches to show that this was not the case. First, we obtained a measure of the degree of laterality for each of the two tasks, and correlated them. This correlation was positive in magnitude, but failed to reach statistical significance, suggesting that the two tasks do not measure the same lateralized process. Second, we performed covariance analyses on the recognition scores for each task, using the scores on the other task as the covariate. When differences in character identification were con-

FIGURE 2. *The faces used in the Ley and Bryden (1979a) study. The expressions vary from very positive in the top row to very negative in the bottom row. From "Hemispheric Differences in Recognizing Faces and Emotions" by R. G. Ley and M. P. Bryden,* Brain and Language, *1979, 7, 127–138. Copyright 1979 by Academic Press. Reprinted by permission.*

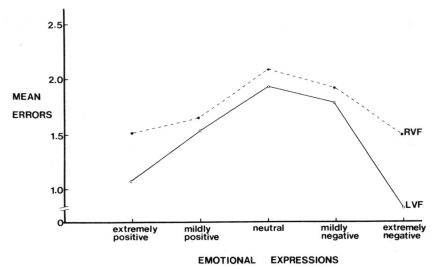

FIGURE 3. *Left-visual-field (LVF) superiority for matching emotional expression, using the cartoon faces shown in Figure 2. RVF, right visual field. Data from Ley and Bryden (1979a).*

trolled, a significant left-visual-field superiority for emotion recognition remained. In contrast, when the emotion differences were controlled, the left-visual-field effect for character recognition dropped below statistical significance. At the very least, this indicates that the left-visual-field effect for emotion recognition is a robust one.

Reflection on this issue, however, suggests that it is extremely difficult to demonstrate that the left-visual-field effect for emotion recognition is not just a complex way of revealing the right hemisphere's well-established superiority in processing complex visuospatial material. The information that permits one to judge whether two different drawings represent the same character is largely contained in the upper part of the face (nose, eyes, and hair) in the drawings we used. On the other hand, the information that permits the recognition of emotion is concentrated in the lower part of the face (primarily the mouth). In both tasks, accurate performance depends on making complex visual discriminations. The two tasks appear to be dissociated because the discriminations relevant to the character-recognition task are different from those relevant to the emotion-recognition task. By this argument, our "emotion-recognition" task may be little more than an elegant way of investigating the right-hemispheric superiority for dealing with complex visuospatial information.

Perhaps, however, this is all we can ever hope to accomplish by a visual study of emotion recognition. So long as there are discriminable differences in affect between the stimuli there must be *some* physical characteristic that permits the discrimination, and any demonstration of a left-visual-field effect for the recognition of affect is also a demonstration of a left-visual-field effect for the recognition of some complex visual pattern.

DICHOTIC LISTENING STUDIES

Rather than trying additional visual experiments in our study of the role of the right hemisphere in emotion processing, we sought convergent evidence from the auditory modality. Similar laterality effects in different sensory modalities, and for both verbal and nonverbal material, would strengthen our conviction that the right hemisphere plays a special role in the perception of emotion.

Our first study (Bryden, Ley, & Sugarman, 1982) took advantage of the fact that people with a Western cultural background generally describe music written in a major key as being bright and gay, while that written in a minor key is described as sad and melancholy (Davies, 1978). We constructed a set of seven-note tonal sequences selected to produce different affective ratings. These sequences all began on the same note, and were matched for rhythm, tempo, and pitch range, but some were in a major mode, some in a minor mode, and some were random tonal sequences. Our original sequences were rated by a set of judges for affective quality, and reduced to three examples of each type of stimulus that could be reliably categorized as being either positive, negative, or neutral in affect.

These nine stimulus sequences were then paired dichotically with one another. The dichotic stimuli were presented to subjects who were instructed to attend to one ear and to judge the affective value of the stimulus heard at that ear. Order of attending was counterbalanced over blocks of trials so that each subject reported on the left ear sequences on half the trials and on the right ear stimuli on the remaining half.

The number of trials on which the affective value of the attended stimulus was correctly identified was very much higher when attending to the left ear than when attending to the right ear. Of the 20 subjects, 19 showed fewer errors on the left ear, and the remaining subject was equally accurate at the two ears. In addition, there were a number of significant interactions involving the ear to which the subject attended, the affect of the target stimulus, and the affect of the competing stimulus. These complex interactions are best understood by examining the ear effect for different combinations of target and competing affect (Figure 4). In three of the pairings employed, the affective value of the two stimuli was the same (++, NN, and −−); in four pairings, the difference was moderate (+N, N+, −N, N−); and in two pairings, the difference was a large one (+−, −+). In general, the left-ear superiority was small when the affective value of the target and competing stimuli was the same, and large when the two stimuli differed maximally in affective value. When the two stimuli were

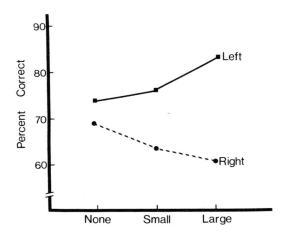

Difference in Affect

FIGURE 4. *Categorization of emotional tone of musical passages as a function of the difference in affect between attended and unattended passages. When the two passages differ considerably in affect (+−, −+), the left-ear superiority is maximal. Small differences in affect include +N, N−, N+, −N combinations; no-difference data are based on NN, ++, and −− combinations. Data from Bryden, Ley, and Sugarman (1982).*

clearly different, the information from the left ear dominated the judgment. Unlike the visual experiments, however, the left-ear effect was similar for all levels of affect: The neutral stimuli produced as great a left-ear advantage as did the positive and negative stimuli (see Figure 5).

Having demonstrated a left-ear effect for affectively toned musical material, we turned to speech material (Ley & Bryden, 1982). To prepare this experiment, we had speakers read sentences in various tones of voice (happy, sad, angry, and neutral). We produced a set of short sentences that judges could reliably classify as to emotional expression when they were heard binaurally. Each of these sentences was then paired with a different sentence, spoken in a neutral tone of voice by a different speaker.

As in the music experiment, subjects listened to a prespecified ear and reported on the content of the sentence arriving at that ear.

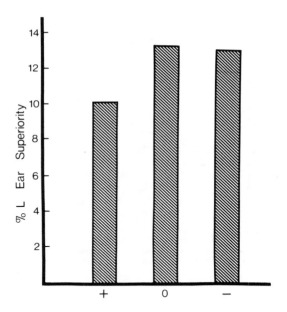

Affective Value of Target

FIGURE 5. *Degree of left-ear superiority on music-recognition task as a function of the affective value of the attended stimulus. Essentially the same left-ear effect is found for all affective values. Data from Bryden, Ley, and Sugarman (1982).*

On each trial, subjects were asked to categorize the affect of the sentence they heard, and also to report on its content. After hearing each trial, the subject turned over a new page in a response booklet, indicated the affective tone in which the sentence had been spoken, and marked the words that had appeared in the target sentence on a multiple-choice sheet (see Figure 6). The alternatives in the multiple-choice set were drawn from the target sentence, the unattended message, and from words having similar sounds and meanings as those in the target sentence. The order of making affective and content judgments was counterbalanced across subjects.

Subjects were most accurate in judging the emotional tone of the sentences when they listened to the left ear, and, at the same time, more accurate in identifying the content of the sentences when listening to the right ear. Of the 31 subjects, 28 showed a right-ear advantage for content recognition, while 24 showed a left-ear advantage for emotional intonation. As in the music study,

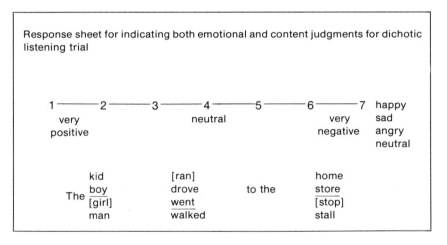

FIGURE 6. *Response sheet used in the Ley and Bryden (1982) study. For half the subjects, the content item was on top. Subjects rated the affect of the sentence on the 7-point scale, indicated what emotion was expressed by checking one of the four items at the right, and then marked the words that had been heard at the attended ear for each of the three probe positions. In the example shown, the underlined words are correct, and the bracketed ones are those heard on the unattended ear.*

the left-ear effect for affect did not vary systematically with the specific affect employed.

These two dichotic listening studies provide further evidence that the right hemisphere has a special role in the perception of emotion. While these results may also be interpreted in terms of a specialization of the right hemisphere for complex pattern recognition, it is noteworthy that the use of affective stimuli produces an extremely robust right-hemispheric superiority. Furthermore, the sentence-intonation study (Ley & Bryden, 1982) provides a clear demonstration that both verbal and nonverbal laterality effects can be obtained simultaneously, and dissociates one from the other within the same stimulus presentation.

Having demonstrated left-ear effects for affective stimuli with both music and speech, our next step was to investigate this phenomenon developmentally (Saxby & Bryden, 1982). In order to do this, we modified the Ley and Bryden (1982) dichotic intonation procedure to test affect and content separately, so as to make the task sufficiently easy for young children.

As in the previous study, a set of short sentences spoken in different tones of voice were prepared. These sentences were paired dichotically with neutral sentences, and presented to the subjects. Following presentation of the dichotic pair, a sentence was presented binaurally. In the affective task, the child had to judge whether or not this binaural sentence was spoken in the same tone of voice as the dichotic sentence heard in the attended ear. In the verbal content task, the child indicated whether or not the binaural sentence had the same content as the dichotic sentence presented at the attended ear. Even with these modifications in procedure, the kindergarten children found the task extremely difficult, and, consequently, it was necessary to present the binaural sentence first, followed by the dichotic pair, with this group.

Eventually, we were able to test 31 kindergarten children (age 5–6 years), 30 fourth-grade children (age 9–10 years), and 29 eighth-grade children (age 13–14 years) on this task, with approximately equal numbers of boys and girls in each group. An analysis of the laterality scores obtained in this experiment, using the laterality index proposed by Bryden and Sprott (1981), revealed a highly significant difference between the affective and content scores (F (1,84) = 95.53, $p < .001$): Performance was much better on the left ear for the affective task and much better on the right ear for the content task (see Figure 7). The only other effect that reached statistical significance was a task by sex interaction: The laterality effects were somewhat more pronounced for the girls than for the boys. Although performance improved with age, there were no signs of any change in either verbal or affective lateralization with age.

These findings were not appreciably influenced by the slight shift of task from the kindergarten children to the older children. When the data from the kindergarten children were analyzed separately, highly significant left-ear effects for the affective judgments and right-ear effects for the content judgments were observed. Likewise, the same effects were seen in an analysis of the two groups of older children, with no interaction of the laterality effects with age.

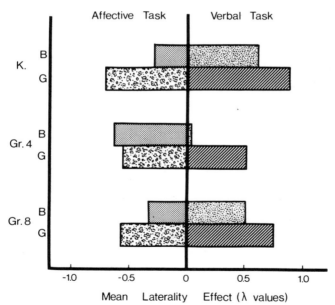

FIGURE 7. *Mean laterality values for sentence content and emotion judgments in kindergarten (age 5–6), fourth-grade (age 9–10), and eighth-grade (age 13–14) children. The bars to the left show the left-ear effect for the affective judgments; those to the right, the right-ear effect for the content judgments. Data from Saxby and Bryden (1982).*

Even in 5- and 6-year-olds, then, judgments of affect lead to a highly significant left-ear advantage. This would suggest that right-hemisphere mechanisms for the recognition of affect are active even in young children, and do not seem to alter significantly with age. The consistency of the effect across ages also provides further support for the robustness of the right-hemisphere involvement in emotion.

Priming Studies

The preceding set of studies provide clear evidence that right-hemispheric effects are obtained for the recognition of affect in a wide variety of situations. Despite this, it is extremely difficult to separate the recognition of affect from the recognition of complex patterns in general. Emotion expressed through facial expression is communicated as a complex visual stimulus, emotion expressed in music is a function of the complex relations between the individual notes, and emotion expressed through tone of voice is communicated through the intonation pattern of the speech sounds. Our experiments have shown that the laterality effects obtained for the recognition of affect are clearly dissociable from left-hemispheric language effects, but it may not be possible to show that the recognition of affect involves processes other than those involved in any complex pattern-recognition task. To make the case for a specialized right-hemisphere involvement in emotion and affect, we decided to turn away from recognition tasks to other procedures.

We reasoned that if there is special right-hemisphere involvement in emotion, then perhaps thinking about emotional material would produce activity in the right hemisphere. Furthermore, such activity could serve to alter the receptivity of the right hemisphere to other incoming information. To test this notion, we had subjects remember lists of affectively loaded words while they were being tested on a laterality task, and examined the effect of remembering these words on performance (Ley & Bryden, 1979b, 1980, 1983).

As the first step in carrying out these experiments, we had a group of judges rate the affective value of a large number of nouns, drawn largely from the list of words used by Paivio,

Yuille, and Madigan (1968) in their study of imagery. Judges rated each word on a 7-point scale, ranging from very negative to very positive. From these ratings, we selected six groups of 20 words, varying in both affect and imagery value. One list of 20 words was comprised of high-imagery positive-affect words (e.g., friend), one of high-imagery negative-affect words (e.g., corpse), and one of high-imagery neutral words (e.g., elephant). Comparable positive, negative, and neutral lists were constructed using low-imagery words.

These word lists were used in two different experiments. In both of these experiments, the subjects were initially tested on a laterality task. In one study, this involved the recognition of laterally presented faces; in the other, it involved the identification of dichotically presented stop–consonant–vowel syllables. Following this initial testing, each subject was presented with one of the word lists, typed on a white card. They were given 5 minutes to study the word list, and were told that they would subsequently be tested for retention of the words. The subjects were encouraged to try to remember the words during the next phase of the study, and were told that they would be given additional remuneration for good performance on the retention test. Following the study period, the subjects were retested on the initial laterality task, and then asked to recall as many of the words from the word list as possible. Of particular interest to us was the change in performance on the laterality task from the initial testing to the retesting when the word list was being held in memory.

The results of these two experiments were remarkably similar. The study of either positive or negative word lists resulted in a relative improvement in performance in the right hemisphere. That is, scores improved in the left visual field in the face-recognition study and in the left ear in the dichotic study when emotional words were studied, but not when neutral words were studied. Furthermore, high-imagery word lists also produced a similar shift in performance toward the right hemisphere (see Figures 8 and 9). Statistically, the effects of affect and imagery were independent, in that the two factors showed no interactions in the analysis of the results of either experiment. Thus, imagery and affect seem to have similar and additive effects on the right hemisphere.

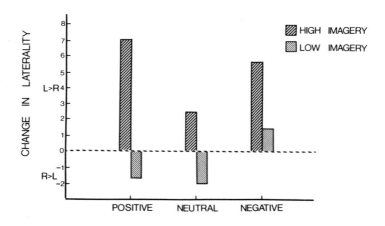

FIGURE 8. *Change in face-recognition laterality effects following the study of 20-item word lists varying in imagery and affective value. From "Right Hemisphere Involvement in Imagery and Affect" by R. G. Ley and M. P. Bryden, in E. Perecman (Ed.),* Cognitive Processing in the Right Hemisphere, *New York: Academic Press, 1983. Copyright 1983 by Academic Press. Reprinted by permission.*

To summarize the priming experiments, then, in the face-recognition study memorization of either high-imagery or affectively loaded word lists resulted in an enhancement of the left-visual-field (right hemisphere) effect that was observed in the initial testing. In the verbal dichotic experiment, the same word lists served to reduce the right-ear effect that was found in the initial testing. Apparently, remembering a list of emotional words can serve to activate the right hemisphere and make it more receptive to incoming stimuli. Similar effects were obtained with both positive and negative word lists. Further, these results cannot be attributed to differences in the ease of remembering the word lists: Although high-imagery words were remembered more easily than low-imagery words, there were no differences in retention as a function of affective value.

As a further point, one should note that this priming effect is quite different from that postulated by Kinsbourne (1973, 1975). He suggested that verbal activity would serve to activate the left hemisphere and thus improve performance on the right ear or right visual field. These experiments have used verbal material, but the effect is one of activating the right hemisphere and improving performance on the left side. We would suggest that it is the affective quality of the verbal material that produces activation of the right hemisphere.

In summary, then, our research has demonstrated two major effects. First, we have found a general right-hemisphere superiority for the recognition of lateralized emotional stimuli. This finding has been evident in studies of face recognition, music, and spoken sentences, and has been observed with children as well as with adults. Further, effects of similar magnitude have been found with both positive and negative material. Second, we have also been able to show that remembering affectively laden word lists can serve to prime or activate the right hemisphere.

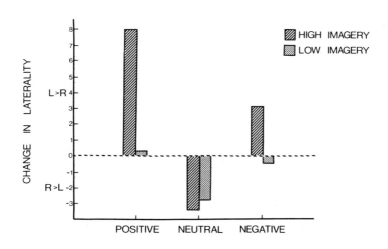

FIGURE 9. *Change in dichotic listening laterality effects following the study of 20-item word lists varying in imagery and affective value. From "Right Hemisphere Involvement in Imagery and Affect" by R. G. Ley and M. P. Bryden, in E. Perecman (Ed.),* Cognitive Processing in the Right Hemisphere, *New York: Academic Press, 1983. Copyright 1983 by Academic Press. Reprinted by permission.*

OTHER RESEARCH ON THE LATERALIZATION OF EMOTIONS

DICHOTIC LISTENING STUDIES

There is a substantial and impressive body of literature investigating the lateralization of emotions in normal subjects. The earliest lateralization studies on emotion date back to the early 1970s. In addition, there is a vast clinical literature on the asymmetry of emotion which we have not the time to review here (see Gruzelier & Flor-Henry, 1979; Ley, 1979; Tucker, 1981). The first studies on the lateralization of emotion in normals involved dichotic listening procedures, although studies of facial expression have become far more commonplace in recent years.

Haggard and Parkinson (1971) paired short sentences with speech babble in a dichotic listening task. The sentences were spoken in one of four emotional tones: angry, bored, happy, or distressed. Subjects were asked to indicate by ticking on a response sheet both the sentence and the emotion they heard. Haggard and Parkinson found that accuracy in identifying the emotion expressed was better on the left ear. When only those trials on which the subject identified the sentence correctly were considered, nine of the ten subjects showed a left-ear advantage for identifying the emotion.

Carmon and Nachshon (1973) used nine different sounds in their experiment: the crying, shrieking, and laughing of an adult male, an adult female, and a child. Subjects listened to a dichotic pair, and then pointed to a cartoon display illustrating the characters and the nine possible sounds. Overall, a highly significant left-ear effect was found, with 19 of the 25 subjects being more accurate in identifying the stimulus presented to the left ear. Carmon and Nachshon indicate that neither speaker nor emotional content interacted with the ear effect, although their data (Table 1, p. 353) suggest that a greater left-ear effect was observed for crying than for any other emotion.

A third relevant dichotic listening study is a rather complex experiment carried out by Beaton (1979). He employed three passages of classical music and three poems as stimuli. These were paired dichotically with white noise. Subjects listened to each of these items in turn, and rated each for pleasantness, cheerfulness, and soothingness. Both music and poetry were judged as more pleasant when heard at the left, rather than the right, ear. Similar, but statistically insignificant, effects were found on the cheerfulness dimension, with left-ear passages being more cheerful. Music, but not poetry, was judged as more soothing at the left ear. These results are not in agreement with those obtained by Bryden *et al.* (1982), who found that left-ear passages were given more extreme ratings, rather than being judged as more positive in affect. However, Beaton's passages were quite long, permitting drifting of attention away from the target stimulus, and he provides no baseline data to indicate how the passages would be rated in the absence of dichotic competition. Thus, in Beaton's study we cannot say whether left-ear input is rated more positively or right-ear input more negatively. Nevertheless, Beaton's results do indicate an effect of ear of presentation on rated affective value, and thus implicate hemispheric asymmetry in the judgment of emotion.

Another experiment in this area that deserves mention, although it involved monaural rather than dichotic listening, is that of Safer and Leventhal (1977). Safer and Leventhal constructed short passages that were either positive, negative, or neutral in content, and spoken in a positive, negative, or neutral tone of voice. They had subjects listen to these passages monaurally, and indicate whether they thought the passage was pleasant, unpleasant, or neutral. Those subjects who listened to the passage at their left ear tended to use intonation cues in making their ratings, while those who listened at the right ear tended to use the content cues. A subsequent experiment indicated that when subjects had to rate the tone of voice and the content separately, those who listened to the right ear were more accurate on both tasks. Thus, the left-ear superiority seems to be present only when the subject has to make an integrated judgment about the affect of the passage as a whole. While the Safer and Leventhal data are highly suggestive, interpretation is clouded by the fact that they chose to test separate groups of subjects on left-ear and right-ear presentation, so that it is impossible to determine what proportion of individuals show a left-ear superiority on their task. Further, they included a high percentage of left-handed subjects, in whom one might expect a rather different lateralization of cerebral function (e.g., Hécaen, DeAgostini, & Monzon-Montes, 1981).

In general, the dichotic and other auditory studies agree with our experiments (Bryden *et al.*, 1982; Ley & Bryden, 1982; Saxby & Bryden, 1982) in showing a left-ear superiority for the judgment of emotion. Like our studies, the majority of these studies show left-ear effects for both positive and negative affects, although Beaton's (1979) study suggests that the right hemisphere produces a more positive evaluation, and the Carmon and Nachshon (1973) study shows some sign of a greater right-hemisphere effect for a negative stimulus (crying).

TACHISTOSCOPIC STUDIES

The majority of visual studies of emotion perception in normal individuals have employed faces as stimuli, and either accuracy or reaction time as a dependent measure. The study most similar to the Ley and Bryden (1979a) study is that of Safer (1981). He reversed our conditions by first presenting a target in central vision and by following this with a brief exposure of a comparison slide in the left or right visual fields, but otherwise he followed much the same procedure. As in our study, subjects were asked to indicate whether the emotion shown in the comparison slide was the same as that in the target or different from it. The targets, in this case photographs of posed expressions, showed six different emotions: anger, surprise, happiness, fear, sadness, and disgust. In addition, as an encoding procedure, some subjects were asked to label the emotion expressed in the target slide, while others were instructed to empathize with it.

In general, Safer (1981) found that accuracy was better in the left visual field than in the right, verifying our findings (Ley & Bryden, 1979a). With the empathy instructions, a strong left-visual-field effect was obtained, but no significant laterality effect was found with the labeling instructions. Furthermore, men showed a large left-visual-field effect, while women did not. The Safer study indicates that the technique used for encoding and remembering the target can influence the observed laterality effect (cf. Bryden, 1978). In addition, it raises the question of possible sex differences, although as we shall see, other studies have obtained contradictory results.

Other researchers have chosen to use reaction time as a dependent measure. Suberi and McKeever (1977) had subjects memorize two target faces, and presented these and comparable nontargets in the lateral visual fields. Those subjects who memorized emotional faces showed a much larger left-visual-field superiority than did those who had memorized nonemotional targets. Those subjects who memorized emotional targets, but were required to discriminate them from nonemotional nontargets showed the same large laterality effect as did those who had memorized nonemotional targets. Those subjects who memorized emotional targets, but were required to discriminate them from nonemotional nontargets, showed the same large laterality effect as did those who saw only emotional faces. This would suggest that it is the affective value of the memorized target set that determined the large left-field effect. In some ways, then, the Suberi and McKeever (1977) finding is comparable to the priming effect found in our studies (Ley & Bryden, 1979b, 1980, 1983).

In a subsequent study, McKeever and Dixon (1981) showed only the neutral faces of the Suberi and McKeever (1977) study, but instructed some of their subjects to imagine that something very sad had just happened to the people represented in two target stimuli. In addition, subjects were asked to rate the emotionality of the targets. As before, subjects were then asked to discriminate the target faces from nontargets when they were laterally presented. Female subjects using emotional imagery during memorization showed a large left-visual-field effect, but males did not; under neutral instructions, only a small left-field advantage was found. In addition, those subjects who rated the target faces as being emotional were faster with left-visual-field presentations, while those who did not consider the targets to express emotion showed a small right-visual-field advantage. Thus the use of emotional imagery enhanced right-hemispheric performance only in women, but the perceived emotionality of the targets (not the nontargets) affected performance in both sexes. The sex difference in the emotional imagery condition is quite different from that reported by Safer (1981), who found that men exhibited a larger left-visual-field superiority when instructed to empathize with the target face. The McKeever and Dixon subjects, however, memorized only two target faces that they were instructed to think of as being sad and were to retain these two faces in memory for the duration of the experiment: Safer presented a new target on every trial, and his subjects were constantly changing their empathized affect from one state to another.

Ladavas, Umilta, and Ricci-Bitti (1980) had subjects respond when the laterally presented face showed a particular specified emotion. They found that women were much faster when a face with the specified emotional expression appeared in the left visual field, but men showed no significant laterality effect. They also found no significant differences in lateralization between the various emotions used (happiness, sadness, anger, disgust, fear, and surprise). A similar experiment was carried out by Buchtel, Campari, DeRisio, and Rota (1978). They required subjects to respond to "happy" rather than "sad" faces (or vice versa); unknown to the subjects, a number of neutral targets were also introduced. Subjects were faster in responding to both positive and negative stimuli in the left visual field. Curiously, however, the unexpected neutral targets were responded to faster in the right visual field. Since the task was a "go/no go" reaction time, responses were made to the neutral stimuli only when they were miscategorized as showing the target emotion: The large increase in left-visual-field response times for neutral as compared with target stimuli could indicate that the categorization of emotion is more precise in the right hemisphere than in the left. It should also be noted that both this study and the Ladavas et al. (1980) study used blocks of trials in each visual field. The fact that subjects knew where the stimulus was to appear may have made it difficult to control fixation adequately.

A left-visual-field effect for the recognition of emotional faces has also been reported by Hansch and Pirozzolo (1980). In this study, both words and faces were presented laterally. Subjects were orally cued with the name of the emotion or a neutral name, and asked whether the stimulus was the same as the cue or not. Left-field effects were obtained for both neutral and emotional faces, and right-field effects for both neutral and emotional words, indicating that the nature of the task had a bigger effect than the emotionality of the stimulus.

Strauss and Moscovitch (1981) have also investigated the lateralization of emotional expression. They presented two faces in one visual field or the other, and required subjects to indicate whether or not the faces showed the same emotional expression, or represented the same character. Both character and expression identification showed faster reaction times in the left visual field, although the detailed pattern of results differed for the two types of judgments. Strauss and Moscovitch (1981) argue, as we have, that emotion judgments and character identification involve somewhat different processes, but, since the task requirements differ somewhat in the two tasks, alternative explanations may be possible.

A somewhat different approach was taken by Reuter-Lorenz and Davidson (1981). Rather than asking subjects to discriminate faces that might differ in emotional expression, they asked their subjects to indicate which of two faces showed the strongest affect. Two faces, one neutral and one either happy or sad, were presented on each trial, one in each visual field. When one of the two faces was happy, subjects were faster when it appeared in the right visual field. Conversely, when one of the faces was sad, response times were faster when the sad face was in the left visual field. Unlike the other studies (Ley & Bryden, 1979a; Safer, 1981; Strauss & Moscovitch, 1981), this investigation yields a direction of affect by visual field interaction.

Emotion effects can be demonstrated with verbal material as well as in face-recognition tasks. Graves, Landis, and Goodglass (1981) investigated visual-field differences between emotional and nonemotional words in a lexical decision task. For men, Graves *et al.* found that the right-visual-field effect for nonemotional abstract words was considerably reduced when emotional words (e.g., love, hate, rage) were used. In women, the right-visual-field effect was enhanced by the use of emotional words, but not significantly so. Graves *et al.* then examined the relation between performance and scores on various predictor variables for all combinations of sex and visual field. For men, emotionality was the best predictor of left-visual-field scores, and word frequency the best predictor of right-field scores. For women, imageability was the best predictor in the left visual field, and emotionality in the right visual field.

The Graves *et al.* (1981) study is important in that it adds evidence that left-visual-field effects for emotional material can be obtained with verbal material as well as with faces. We have now seen that right-hemisphere emotionality effects can be obtained with both verbal and nonverbal procedures in both auditory and visual domains. However, the Graves *et al.* data also leave the state of affairs with respect to sex differences quite confused. Like Safer (1981), Graves *et al.* (1981) found greater right-hemisphere effects in men than in women. In contrast, McKeever and Dixon (1981) and Ladavas *et al.* (1980) reported greater effects for women than for men. While sex differences in laterality studies are notoriously unstable (Bryden, 1979), the idea that men show more predictable and consistent effects than women is in line with the observation that cerebral lateralization is more clearly established in men than in women (McGlone, 1980). In this sense, the Safer (1981) and Graves *et al.* (1981) studies are more consistent with the general body of knowledge than those reporting greater laterality effects in women.

The visual studies on emotion perception are in general agreement in showing right-hemisphere effects for both positive and negative emotions. While other studies have not investigated the degree of emotionality as we did (Ley & Bryden, 1979a), similar effects have been obtained for the six differentiable emotions identified by Ekman and Friesen (1975), including both positive (happiness) and negative (anger, sadness) states.

Conjugate Lateral Eye Movements

A quite different approach is seen in studies examining the direction of the initial lateral eye movement made in response to a reflective question. It has been observed that when people are asked a question requiring momentary reflection, they will typically avert their gaze before answering, looking briefly to either the left or the right (Bakan, 1971; Day, 1968). Individuals differ in the extent to which they tend to look in one direction or the other. It is often hypothesized that left-lookers are people who tend to make use of their right hemispheres, while right-lookers are more likely to utilize their left hemispheres. Constellations of behavioral characteristics and personality traits have been described for people who are consistent left-lookers or right-lookers (Ley, 1979, 1982). Thus, Bakan (1969) found that, in comparison with right-looking men, left-looking men were more likely to show a greater use of imagery and tended to rate their visual imagery as clearer. Similarly, Harnad (1972) found that left-looking mathematicians tend to utilize imagery to a greater degree than right-lookers in solving problems.

At the same time, different types of questions have been shown to lead to different types of lateral eye movement (Richardson, 1978). Kinsbourne (1972) found that most right-handed individuals tended to look to the left when asked a question dealing with spatial relations or imagery, while looking to the right when asked a question that involved verbal thought. Much debate has focused on the appropriate conditions for obtaining a large "subject effect"—the categorization of individuals into left and right lookers—and those for obtaining a "question effect"—a clear within-subject distinction between spatial and verbal questions. Gur, Gur, and Harris (1975) reported that the subject effect was most readily obtained when the interviewer and subject were in direct face-to-face contact, while the question effect was found when eye movements were monitored while the questioner was out of sight of the subject. They suggested that the face-to-face situation leads to higher anxiety on the part of the subject, and causes her or him to fall back on a more habitual mode of responding. However, Berg and Harris (1980) have failed to replicate these findings, and have concluded that the validity of the lateral eye movement procedure as a measure of hemispheric activation has yet to be established. In a thorough review of the literature, Ehrlichman and Weinberger (1978) also concluded that there was questionable justification for using lateral eye movements for studying hemispheric function.

Nevertheless, many researchers have continued to use the procedure, and their findings may be considered as at least suggestive (see Ley, 1979, 1982). Schwartz, Davidson, and Maer (1975), for example, recorded lateral eye movements to emotional or neutral questions and also varied the spatial or verbal nature of the questions. They found significantly more left lateral eye movements to emotional than to nonemotional questions, suggesting the possibility of a greater activation of the right hemisphere in responding to emotional questions. Tucker, Roth, Arneson, and Buckingham (1977) have subsequently replicated this finding. In contrast, Ahern and Schwartz (1979) claim that positive emotion questions evoked right lateral eye movements, while negative emotion questions led to left lateral eye movements. An examination of the data presented in their Table 2 (Ahern & Schwartz, 1979, p. 695) suggests that this may be an oversimplification. They observed a significant statistical interaction between emotion and eye movement direction. However, their analysis included "no eye movement" as one of the categories of eye movement and analyzed the five emotions of happiness, excitement, sadness, fear, and neutral as separate categories. The result is to make the nature of the interaction much more difficult to interpret. Their conclusions about the differences between positive and negative affect seem to be based on visual inspection of the data.

We have reexamined the Ahern and Schwartz (1979) data, taking into account only those trials on which a lateral eye movement was observed. If we collapse over the spatial/verbal dimension, which Ahern and Schwartz indicate had only a minor effect on their data, we find the results shown in Figure 10. While it is true that fear leads to the highest proportion of left lateral eye movements, both happiness and excitement lead to more left movements than does sadness, the other negative emotion. Furthermore, *all* of the affective questions lead to a lower proportion of left eye movements than do the neutral questions. Despite their conclusions, then, the Ahern and Schwartz (1979) data fail to show any clear difference in eye movement direction between positive and negative emotional questions. On the other hand, their data also indicate that emotional questions lead to more right eye movements, in direct contradiction to the studies of Schwartz *et al.* (1975) and Tucker *et al.* (1977). The problems of replicability pointed out by Ehrlichman and Weinberger (1978) are clearly evident here.

ASYMMETRIES OF EMOTIONAL EXPRESSION

In many situations, we communicate our emotions by changes in facial expression. Ekman and Friesen (1975) have demonstrated that we can reliably discriminate at least six different emotions in the human face. Since it has long been recognized that the human face is asymmetric, it was only natural that researchers should ask

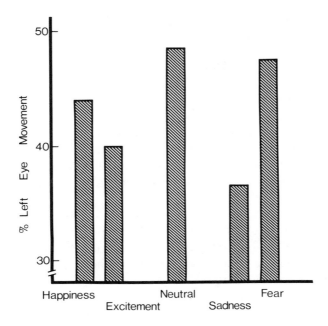

Affect of Question

FIGURE 10. *Proportion of left lateral eye movements to emotional questions, excluding "no-movement" trials. Data from Ahern and Schwartz (1979). Note the lack of systematic relationship between direction of affect and proportion of left eye movements.*

whether or not emotions were expressed more on one side of the face than on the other.

The most common approach to this question has been to have subjects pose for photographs depicting various emotions. These photographs are then cut down the midline, and the left and right halves each mirror-reversed and joined to produce two composite pictures. Such composites are bilaterally symmetric, one formed from the left half of the subject's face and one from the right half. In most studies using this procedure, the left-half composite is judged as expressing a more intense emotion than the right-half composite (Sackeim & Gur, 1978; Sackeim, Gur, & Saucy, 1978; Campbell, 1978, 1979). Campbell (1979), however, found that left-handers also exhibited a more positive smile with the left side of the face, a somewhat unexpected finding if we expect the lateralization of emotional expression to be related to conventional ideas about hemispheric asymmetry. Further, Campbell (1979) also found that the right-side composite of left-handers appeared sadder than the left-side composite when the subjects were photographed in a relaxed (neutral) state. This pattern was reversed in right-handers (Campbell, 1978). Finally, Strauss and Kaplan (1980) reported no differences between left- and right-half composites in which faces appeared happier or sadder when subjects judged photographs of themselves. Subjects did judge the left happy composite and the right sad composite to be "more like themselves."

Cacioppo and Petty (1981) also used the composite procedure to investigate the difference between spontaneous and posed expressions. They had actors produce expressions of grief, thoughtfulness, and relaxed neutrality, and were also photographed while reading material designed to elicit sad and thoughtful expressions. They report that judges considered the right side more expressive in the posed photographs, and the left side more expressive in the spontaneous pictures. In the spontaneous pictures, the left-side composite was considered to be sadder than the right-side composite. Unfortunately, Cacioppo and Petty (1981) used only four posers, with the result that the statistical effects across different posers (as opposed to judges) are very weak. Their results do indicate an interaction between side of face and spontaneity of expression, but it is impossible to break down the details of this interaction. Furthermore, they employed only a single affective expression, and thus their data do not address the question of whether different emotions are expressed in different parts of the face.

Unlike most other experimenters using composite stimuli, Heller and Levy (1981) produced composites in which one-half of the face was smiling and the other half was expressionless or neutral. They found that the composites were judged as happier when it was the left half of the face that was smiling, regardless of whether the poser was left-handed or right-handed. Furthermore, right-handed, but not left-handed, subjects saw the faces as being happier when they appeared in the left visual field, thus corroborating the tachistoscopic work of Ley and Bryden (1979a) and Safer (1981).

Borod and her colleagues have approached the question of facial asymmetry somewhat differently. Rather than using static photographs and artificial composites, they videotaped people posing various emotions, and then selected the still frames best representing the emotions. Borod and Caron (1980) rated the relative intensity of emotion on the two sides of the face while subjects posed for nine different expressions: greeting, disapproval, confusion, toughness, horror, flirtation, grief, clowning, and disgust. For both right- and left-handed posers, the left side of the face was judged to be more expressive, with little difference between positive and negative expressions. In the combined judgments, summed over all expressions, 77% of right-handers and 65% of left-handers were judged to be more expressive on the left side. Borod, Caron, and Koff (1981a) found that facial asymmetry was positively related to eye dominance, but not to handedness or footedness. Not only does this finding seem to contradict the distinction between left- and right-handers reported in the earlier study (Borod & Caron, 1980), but, in light of the questions surrounding the interpretation of eye dominance (Coren & Porac, 1977), the significance of a relation between eye dominance and facial asymmetry is not clear. In a further study, Borod, Caron, and Koff (1981b) found that facial asymmetry did correlate with lateral dominance, but only for males and only for positive expressions.

Moscovitch and Olds (1982) have carried out a naturalistic investigation of spontaneous emotional expression. They had an investigator observe people in restaurants, parks, and other field settings, and again found that emotional expressions were more likely to appear on the left side of the face. Under more controlled laboratory conditions, they replicated these findings, and also showed that the tendency to use the right hand in manual gesturing (Kimura, 1973a, 1973b) was observed only when the gesture was not accompanied by a change in facial expression.

In general, then, the research on facial asymmetries indicates that the left side of the face is more expressive than the right side, for both posed and spontaneous expressions. Left-handers may not show as marked an asymmetry as right-handers, but the data remain somewhat equivocal on this point (see Campbell, 1979; Borod *et al.*, 1981a).

SOME GENERAL CONSIDERATIONS

The research we have reviewed, both that of others and that of our own, leads to several major conclusions about the lateralization of emotion in the normal individual. Perceptual tasks involving lateralized presentation, such as is used in tachistoscopic recognition or dichotic listening, lead to a general superiority of performance in the left visual field or on the left ear. This is indicative of a predominant right-hemispheric involvement. Furthermore, the study and retention of lists of emotional words can bias performance on a perceptual laterality task, and lead to better performance in the right, as opposed to the left, hemisphere. At the same time, this asymmetry of emotion is not confined to the perceptual end, but also appears in the expression of emotion. The left side of the face is more involved than the right in the expression of emotion, and there are also some signs that emotional questions lead to an increased incidence of conjugate lateral eye movements to the left.

Unfortunately, this is a relatively cursory summary of the existing state of knowledge about the lateralization of emotion, and fails to highlight a number of problems that must be solved before achieving a comprehensive theoretical understanding of hemispheric asymmetries in emotion. Before we go further, then, we will examine these problems. It is convenient to consider initially the perceptual studies showing an asymmetry of emotion recognition, then to deal with the priming studies, and finally to consider the studies of emotional expression.

Current evidence indicates that a right-hemispheric superiority exists for the recognition of emotion in studies using lateralized stimulus presentation. Results of this sort have been found both visually and auditorily, and with both verbal and nonverbal material. Although it is often claimed that positive and negative emotions are lateralized quite differently (e.g., Reuter-Lorenz & Davidson, 1981), there is remarkably little evidence to support this assertion in the perceptual literature. That which does exist comes primarily from the clinical literature, and is concerned with the expression, rather than the perception, of affect (Ley, 1979; Tucker, 1981).

In the Reuter-Lorenz and Davidson (1981) study, subjects were required to judge which of two faces was showing an emotional expression. In most of the other visual studies, however, the task has been one of deciding whether or not two faces, one of which has been presented laterally, show the same emotional expression. It is possible that this difference in task requirements could account for the differences between the results of Reuter-Lorenz and Davidson (1981) and those of Ley and Bryden (1979a) and Safer (1981). On the other hand, Reuter-Lorenz and Davidson (1981) used exposure durations on the order of 300–350 msec, far longer than those used in the other studies. Sergent and Bindra (1981) have indicated that exposure duration may be a critical variable in face recognition studies. Despite the Reuter-Lorenz and Davidson findings, the general pattern found in the perceptual studies of emotion recognition is one of both positive and negative stimuli manifesting similar right-hemispheric effects.

It is also generally accepted that the right hemisphere plays a preeminent role in the recognition of complex visuospatial and auditory patterns (Bradshaw & Nettleton, 1981; Gates & Bradshaw, 1977a, 1977b). Although both Ley and Bryden (1979a) and Safer (1981) tried to show that the lateralization of emotion was separate from that for complex pattern recognition, their control conditions may not have been fully adequate. In determining whether two sets of facial features represent the same character, it is possible that subjects pay more attention to the eyes and hairline, while emphasizing the mouth and the lower part of the face in judging whether two stimuli represent the same emotion. Thus, one would not expect to find exactly the same results with emotion judgments as with character judgments, although they still might be mediated by the same mechanism. The question of whether emotion judgments represent nothing more than a special case of complex pattern discriminations may be little more than a semantic issue: Ekman and Friesen (1975) could not have shown that six universal emotions could be reliably discriminated from facial photographs unless there were some stimulus difference, however complex, between representations of various emotions. Similarly, there are certainly complex differences in stimulus pattern between musical sequences in major and minor keys (Bryden *et al.*, 1982), and between similar sentences spoken in different tones of voice (Haggard & Parkinson, 1971; Ley & Bryden, 1982; Saxby & Bryden, 1982).

One might also ask whether the right-hemispheric dominance observed in the perceptual studies is due to the specific stimuli employed, or to the general nature of the task. If the former, it would mean that a particular emotional stimulus would have an immediate perceptual effect such that it is better identified or discriminated because it has been presented in the left visual field or to the left ear. If the latter, it would suggest that the right-hemispheric effect arises simply because the subject is doing a task that includes emotional stimuli. In our own original work on face recognition (Ley, 1978; Ley & Bryden, 1979a), much stronger right-hemispheric effects were obtained for emotionally positive or negative stimuli than for the neutral stimuli used in the same experiment. This would suggest that each individual stimulus has an effect on some lateralized processes, such that emotional stimuli are facilitated when they are first registered in the right hemisphere. Zajonc (1980) has recently argued that stimulus events have affective as well as connotative meaning, and that the affective component may exert its own distinct effects. One might argue that a stimulus could excite some affective representation in the right hemisphere, which would serve to facilitate identification or categorization of the stimulus.

Our later work, however, has not been so clear on this point. In the Bryden *et al.* (1982) study of musical affect, for example, roughly equivalent left-ear effects were found for all stimuli, whether the individual stimulus was rated as emotional or not. Likewise, in our study of emotion in spoken sentences (Ley & Bryden, 1982), a robust left-ear superiority was found for the neutral sentences as well as for the emotional ones. These findings would suggest that it was the task, and not the individual stimulus, that led to the left-ear effect. By this argument, doing any emotional task would serve to produce general activation within the right hemisphere, and this activation would serve to facilitate performance. Of course, such an argument could also account for the results of our priming studies (Ley & Bryden, 1979b, 1980, 1983).

At present, there are no clear data to permit us to distinguish between these two possibilities. Relatively few studies of emotion perception employ very many different types of emotional stimuli, and those that do often fail to include neutral stimuli. If the individual stimuli are having their own specific effect on the right hemisphere, one would expect to obtain larger laterality effects with more extreme emotions, and the smallest laterality effect with the neutral stimuli. While this is the pattern observed in our study of facial expression (Ley & Bryden, 1979a), it is important to have a replication of this finding. However, the fact that Graves *et al.* (1981) were able to demonstrate a clear laterality effect for emotional words biases us in favor of the argument that any emotional stimulus can immediately activate right-hemispheric affective mechanisms.

The priming studies represent a rather different approach to the study of the lateralization of emotion, for they indicate that the cumulated impact of an emotional word list serves to alter responsivity in such a way that right-hemisphere performance is enhanced. The pioneer of priming studies was Kinsbourne (1970, 1973, 1975). He has argued that verbal thought leads to a general activation of the left hemisphere, thereby making it more receptive to incoming sensory information. Conversely, spatial thought activates the right hemisphere, and makes one more receptive to information coming from the left ear or the left visual field. In his initial priming study, Kinsbourne (1970) showed that remembering a list of words led to a right-visual-field superiority on an otherwise unlateralized gap-detection task. While there have been some problems in replicating the details of this study (Gardner & Branski, 1976; Boles, 1979), the idea that performance of one hemisphere can be enhanced relative to that of the other has proven to be an attractive one (see Hellige & Cox, 1976).

Our priming results, obtained in both tachistoscopic and dichotic studies, indicate that right-hemisphere performance is improved by studying word lists that are high in imagery or high in affective valence. Similar results were obtained with both positive and negative emotional word lists. In one sense, our results are precisely the opposite of what would be predicted from Kinsbourne's model: Studying particular types of verbal material has enhanced, not the *left* hemisphere, but the *right*. To what, then, can we attribute the priming effect we observed?

Paivio's work (see Paivio, 1978) on dual coding has amply illustrated the fact that verbal material can be encoded in memory in different ways: Paivio argues for a distinction between verbal codes and imagery-based codes. He shows, for example, that high-imagery words are better remembered than low-imagery words, presumably because high-imagery words have ready access to both verbal and imagery-based representations, while low-imagery words can only be represented as verbal codes. If we then add Zajonc's (1980) notion that stimuli have affective components as well, and attribute the imagery and affective components to the right hemisphere, the priming results become quite explicable (see Ley, 1982). Study of a high-imagery list of emotional words leads to a representation of the word list that includes not only verbal coding mechanisms that presumably are represented in the left hemisphere, but also imagery-based and affective components that are localized to the right hemisphere. Thus, relative to a neutral word list, there is greater activity in the right hemisphere than in the left when either high-imagery or highly emotional words have been presented. This increased right-hemispheric activity makes the right hemisphere more receptive to incoming stimuli, and consequently produces relatively better performance in the left visual field or at the left ear, performance better than that which is observed when word lists not having imagery or affective components are studied.

One might further expect that studying a list of highly emotional words might produce a slight shift in the subject's mood. In our dichotic priming study, we attempted to assess this possibility. Subjects were given a Mood Adjective Check List (Nowlis, 1965) and a modified Rorschach procedure after completing the dichotic retesting. There was no evidence that studying emotionally positive word lists made the subjects momentarily any happier, or that negative word lists made them more depressed. However, neither of our measures may have been sufficiently sensitive, and it remains entirely possible that the priming studies generated a slight shift in mood.

Finally, the general picture which emerges from the studies of facial asymmetry is also one of a right-hemispheric involvement in emotion. It is the left side of the face that is seen as more responsive in producing emotional expression. One possible problem in this literature is that the distinction between right- and left-handers is not as clear-cut as one might expect on the basis of knowledge about the influence of handedness on speech lateralization (Campbell, 1979; Borod et al., 1981a). However, it is entirely possible that different factors influence the lateralization of emotional processes and the lateralization of speech: Our dichotic study of sentence intonation (Ley & Bryden, 1982) did not indicate that they were related in a complementary fashion, but that they were independent. Similarly, Hécaen et al. (1981) have shown that the differences between right- and left-handers in visuospatial ability are not as pronounced as those in language, suggesting that different components of behavior may be lateralized independently to one hemisphere or the other.

CONCLUSIONS

What conclusions can we reach from this research? In general, perception of emotional stimuli seems to be more accurate when the stimuli are presented in such a way as to first reach the right hemisphere. Likewise, the display of emotion also appears to be more striking on the left side of the face than on the right. These effects, for the most part, are observed whether the emotions under consideration are positive or negative. These findings are commensurate with the view that there are specialized processes in the right hemisphere that are particularly concerned with the reception and expression of emotion.

It seems that any emotional stimulus or thought can activate some affective component that is more likely to be represented in the right hemisphere than in the left. Repeated or strong activation of these affective components can have an effect that will spread to adjacent regions of the cortex, thus resulting in the priming effects observed in our studies, and possibly leading to the conjugate lateral eye movements reported by others. We speculate that the affective component of a stimulus represents an alternative way of encoding incoming information, and is in some way related to Paivio's (1978) dual coding hypothesis and to the affective representations discussed by Zajonc (1980). The components may be primarily right-hemispheric because they may well represent the integration and encoding of multidimensional aspects of the stimulus (Gazzaniga & Le Doux, 1978) and thus take advantage of the integrative and holistic properties of the right hemisphere (Semmes, 1968).

ACKNOWLEDGMENTS

Preparation of this chapter was aided by a grant from the Natural Sciences and Engineering Research Council of Canada to M. P. Bryden. We should like to thank Marion Tapley for her excellent editorial and bibliographic assistance, and Lorie Saxby for her comments on an initial draft.

REFERENCES

Ahern, G. L., & Schwartz, G. E. Differential lateralization for positive versus negative emotion. *Neuropsychologia*, 1979, *17*, 693–698.

Bakan, P. Hypnotizability, laterality of eye movement and functional brain asymmetry. *Perceptual and Motor Skills*, 1969, *28*, 927–932.

Bakan, P. Birth order and handedness. *Nature*, 1971, *229*, 195.

Beaton, A. A. Hemisphere function and dual task performance. *Neuropsychologia*, 1979, *17*, 629–636.

Berg, M. R., & Harris, L. J. The effect of experimenter location and subject anxiety on cerebral activation measured by lateral eye movements. *Neuropsychologia*, 1980, *18*, 89–94.

Boles, D. Laterally biased attention with concurrent verbal load: Multiple failures to replicate. *Neuropsychologia*, 1979, *17*, 353–362.

Borod, J. C., & Caron, H. S. Facedness and emotion related to lateral dominance, sex and expression type. *Neuropsychologia*, 1980, *18*, 237–241.

Borod, J., Caron, H. S., & Koff, E. Asymmetry of facial expression related to handedness, footedness, and eyedness: A quantitative study. *Cortex*, 1981, *17*, 381–390. (a)

Borod, J., Caron, H. S., & Koff, E. Asymmetry in positive and negative facial expressions: Sex differences. *Neuropsychologia*, 1981, *19*, 819–824. (b)

Bradshaw, J. L., & Nettleton, N. C. The nature of hemispheric specialization in man. *The Behavioral and Brain Sciences*, 1981, *4*, 51–91.

Bryden, M. P. Strategy effects in the assessment of hemispheric asymmetry. In G. Underwood (Ed.), *Strategies of information processing*. London: Academic, 1978.

Bryden, M. P. Evidence for sex-related differences in cerebral organization. In M. Wittig & A. C. Petersen (Eds.), *Sex-related differences in cognitive functioning: Developmental issues*. New York: Academic, 1979.

Bryden, M. P. *Laterality: Functional asymmetry in the intact brain*. New York: Academic, 1982.

Bryden, M. P., & Sprott, D. A. Statistical determination of degree of laterality. *Neuropsychologia*, 1981, *19*, 571–581.

Bryden, M. P., Ley, R. G., & Sugarman, J. H. A left ear advantage for identifying the emotional quality of tonal sequences. *Neuropsychologia*, 1982, *20*, 83–87.

Buchtel, H. A., Campari, F., DeRisio, C., & Rota, R. Hemispheric differences in discriminative reaction time to facial expressions. *Italian Journal of Psychology*, 1978, *5*, 159–169.

Cacioppo, J. T., & Petty, R. E. Lateral asymmetry and expression of cognition and emotion. *Journal of Experimental Psychology: Human Perception and Performance*, 1981, *7*, 333–341.

Campbell, R. Asymmetries in interpreting and expressing a posed facial expression. *Cortex*, 1978, *14*, 327–342.

Campbell, R. Left-handers' smiles: Asymmetries in the projection of a posed expression. *Cortex*, 1979, *15*, 571–580.

Carmon, A., & Nachshon, I. Ear asymmetry in perception of emotional nonverbal stimuli. *Acta Psychologica*, 1973, *37*, 351–357.

Coren, S., & Porac, C. Fifty centuries of right-handedness: The historical record. *Science*, 1977, *198*, 631–632.

Davies, J. B. *The psychology of music*. London: Hutchinson, 1978.

Day, M. E. Attention, anxiety and psychotherapy. *Psychotherapy: Theory, Research and Practice*, 1968, *5*, 146–149.

Ehrlichman, H., & Weinberger, A. Lateral eye movements and hemispheric asymmetry: A critical review. *Psychological Bulletin*, 1978, *85*, 1080–1101.

Ekman, P., & Friesen, W. V. Measuring facial movement. *Journal of Environmental Psychology and Nonverbal Behavior*, 1975, *1*, 56–75.

Gardner, E. B., & Branski, D. M. Unilateral cerebral activation and perception of gaps: A signal detection analysis. *Neuropsychologia*, 1976, *14*, 43–53.

Gates, A., & Bradshaw, J. L. The role of the cerebral hemispheres in music. *Brain and Language*, 1977, *4*, 403–431. (a)

Gates, A., & Bradshaw, J. L. Music perception and cerebral asymmetries. *Cortex*, 1977, *13*, 390–401. (b)

Gazzaniga, M. S., & LeDoux, J. E. *The integrated mind*. New York: Plenum, 1978.

Graves, R., Landis, T., & Goodglass, H. Laterality and sex differences for visual recognition of emotional and nonemotional words. *Neuropsychologia*, 1981, *19*, 95–102.

Gruzelier, J., & Flor-Henry, P. (Eds.). *Hemisphere asymmetries of function in psychopathology*. Amsterdam: Elsevier/North Holland, 1979.

Gur, R. E., Gur, R. C., & Harris, L. J. Cerebral activation, as measured by subjects' lateral eye movements, is influenced by experimenter location. *Neuropsychologia*, 1975, *13*, 35–44.

Haggard, M. P., & Parkinson, A. M. Stimulus and task factors in the perceptual lateralization of speech signals. *Quarterly Journal of Experimental Psychology*, 1971, *23*, 168–177.

Hansch, E. C., & Pirozzolo, F. J. Task relevant effects on the assessment of cerebral specialization for facial emotion. *Brain and Language*, 1980, *10*, 51–59.

Harnad, S. R. Creativity: Lateral saccades and the nondominant hemisphere. *Perceptual and Motor Skills*, 1972, *34*, 653–654.

Hécaen, H., DeAgostini, M., & Monzon-Montes, A. Cerebral organization in left-handers. *Brain and Language*, 1981, *12*, 261–284.

Heller, W., & Levy, J. Perception and expression of emotion in right-handers and left-handers. *Neuropsychologia*, 1981, *19*, 263–272.

Hellige, J. B., & Cox, P. J. Effects of concurrent verbal memory on recognition of stimuli from the left and right visual fields. *Journal of Experimental Psychology: Human Perception and Performance*, 1976, *2*, 210–221.

Kimura, D. Dual functional asymmetry of the brain in visual perception. *Neuropsychologia*, 1966, *4*, 275–285.

Kimura, D. Functional asymmetry of the brain in dichotic listening. *Cortex*, 1967, *3*, 163–178.

Kimura, D. Manual activity during speaking—I: Right-handers. *Neuropsychologia*, 1973, *11*, 45–50. (a)

Kimura, D. Manual activity during speaking—II. Left-handers. *Neuropsychologia*, 1973, *11*, 51–56. (b)

Kinsbourne, M. The cerebral basis of lateral asymmetries in attention. *Acta Psychologica*, 1970, *33*, 193–201.

Kinsbourne, M. Eye and head turning indicate cerebral lateralization. *Science*, 1972, *176*, 539–541.

Kinsbourne, M. The control of attention by interaction between the cerebral hemispheres. In S. Kornblum (Ed.), *Attention and performance IV*. New York: Academic, 1973.

Kinsbourne, M. The mechanism of hemispheric control of the lateral gradient of attention. In P. M. A. Rabbitt & S. Dornic (Eds.), *Attention and performance V*. London and New York: Academic, 1975.

Ladavas, E., Umilta, C., Ricci-Bitti, P. E. Evidence for sex differences in right-hemisphere dominance for emotions. *Neuropsychologia*, 1980, *18*, 361–366.

Ley, R. G. *Asymmetry of hysterial conversion symptoms*. Paper presented at the annual meeting of the Canadian Psychological Association, Ottawa, June 1978.

Ley, R. G. Cerebral asymmetries, emotional experience, and imagery: Implications for psychotherapy. In A. Sheikh & J. T. Shaffer (Eds.), *The potential of fantasy and imagination.* New York: Brandon House, 1979.

Ley, R. G. Cerebral laterality and imagery. In A. Sheikh (Ed.), *Imagery: Theory, research, and current application.* New York: Wiley, 1982.

Ley, R. G., & Bryden, M. P. Hemispheric differences in recognizing faces and emotions. *Brain and Language,* 1979, *7,* 127–138. (a)

Ley, R. G., & Bryden, M. P. *Right hemisphere emotional effect for emotional, imagic words.* Paper presented at the annual meeting of the Psychonomic Society, Phoenix, November 1979. (b)

Ley, R. G., & Bryden, M. P. *A dichotic listening investigation of hemispheric differences for positive and negative emotional stimuli.* Paper presented at the annual conference of the American Association for the Advancement of Science, San Francisco, January 1980.

Ley, R. G., & Bryden, M. P. A dissociation of right and left hemispheric effects for recognizing emotional tone and verbal content. *Brain and Cognition,* 1982, *1,* 3–9.

Ley, R. G., & Bryden, M. P. Right hemisphere involvement in imagery and affect. In E. Perecman (Ed.), *Cognitive processing in the right hemisphere.* New York: Academic, 1983, in press.

McGlone, J. Sex differences in human brain organization: A critical survey. *The Behavioral and Brain Sciences,* 1980, *3,* 215–227.

McKeever, W. F., & Dixon, M. S. Right-hemisphere superiority for discriminating memorized from nonmemorized faces: Affective imagery, sex, and perceived emotionality effects. *Brain and Language,* 1981, *12,* 246–260.

Moscovitch, M. Information processing and the cerebral hemispheres. In M. S. Gazzaniga (Ed.), *Handbook of behavioral neurobiology* (Vol. 2: *Neuropsychology*). New York: Plenum, 1979.

Moscovitch, M., & Olds, J. Asymmetries in emotional facial expressions and their possible relation to hemispheric specialization. *Neuropsychologia,* 1982, *20,* 71–81.

Nowlis, V. Research with the Mood Adjective Check List. In S. Tompkins & C. Izard (Eds.), *Affect, cognition, and personality.* New York: Springer, 1965.

Paivio, A. The relationship between verbal and perceptual codes. In E. C. Carterette & M. P. Friedman (Eds.), *Handbook of Perception* (Vol. VIII). *Perceptual coding.* New York: Academic, 1978.

Paivio, A. Yuille, J. C., & Madigan, S. A. Concreteness, imagery and meaningfulness values of 925 nouns. *Journal of Experimental Psychology Monograph Supplements,* 1968, *76* (1, Pt. 2).

Reuter-Lorenz, P., & Davidson, R. J. Differential contributions of the two cerebral hemispheres to the perception of happy and sad faces. *Neuropsychologia,* 1981, *19,* 609–614.

Richardson, A. Subject, task, and tester variables associated with initial eye movement responses. *Journal of Mental Imagery,* 1978, *2,* 85–100.

Sackeim, H. A., & Gur, R. C. Lateral asymmetry in intensity of emotional expression. *Neuropsychologia*, 1978, *16*, 473–482.

Sackeim, H. A., Gur, R. C., & Saucy, M. C. Emotions are expressed more intensely on the left side of the face. *Annals of the New York Academy of Science*, 1978, *202*, 424–435.

Safer, M. A. Sex and hemisphere differences in access to codes for processing emotional expressions and faces. *Journal of Experimental Psychology: General*, 1981, *110*, 86–100.

Safer, M., & Leventhal, H. Ear differences in evaluating emotional tones of voice and verbal content. *Journal of Experimental Psychology: Human Perception and Performance*, 1977, *3*, 75–82.

Saxby, L., & Bryden, M. P. *Left ear superiority in children for processing emotional material.* Paper presented at the annual meeting of the International Neurospychology Society, Pittsburgh, February 1982.

Schwartz, G., Davidson, R., & Maer, F. Right hemispheric lateralizations for emotion in the human brain: Interactions with cognition. *Science*, 1975, *190*, 286–288.

Semmes, J. Hemispheric specialization: A possible clue to mechanism. *Neuropsychologia*, 1968, *6*, 11–26.

Sergent, J., & Bindra, D. Differential hemispheric processing of faces: Methodological considerations and reinterpretation. *Psychological Bulletin*, 1981, *89*, 541–554.

Springer, S. Speech perception and the biology of language. In M. Gazzaniga (Ed.), *Handbook of behavioral neurobiology*. New York: Plenum, 1979.

Strauss, E., & Kaplan, E. Lateralized asymmetries in self-perception. *Cortex*, 1980, *16*, 289–294.

Strauss, E., & Moscovitch, M. Perception of facial expressions. *Brain and Language*, 1981, *13*, 308–332.

Suberi, M., & McKeever, W. F. Differential right hemispheric memory storage of emotional and non-emotional faces. *Neuropsychologia*, 1977, *5*, 757–768.

Tucker, D. M. Lateral brain function, emotion, and conceptualization. *Psychological Bulletin*, 1981, *89*, 19–46.

Tucker, D. M., Roth, R. S., Arneson, B. A., & Buckingham, V. Right hemisphere activation during stress. *Neuropsychologia*, 1977, *15*, 697–700.

White, M. J. Hemispheric asymmetries in tachistoscopic information processing. *British Journal of Psychology*, 1972, *63*, 497–508.

Zajonc, R. B. Feeling and thinking: Preferences need no inferences. *American Psychologist*, 1980, *35*, 151–175.

AFFECTIVE DISORDERS ASSOCIATED WITH HEMISPHERIC DISEASE

Kenneth M. Heilman
Robert T. Watson
Dawn Bowers

INTRODUCTION

Babinski (1914) noted that patients with right-hemisphere disease often appear indifferent or euphoric. Hécaen, Ajuriaguerra, and Massonet (1951) and Denny-Brown, Meyer, and Horenstein (1952) also noted that patients with right-hemisphere lesions often appeared inappropriately "indifferent." Goldstein (1948) noted that patients with left-hemisphere lesions and aphasia often showed a profound depression, which he termed the "catastrophic reaction."

Gainotti (1972) studied 160 patients with lateralized brain damage, and his findings supported the earlier clinical observations of Goldstein (1948) and Babinski (1914) that left-hemisphere disease was frequently associated with the catastrophic reactions, and right-hemisphere lesions were often associated with indifference. Terzian (1964) and Rossi and Rosadini (1967) have studied the emotional reactions of patients recovering from barbiturate-induced hemispheric anesthesia produced by left or right carotid artery injections (Wada test). They observed that injections into the left carotid artery were associated with a depressed–catastrophic

Kenneth M. Heilman, Robert T. Watson, and Dawn Bowers. College of Medicine, University of Florida, and Veterans Administration Medical Center, Gainesville, Florida.

reaction, whereas right carotid injections were associated with a euphoric–maniacal response. Milner (1974), however, was unable to replicate these findings.

Both Goldstein (1948) and Gainotti (1972) postulated that the catastrophic reaction was a normal response to a serious cognitive and physical defect. Gainotti thought the indifference reaction was an abnormal mood associated with denial of illness (anosognosia). Although the asymmetrical moods with hemispheric disease may be related to the reaction of patients to their illness, recent research has offered alternative hypotheses.

RECEPTION (PERCEPTUAL AND COGNITIVE DEFECTS)

AUDITORY–VERBAL PROCESSES

Patients with right-hemisphere lesions might have a defect in the comprehension or expression of affect or both. Developing an appropriate emotional tone depends, in part, on comprehending speech. Speech can simultaneously carry at least two different types of information—the linguistic content (what is said) and the affective content (how it is said). The linguistic content is conveyed by a complex code that requires semantic and phonemic decoding. In contrast, the affective content is conveyed by the pitch, tempo, and tonal contours of speech (Paul, 1909), and consequently requires a different type of processing.

The left hemisphere is clearly more adept than the right in decoding the linguistic content of speech in the vast majority of individuals (particularly right-handers). Until several years ago little was known about how affective intonations were being mediated. We therefore attempted to determine whether the right hemisphere is more adept than the left in decoding the affective components of speech. In one study (Heilman, Scholes, & Watson, 1975), sentences with semantically neutral content (e.g., "The boy went to the store."), were read in four different emotional intonations (happy, sad, angry, indifferent) to patients with right temporoparietal infarctions and to those with aphasia and left temporoparietal infarctions. The patient's task was to identify the emotional tone of the speaker (how the sentence was read). Patients with right-hemisphere lesions performed worse on this task than those with left-hemisphere lesions, suggesting that the right hemisphere is more critically involved in processing the affective intonations of speech.

Schlanger, Schlanger, and Gerstmann (1976) performed a similar study in patients with right- or left-hemisphere damage. Although they found that brain-damaged subjects performed more poorly than did controls, these investigators did not find any differences in whether the damage was in the right or the left hemisphere. However, only 3 of their 20 subjects with right-hemisphere disease had temporoparietal lesions.

Further support for the hypothesis that the two hemispheres process different aspects of speech (semantic content vs. affective intonations) has been drawn from dichotic listening studies with normal adults. For further details see Chapter 1, this volume, by Bryden and Ley.

The neuropsychological defect underlying the impaired ability of patients with right-hemisphere disease to identify affective intonations in speech is not entirely clear. This defect may be related to a cognitive inability to denote and classify affective stimuli. This defect could also be related to an inability to discriminate perceptually between affective intonations in speech. In a subsequent study, we (Tucker, Watson, & Heilman, 1977) replicated our previous finding and attempted to determine whether patients with right-hemisphere disease could, in fact, discriminate between affective intonations of speech without having to classify or denote these intonations. Patients were required to listen to identical pairs of sentences spoken in either the same or different emotional tones. The patients did not have to identify the emotional intonation, but had to tell whether the intonations associated with the sentences sounded the same or different. Patients with right-hemisphere disease performed more poorly on this task than did patients with left-hemisphere disease, which suggests that the perceptual discrimination between affectively intoned stimuli was impaired in the patients with right-hemisphere damage. An alternative explanation for these findings is that the patients with right-hemisphere disease can discriminate between and classify affective intonations because the left hemisphere may also have the capacity to process affective intonations. However, with the presentation of affectively intoned speech, the patients with right-hemisphere disease were distracted by and listened to the propositional message rather than listening to the affective message.

The ability of the intact right hemisphere to comprehend affective intonations of speech has not been fully explored. Recently, however, we examined a patient with pure word deafness (normal speech output and reading but impaired speech comprehension) from a left-hemisphere lesion. In patients with pure word deafness the left auditory cortex is thought to have been destroyed and the right disconnected from Wernicke's area on the left; however, the right auditory area and its connections to the right hemisphere are intact. Although this patient comprehended speech very poorly, he had no difficulty recognizing either environmental sounds or emotional intonations of speech. We also studied five patients with global aphasia by giving them propositional commands like "Point to the happy face" (Heilman, Cobb, & Rothi in preparation). These commands were either neutrally intoned or intoned with the appropriate affective intonations. In the happy condition, these patients pointed to the correct face more often when the appropriate intonations were present than when the sentences were not intoned. In the sad and angry conditions, they were not aided by intonations. Boller, Cole, Urtunski, Patterson, and Kim (in press) presented sentences to eight patients with severe aphasia. These sentences had either neutral or emotional content. The sentences with emotional content produced a greater number of responses than did neutral sentences.

Emotional messages may be conveyed by propositional speech. Graves, Landis, and Goodglass (1980) visually presented emotional and nonemotional words to aphasic patients with left-hemisphere lesions. Their task was to read the words. Unlike speech, which can be affectively intoned, the written word carries no prosody. Nevertheless, Graves and co-workers (1980) found that emotional words were read better than were nonemotional words. These authors also performed a study with normal adults in which emotional and nonemotional words were tachistoscopically presented to the left and right visual half-fields. In the left visual half-field, there was a relative superiority for the recognitional of emotional words over nonemotional words. The right hemisphere therefore appears to be important in processing not only affective intonations but also emotional propositional language.

Several years ago we presented the Token Test (a sensitive instrument for measuring language comprehension) to aphasic patients with left-hemisphere disease (Heilman, Gold, & Tucker, 1975). This test was administered in two conditions—one in the usual manner (normal speech); in the other condition, the intensity and prosody of the commands were varied, and many of the commands were affectively intoned. In the high-prosody condition, comprehension was greatly improved. It is not clear, however, whether the novelty or the emotional prosody was responsible for improved performance. Our original interpretation of these data was that novelty increased arousal, which then facilitated language processing. There are, however, multiple explanations, including the possibility that emotional stimuli activated the right hemisphere and that increased right-hemisphere processing of the affective stimuli contributed to the improved performance. It is not known how the processing of affective and propositional messages interacts in the normal and brain-damaged populations, and we are currently performing studies to clarify this question.

VISUAL–NONVERBAL PROCESSES

The development of an appropriate emotional state depends on perceiving and comprehending auditory stimuli (e.g., intonations) and also visual stimuli (e.g., facial expression, gesture). Gardner, Ling, Flam, and Silverman (1975) found that patients with right-hemisphere disease and those with left-hemisphere disease were equally impaired in selecting the most humorous of a group of cartoons. Patients with left-hemisphere disease performed better on cartoons without captions. Patients with right-hemisphere disease performed better with captions.

We gave a variety of affective visual tasks to patients with left- or right-hemisphere lesions, as well as to neurologic controls without hemispheric disease (DeKosky, Heilman, Bowers, & Valenstein, 1980). We asked our subjects to: discriminate between a pair of neutral faces (e.g., "Are these two faces the same person or two different people?"); name the emotion expressed by a face (happy, sad, angry, indifferent); select from a multiple-choice array of faces a "target" emotion (e.g., "Point to the happy face."); determine whether two pictures of the same person's face expressed the same or a different emotion.

Compared with other groups, patients with right-hemisphere disease were markedly impaired in their ability to discriminate between pairs of neutral faces, as has been previously reported by Benton and Van Allen (1968). Although both hemisphere-damaged groups had difficulty naming and selecting emotional faces, there was a trend for patients with right-hemisphere disease to perform more poorly on these two tasks than patients with left-hemisphere disease. In addition, patients with right-hemisphere disease were more impaired in making same–different discriminations between emotional faces.

When performance across these various affect tasks was co-varied for neutral facial discrimination (a visuospatial nonemotional task), differences between the two groups disappeared. This finding suggests that the defect underlying poor discrimination of neutral faces observed in the group with right-hemisphere disease might also underlie their inability to recognize and discriminate between emotional faces. However, the poor facial discrimination by the group with right-hemisphere disease did not entirely correlate with their ability to recognize and discriminate between emotional faces. Retrospective review of the data revealed that about one-third of the patients with right-hemisphere disease performed poorly on both the neutral facial discrimination task and the emotional faces tasks, whereas about one-third performed well on both. The remaining patients with right-hemisphere disease, however, performed relatively well on neutral facial discrimination but poorly on the emotional faces tasks.

We therefore believe that the right hemisphere might be important for perceiving both faces and facial expressions. These processes may be either interdependent (i.e., one must perceive faces before perceiving the emotions expressed by the face), or they may be independent, but share the same or a contiguous anatomic locus. Cicone, Waper, and Gardner (1980) also presented emotional faces to patients with right- or left-hemisphere damage and also found that right-hemisphere-damaged patients were impaired in recognizing emotional faces. Recently, we (Bowers & Heilman,

1981) examined a patient with a large right-hemisphere tumor. The tumor was in the posterior region and did not appear to involve cortical structures, but did involve subcortical association fibers, some of which may have been commisural fibers that course to and from the left hemisphere. This patient performed flawlessly on the neutral and emotional facial discrimination task, but had great difficulty naming and selecting emotional faces. His test performance suggested that the ability to recognize or match faces can be dissociated from the ability to recognize emotional faces. A right-hemisphere disconnection from the left hemisphere may have caused his inability to name emotional faces or to point to a face named by the examiner. Because this patient could, however, name the emotion associated with affectively intoned, propositionally neutral sentences, he may have been able to cross the callosum more anteriorly.

We recently examined a patient who had most of the callosum destroyed excluding the splenium by an extensive hemorrhage with possible infarction (Bowers, Watson, & Heilman, in preparation). The cause of the hemorrhage and infarction could not be elucidated. Unlike our previous patient, when presented with emotional faces she could name the emotion and point to the face named by the examiner. However, unlike the patient with a posterior tumor, she also could not correctly name affectively intoned speech.

Tachistoscopic studies with normal adults have also implicated the role of the right hemisphere in the processing of affective faces. For a review see Chapter 1, this volume, by Bryden and Ley.

Although the right hemisphere appears to have a special role in discriminating and recognizing emotional faces, the left hemisphere also has a role. In the visual affect study by DeKosky et al. (1980), impairment was greater in patients with left-hemisphere disease compared with that in neurologic controls without hemispheric lesions. The neuropsychological mechanisms underlying the defect of the group with left-hemisphere disease in identifying emotional faces is not immediately apparent. This group was aphasic with relatively spared comprehension, and when compared with control did not have problems discriminating between neutral faces per se. Berent (1977) tested a group of depressed women before and after electroconvulsive therapy (ECT) to either

the left or right hemisphere. The ECT to the right hemisphere
induced a deficit in recognizing faces, whereas ECT to the left
hemisphere induced difficulty in recognizing emotional faces.
Berent speculated that verbal mediation and verbal labeling might
underlie the recognition of emotional faces. Berent's hypothesis is
compatible with the performance of the patients with left-hemisphere disease in the study by DeKosky *et al.* (1980). With the
exception of the neutral facial discrimination task, the test on
which the aphasic patients with left-hemisphere disease performed
best (and significantly better than the group with right-hemisphere
disease) was matching emotional faces, a task that does not require
verbal labeling or mediation.

EXPRESSION

VERBAL

Previous research with normal and with brain-damaged subjects
has suggested that there are hemispheric differences in the ability
to comprehend affectively intoned speech. Hemispheric differences
may also exist in the ability to *express* various emotions in speech.
Patients with left-hemisphere disease are often aphasic and thus
have difficulty using propositional speech. They are impaired in
ability to convey emotional content within a semantic–propositional context. However, as noted by Hughlings Jackson (Taylor,
1932), some aphasic patients can, by varying tempo, pitch, and
timbre, convey a rich variety of emotional feeling, despite their
inability to produce propositional speech.

Patients with left-hemisphere lesions who have severe non-
fluent aphasia and limited ability to express propositional speech
not only can affectively intone words and sounds but also may be
very fluent when using emotional words, especially expletives.

We attempted to determine whether patients with right-
hemisphere disease can express emotionally intoned speech (Tucker
et al., 1977). The patients were asked to say semantically neutral
sentences (e.g., "The boy went to the store.") using a happy, sad,
angry, or indifferent tone of voice. These patients were severely
impaired. Typically, they spoke the sentences in a flat monotone
and often denoted the target affect (e.g., "The boy went to the

store, and he was sad.") Ross and Mesulam (1979) described two patients who could not express affectively intoned speech but could comprehend affective speech. Ross (1981) has also described patients who could not comprehend affective intonations but could repeat affectively intoned speech. Ross (1981) has postulated that right-hemisphere lesions may disrupt affective speech (i.e., in terms of comprehension, repetition, and production) in the same manner that left-hemisphere lesions disrupt propositional speech.

FACES

Buck and Duffy (1980) studied the ability of right- and left-hemisphere-damaged patients to make emotional faces in response to viewing slides such as those of familiar people, an unpleasant scene (e.g., a starving child, a crying woman), and unusual pictures (e.g., double exposures). The subjects' faces were videotaped as they viewed the slides and were later judged. The results showed that compared with left-hemisphere-injured subjects, right-hemisphere-damaged patients were less facially expressive.

We asked five left-hemisphere-damaged and five right-hemisphere-damaged aphasic patients to make happy, sad, or angry faces. We photographed their faces, and submitted these photographs to judges. When we compared the ability of right- and left-hemisphere-damaged patients to make emotional faces, we found no significant differences.

One possibility to account for the differences between studies is that right-hemisphere-damaged patients have visuospatial and visuoperceptive disorders and the slides may not have had the same meaning for them as for the left-hemispheric aphasic patients. However, responding to a slide also differs from posing. Posing is a skilled task that requires the subject to have not only an internal model of the proposed face but also the motor skills to approximate the model. Left-hemisphere lesions are frequently associated with apraxia, including buccofacial apraxia. One reason that we found no difference between right- and left-hemisphere-damaged patients may be that the right-hemisphere patients could not recall the model and the left-hemisphere patients lost the motor skill needed to carry out the pose.

Unlike our study which required poses, Buck and Duffy's (1980) study photographed (videotaped) subjects spontaneously responding to a slide. Unfortunately, we did not study our patients' spontaneous emotions, and Buck and Duffy did not ask their subjects to pose to learn whether there was a dissociation. Our observations in the clinic, however, suggest that posing versus spontaneous emotions may be mediated by different systems. It is not unusual in clinic for us to see patients with a hemiparesis who, when asked to smile or to show their gums, cannot fully contract the contralateral facial muscles. However, when the examiner tells the patient a funny story, the mouth will contract normally. Similarly, posing may rely more heavily on left-hemisphere praxic processes than does the response to pictures, which relies more on right hemisphere, subcortical, or both processes.

Occasionally, patients who cannot move their faces normally to command can have outbursts of crying or laughing (pathological crying or laughing). Usually these emotional outbursts are not under volitional control, and the patient will often tell the examiner that his facial expressions are not always consistent with his mood. Most patients with pathological laughing or crying have bilateral subcortical lesions (Poeck, 1969). Most observers have proposed that this laughing or crying may be induced by disinhibition of a subcortical region where these behaviors are programmed. Recently, Sackeim, Greenberg, Weiman, Gur, Hungerbuhler, and Geschwind (1982) retrospectively analyzed such cases and noted that although most of these patients have bilateral lesions, patients with pathological laughing have larger lesions on the right side and those with pathological crying have larger lesions on the left side.

MEMORY

In one of the few studies of affective memory, Wechsler (1972) presented right- and left-hemisphere-damaged patients with two stories—one designed to elicit an affective response, the other neutral. For example, the emotional story told of a king "who was very sick and his doctors were unable to cure him. He sent for his wise men who told him he would get well if he wore the shirt of a truly happy man." Immediately after a story was read to the patients, they were asked to reproduce it verbally. The score was based on the total units recalled (i.e., similar to the logical memory subtest of the Wechsler Memory Scale). The patients with left-hemisphere lesions made fewer errors on the emotionally charged story than did patients with right-hemisphere disease; there were no differences in their performance on the neutral story. However, it was also noted that even left-hemisphere-damaged subjects, compared with normal controls, had more difficulty with the emotionally charged stories than with neutral stories. In normals, affectively charged facts are recalled better than neutral stories.

The nature of the defect described by Wechsler (1972) needs further clarification. It is not clear whether the stories were read with affective intonations, which may have aided one group more than another. In addition, since some emotional propositional messages appear, at least in part, to be mediated by the right hemisphere, we do not know whether the subject fully comprehended the emotional story. The defect therefore may not have been a memory defect but rather a defect in comprehension of emotionally laden propositional language. A delay procedure may have been useful in distinguishing whether there was a defect in comprehension or in affective memory.

UNDERLYING AFFECT

The studies reviewed thus far have suggested that patients with right-hemisphere disease have more difficulty than patients with left-hemisphere disease in comprehending and expressing affectively intoned speech as well as comprehending emotional facial expressions. Patients with right-hemisphere disease may also have more difficulty comprehending or remembering emotionally charged speech. These perceptual, cognitive, and expressive deficits might underlie and account for the different emotional reactions of patients with right- versus left-hemisphere lesions (i.e., indifference vs. catastrophic reactions), as previously described by clinical investigators (Denny-Brown et al., 1952; Gainotti, 1972; Goldstein, 1948; Hécaen et al., 1951). Alternatively, these perceptual, cognitive, and expressive deficits may be independent of and not contribute to the different patterns of emotional reactivity after unilateral hemispheric lesions.

To lean more about mood, we (Gasparrini, Satz, Heilman, & Coolidge, 1978) administered the Minnesota Multiphasic Personality Inventory (MMPI) to patients with unilateral hemisphere lesions. The patients were matched for severity of cognitive (e.g., IQ) and motor defects (e.g., motor tapping). The MMPI has been widely used as an index of underlying affective experiences, and the completion of this inventory does not require the perception or expression of affectively intoned speech or the perception of facial expression. Patients with left-hemisphere disease showed a marked elevation on the depression scale of this inventory, whereas patients with right-hemisphere disease did not. This finding suggests that the differences in emotional reactions of patients after right- versus left-hemisphere disease cannot be attributed entirely to difficulties in perceiving or expressing affective stimuli. Equally important, the difference in "depression" between the left- and right-hemisphere-damaged groups appears unrelated to differences in the severity of cognitive or motor defects.

Because of the nature of the particular subscales constituting the MMPI used in the aforementioned study (Gasparrini *et al.*, 1978), we could not determine whether patients with right-hemisphere disease have a flattening of their underlying affect. For example, many patients with right-hemisphere disease who have the indifference reaction may not appear depressed because they have anosognosia and do not recognize that they are disabled; that is, they have no reason to be depressed. The critical test of "flattening" in patients with right-hemisphere disease would involve assessing the emotions of these patients in a situation that normally evokes an emotional response and when the patients clearly recognize the meaning of the situation. To our knowledge, this type of study has not yet been performed. In the clinic, however, we see patients who do not explicitly deny illness, in that they recognize that they have had a stroke, are in the hospital, and have a left hemiparesis. These patients often appear unconcerned about their hemiparesis (anosodiaphoria) (Critchley, 1953). A portion of this flattening and unconcern may be induced by a loss of ability to express affective intonations in speech or to use affective facial expressions. Nevertheless, even when one uses propositional speech to assess affect, these patients still convey a lack of concern about their illness.

Pathophysiology Underlying the Indifference Response

Cannon (1927) regarded the thalamus as an important central structure responsible for mediating emotions. It can be stimulated either by peripheral sensory inputs or by cortical impulses. He proposed that thalamic activity could excite both the cortex and the viscera. Cortical activation induces the conscious emotional state, and visceral changes occurred simultaneously and served adaptive purposes. Bard (1934) suggested that the hypothalamus was, in fact, the major effector of emotional expression, since it regulates both the endocrine system and the autonomic nervous system. Papez (1937), in turn, proposed that the limbic system, which has important connections with the hypothalamus, cortex, and thalamus, is important in regulating emotion.

The concept of cortical activation or arousal was central to Cannon's theory. Subsequent research lead to a better understanding of the physiology of arousal. Berger (1933) noted that the electroencephalographic pattern decreased in amplitude and increased in frequency during behavioral arousal. This was termed "electroencephalographic desynchronization." Desynchronization also occurs during emotional states (Lindsley, 1970).

Animals stimulated in the nonspecific thalamic nuclei, as well as in the mesencephalic reticular formation, also show behavioral indices of arousal and electroencephalographic desynchronization (Moruzzi & Magoun, 1949). In addition, stimulation of certain cortical areas like the frontal or temporoparietal regions activates the mesencephalic reticular formation (French, Hernandez-Peon, & Livingston, 1955) and elicits an arousal response (Segundo, Naguet, & Buser, 1955). The limbic system, which has strong input into the reticular formation, is another pathway by which cortical stimulation can produce arousal (Heilman & Valenstein, 1972; Watson, Heilman, Cauthen, & King, 1973).

The relationship between arousal and the "experience" of emotion has been studied in normal human subjects. In 1924, Maranon (see Fehr & Stern, 1970) induced physiological arousal by administering sympathomimetic drugs to normal subjects. He states that most of his subjects reported feeling "no emotions," although many reported that they experienced "as if" feelings. When Maranon induced an affective memory that was not strong enough to produce an emotion in the normal state, emotional reactions then occurred if there was concomitant pharmacological arousal. Similarly, Schachter (1970) aroused normal subjects pharmacologically, placed them in a stressful situation, and found both subjective and objective evidence of emotional states. Pharmacological arousal alone did not produce such emotional states. Likewise, the stressful situation alone produced less emotion when the subjects were not pharmacologically aroused.

Maranon's (Fehr & Stern, 1970) and Schachter's (1970) studies support the hypothesis that in order to experience an emotion, one must have the appropriate cognitive state plus a certain degree of *arousal*. Arousal depends on the brainstem reticular formation, nonspecific thalamic nuclei, and certain regions of the neocortex. Emotions are accompanied by visceral changes mediated by the hypothalamus. The hypothalamus is strongly influenced by the limic system which, in turn, has considerable input from the neocortex (especially the frontal lobes). An emotion thus depends on varied anatomic structures, including: cortical systems for producing the appropriate cognitive set, limbic structures for activating the brainstem and thalamic activating centers and for controlling the hypothalamic output, the hypothalamus for regulating endocrine and autonomic responses, and the brainstem and thalamic activating systems for producing cortical arousal.

Studies in our laboratory have suggested that patients with right-hemisphere disease have difficulty comprehending affectively intoned speech and affective facial expressions. Such deficits might therefore interfere with the development of an appropriate *cognitive state* (thought to be an essential component of emotion), thereby resulting in emotional flattening in patients with right-hemisphere disease. In addition, patients with right-hemisphere disease and the indifference reaction might also be inadequately aroused. To determine whether such patients had normal arousal, we (Heilman, Schwartz, & Watson, 1978) stimulated the normal side of patients with right- or left-hemisphere disease with an electrical stimulus and simultaneously recorded galvanic skin responses. The galvanic skin response is a measure of peripheral sympathetic activity which correlates well with other central measures of arousal, such as the electroencephalogram. We found that patients with right-hemisphere disease and the indifference reaction had dramatically smaller arousal responses (galvanic skin response) than aphasic patients with left-hemisphere disease or control patients without hemispheric lesions.

Recently, Morrow, Urtunski, Kim, and Boller (1981) presented neutral and emotionally loaded stimuli to right- or left-hemisphere-damaged patients. These investigators found that the patients with right-hemisphere disease had reduced galvanic skin responses to both neutral and emotional stimuli. These findings provide further evidence that the indifference reaction is associated with hypoarousal.

Patients with the indifference reaction from right-hemisphere disease typically have unilateral neglect (Denny-Brown *et al.*, 1952; Gainotti, 1972; Heilman & Valenstein, 1972). We have proposed that unilateral neglect is an attention–arousal–activation defect caused by dysfunction in a corticolimbic–reticular loop (Heilman, 1979). Since neglect occurs more often after right-hemisphere lesions, we have also proposed that the right hemisphere may be dominant for mediating an attention–arousal response (Heilman *et al.*, 1978).

Supportive evidence for the importance of the right hemisphere in mediating attention and cerebral activation has been recently documented in our laboratory with normal right-handed adults (Heilman & Van Den Abell, 1979). It is therefore possible that the right hemisphere may have a special role in mediating emotional behavior. Not only can the right hemisphere process affective stimuli and program emotional behavior, but it also appears to have a special relationship to those subcortical structures important for mediating cerebral arousal and activation.

PATHOPHYSIOLOGY UNDERLYING THE DEPRESSIVE REACTION

The mechanisms underlying the depressive reaction have not been elucidated. There are several possibilities. Since patients with left-hemisphere lesions are aware of their deficits (cognitive state) and can become aroused, they might react to their motor and cognitive deficits by becoming depressed. Furthermore, because many patients with left-hemisphere disease are aphasic and have difficulty using propositional language systems mediated in the left hemisphere, they may rely more on right-hemisphere nonpropositional affective systems and therefore more heavily intone their speech and use more facial expressions.

In the study in which we measured arousal by using the galvanic skin response, we found not only that patients with right-hemisphere lesions were hypoaroused (Heilman *et al.*, 1978) but also that our data suggested patients with left-hemisphere disease had an increased arousal response compared with that of normal controls. Trexler and Schmidt (1981) found similar behavior. Morrow *et al.* (1981) did not find hyperarousal in their patients with left-hemisphere disease, but these investigators used different stimuli.

Several authors have proposed that the right hemisphere is more critically involved in processing negative emotions, whereas the left hemisphere processes positive emotions (see Tucker, 1981). The catastrophic reaction would therefore be induced by a left-hemisphere lesion and result in a predominance of right-hemisphere "negative" emotion. This hypothesis that each hemisphere processes different aspects of emotion, however, has not been consistently substantiated (Ley, 1980).

Although many patients with left-hemisphere lesions are depressed, there is intrahemispheric variability. Many patients with posterior perisylvian temporoparietal lesions (e.g., Wernicke and transcortical sensory aphasia) do not appear to be as severely depressed as patients with anterior perisylvian lesions (Benson, 1979). Patients with thalamic aphasia also seem to be less depressed (Alexander & LoVerme, 1980). Patients with posterior neocortical lesions may be less depressed because they have a comprehension defect and are anosognostic for their language disturbance and are not hemiparetic. Patients with thalamic lesions may have a defect in arousal, and similarly patients with posterior neocortical lesions may also have defective arousal. Future systematic studies directed toward comparing the intrahemispheric locus of lesions with the resultant affective changes should provide valuable information about the role of various portions of the cortex in the mediation of affect.

REFERENCES

Alexander, M. P., & LoVerme, S. R. Aphasia after left hemispheric intra-cerebral hemorrhage. *Neurology (NY)*, 1980, *30*, 1193–1202.

Babinski, J. Contribution à l'étude des troubles mentaux dans l'hémi-plégie organique cérébrale (anosognosie). *Revue Neurologique*, 1914, *27*, 845–848.

Bard, P. Emotion: I. The neuro-humoral basis of emotional reactions. In C. Murchison (Ed.), *Handbook of general experimental psychology*. Worcester, Mass.: Clark University Press, 1934.

Benson, D. F. Psychiatric aspects of aphasia. In D. F. Benson (Ed.), *Aphasia, alexia, and agraphia*. New York: Churchill Livingstone, 1979.

Benton, A. L., & Van Allen, M. W. Impairment in facial recognition in patients with cerebral disease. *Cortex*, 1968, *4*, 344–358.

Berent, S. Functional asymmetry of the human brain in the recognition of faces. *Neuropsychologia*, 1977, *15*, 829–831.

Berger, H. Uber das Electroenkephalogramm des Menschen. *Archiv fuer Psychiatrie und Nervenkrankheiten*, 1933, *99*, 555–574.

Boller, F., Cole, M., Urtunski, P. B., Patterson, M., & Kim, Y. Paralin-guistic aspects of auditory comprehension in aphasia. *Brain and Language*, in press.

Bowers, D., & Heilman, K. M. *A dissociation between the processing of affective and nonaffective faces.* Paper presented before the Inter-national Neuropsychological Society, Atlanta, 1981.

Bowers, D., Watson, R. T., & Heilman, K. M. *Verbal affective disconnec-tion.* Manuscript in preparation.

Buck, R., & Duffy, R. J. Nonverbal communication of affect in brain damaged patients. *Cortex*, 1980, *16*, 351–362.

Cannon, W. B. The James–Lange theory of emotion: A critical examina-tion and an alternative theory. *American Journal of Psychology*, 1927, *39*, 106–124.

Cicone, M., Waper, W., & Gardner, H. Sensitivity to emotional expres-sions and situation in organic patients. *Cortex*, 1980, *16*, 145–158.

Critchley, M. *The parietal lobes*. London: E. Arnold, 1953.

DeKosky, S., Heilman, K. M., Bowers, D., & Valenstein, E. Recognition and discrimination of emotional faces and pictures. *Brain and Lan-guage*, 1980, *9*, 206–214.

Denny-Brown, D., Meyer, J. S., & Horenstein, S. The significance of perceptual rivalry resulting from parietal lesions. *Brain*, 1952, *75*, 434–471.

Fehr, F. S., & Stern, J. A. Peripheral psychological variables and emotion: The James–Lange theory revisited. *Psychological Bulletin*, 1970, *74*, 411–424.

French, J. E., Hernandez-Peon, R., & Livingston, R. Projections from the cortex to cephalic brainstem (reticular formation) in monkeys. *Brain*, 1955, *18*, 74–95.

Gainotti, G. Emotional behavior and hemispheric side of lesion. *Cortex*, 1972, *8*, 41–55.

Gardner, H., Ling, P. K., Flam, I., & Silverman, J. Comprehension and appreciation of humorous material following brain damage. *Brain*, 1975, *98*, 399–412.

Gasparrini, W. G., Satz, P., Heilman, K. M., & Coolidge, F. L. Hemispheric asymmetries of affective processing as determined by the Minnesota Multiphasic Personality Inventory. *Journal of Neurology, Neurosurgery and Psychiatry*, 1978, *41*, 470–473.

Goldstein, K. *Language and language disturbances*. New York: Grune & Stratton, 1948.

Graves, R., Landis, T., & Goodglass, H. *Laterality and sex differences for visual recognition of emotional and nonemotional words*. Paper presented before the Academy of Aphasia, Cape Cod, Mass., 1980.

Hécaen, H., Ajuriaguerra, J. de., & Massonet, J. Les troubles visuo-constructifs par lésion pariéto-occipitale droit. *Encephale*, 1951, *40*, 122–179.

Heilman, K. M. Neglect and related syndromes. In K. M. Heilman & E. Valenstein (Eds.), *Clinical neuropsychology*. New York: Oxford University Press, 1979.

Heilman, K. M., Cobb, S., & Rothi, L. J. *Comprehension of affective intonations in global aphasics*. Manuscript in preparation.

Heilman, K. M., Gold, M. S., & Tucker, D. M. Improvement in aphasics' comprehension by use of novel stimuli. *Transactions of the American Neurological Association*, 1975, *100*, 201–202.

Heilman, K. M., Scholes, R., & Watson, R. T. Auditory affective agnosia: Disturbed comprehension of affective speech. *Journal of Neurology, Neurosurgery and Psychiatry*, 1975, *38*, 69–72.

Heilman, K. M., Schwartz, H., & Watson, R. T. Hypoarousal in patients with the neglect syndrome and emotional indifference. *Neurology (Minneapolis)*, 1978, *28*, 229–232.

Heilman, K. M., & Valenstein, E. Frontal lobe neglect. *Neurology (Minneapolis)*, 1978, *22*, 660–664.

Heilman, K. M., & Van Den Abell, T. Right hemispheric dominance for mediating cerebral activation. *Neuropsychologia*, 1979, *17*, 315–321.

Ley, R. G. *Emotion and the right hemisphere*. PhD thesis, University of Florida, 1980.

Lindsley, D. The role of nonspecific reticulo-thalamo-cortical systems in emotion. In P. Black (Ed.), *Physiological correlates of emotion*. New York: Academic, 1970.

Milner, B. Hemispheric specialization: Scope and limits. In F. O. Schmitt & F. G. Worden (Eds.), *The neurosciences: Third study program*. Cambridge, Mass.: MIT Press, 1974.

Morrow, L., Urtunski, P. B., Kim, Y., & Boller, F. Arousal responses to emotional stimuli and laterality of lesion. *Neuropsychologia*, 1981, *19*, 65–72.

Moruzzi, G., & Magoun, H. W. Brainstem reticular formation and activation of the EEG. *Electroencephalography and Clinical Neurophysiology*, 1949, *1*, 455–475.

Papez, J. W. A proposed mechanism of emotion. *Archives of Neurology and Psychiatry*, 1937, *38*, 725–743.

Paul, H. *Principien der Sprachgeschichte* (4th ed.). Niemeyer, 1909.

Poeck, K. Pathophysiology of emotional disorders associated with brain damage. In P. S. Vinken & G. W. Bruyn (Eds.), *Handbook of clinical neurology* (Vol. 13). Amsterdam: North-Holland, 1969.

Ross, E. D. The aprosodias: Functional-anatomic organization of the affective components of language in the right hemisphere. *Archives of Neurology*, 1981, *38*, 561–589.

Ross, E. D., & Mesulam, M. M. Dominant language functions of the right hemisphere? Prosody and emotional gesturing. *Archives of Neurology*, 1979, *36*, 144–148.

Rossi, G. F., & Rosadini, G. Experimental analysis of cerebral dominance in man. In C. H. Millikan & F. L. Darley (Eds.), *Brain mechanisms underlying speech and language*. New York: Grune & Stratton, 1967.

Sackeim, H. A., Greenberg, M. A., Weiman, A. L., Gur, R. C., Hungerbuhler, J. P., & Geschwind, N. Hemispheric asymmetry in the expression of positive and negative emotions. *Archives of Neurology*, 1982, *39*, 210–218.

Schachter, S. The interaction of cognitive and physiological determinants of emotional state. In L. Berkowitz (Ed.), *Advances in experimental social psychology* (Vol. 1). New York: Academic, 1970.

Schlanger, B. B., Schlanger, P., & Gerstmann, L. J. The perception of emotionally toned sentences by right hemisphere-damaged and aphasic subjects. *Brain and Language*, 1976, *3*, 396–403.

Segundo, J. P., Naguet, R., & Buser, P. Effects of cortical stimulation on electrocortical activity in monkeys. *Journal of Neurophysiology*, 1955, *18*, 236–245.

Taylor, J. (Ed.). *Selected writings of John Hughlings Jackson* (Vol. 2). London: Hodder & Stoughton, 1932.

Terzian, H. Behavioral and EEG effects of intracarotid sodium amytal injections. *Acta Neurochirurgica (Vienna)*, 1964, *12*, 230–240.

Trexler, L. E., & Schmidt, N. D. *Autonomic arousal associated with complex affective stimuli in lateralized brain injury*. Paper presented before International Neuropsychological Society, Bergen, Norway, June 30, 1981.

Tucker, D. M. Lateral brain function, emotion, and conceptualization. *Psychological Bulletin*, 1981, *89*, 19–46.

Tucker, D. M., Watson, R. T., & Heilman, K. M. Affective discrimination and evocation in patients with right parietal disease. *Neurology (Minneapolis)*, 1977, *27*, 947–950.

Watson, R. T., Heilman, K. M., Cauthen, J. C., & King, F. A. Neglect
    after cingulectomy. *Neurology (Minneapolis)*, 1973, *23*, 1003–1007.
Wechsler, A. F. The effect of organic brain disease on recall of emo-
    tionally charged versus neutral narrative texts. *Neurology (Minneap-
    olis)*, 1973, *23*, 130–135.

ANIMAL STUDIES
OF LATERALITY

Victor H. Denenberg

INTRODUCTION

This chapter will review animal studies involving lateralization
for emotional behaviors. It will show that the brains of the few
species which have been studied so far are lateralized, and that the
addition of extra experience in early life can enhance already
present laterality or induce lateralization in brains which would
not otherwise have been lateralized. The findings will also be
shown to be congruent with what we know about the nature of
lateralized emotional processes in the human brain, therefore
suggesting that lateralization has a long evolutionary history and
that the lateralized human brain is the end-product of a lengthy
phylogenetic parade.

In discussing the nature of laterality, it is necessary to intro-
duce the concepts of activation and inhibition (Denenberg, 1980).
Activation is brought about by hemispheric specialization. The
word "dominance" is commonly used in the literature when
referring to this process (e.g., the left hemisphere is said to be
dominant for language). Activation pertains to one hemisphere,
independent of what is taking place in the other. Inhibition is our
simplest concept for dealing with relationships between the hemispheres. Inhibition means that one hemisphere is able to either
partially or fully block the action of the other. Although more
constructs than this are needed to explain the workings of the
brain (Denenberg, 1980, 1981), these two will be sufficient for the
material reviewed in this chapter.

Victor H. Denenberg. Departments of Biobehavioral Sciences and Psychology,
University of Connecticut, Storrs, Connecticut.

INDIVIDUAL VERSUS POPULATION ASYMMETRY

Many individual animals, when observed long enough under systematic conditions, have been found to exhibit laterality. For example, mice prefer to use either one or the other of their front paws in a situation in which only one paw can be used to obtain food (Collins, 1977); while individual rats, mice, gerbils, and cats have a preferred direction of rotation, either consistently clockwise or counterclockwise (Glick, Weaver, & Meibach, 1981; Glick, Zimmerberg, & Jerussi, 1977; Jerussi & Glick, 1976).

These findings suggest that an asymmetrical nervous system is favored in nature. A reason for such a bias toward asymmetry is not difficult to find. In order to survive, animals must know their spatial domain, which would include recognizing spatial markers (e.g., to delimit territories) and having spatial memory (e.g., to remember where food was stored). Since the exterior world is chaotic with respect to the left–right dimension, the only way an animal can deal effectively with space is by having internal cues that indicate rightwardness or leftwardness. Thus, in theory, internal asymmetry would provide the appropriate information that would enable an animal to learn and remember key features of its spatial world. (See Corballis & Beale, 1970, and Webster, 1977, for further discussions of this topic.)

Indeed, there are now two experiments consistent with this argument. The first, by Zimmerberg, Strumpf, and Glick (1978), classified animals into two groups based upon their rotational behavior: those who were asymmetrical in terms of having a bias either rightward or leftward and those who showed no asymmetry. These two groups were then compared on the spatial task of learning to escape from electric shock in a T-maze. The asymmetrical animals learned to escape in fewer trials than did those who were not asymmetrical. Furthermore, when retested the next day to see how much of this habit had been retained, the asymmetrical rats had good retention, but those who were symmetrical showed no retention.

The second experiment also classified animals with respect to spatial asymmetry using the measure of bias on rotation (Camp, Therrien, & Robinson, 1981). These researchers first had the rats swim to a platform placed just below the surface of opaque water. Once that skill had been learned, the platform was moved to another position in the tank and the rats had to learn to swim to the new location. After this, their rotational asymmetry was determined. The animals who were asymmetrical were better able to find the platform in its new site than were those who were not asymmetrical.

There is, therefore, good reason to understand why *individual* animals are asymmetrical. However, nothing has been discussed so far which suggests that *populations* may also have a need for asymmetry. Yet we know that there are populations in which the majority of organisms are biased in the same direction. The most obvious example, of course, is the very heavy predominance of right-handedness in human populations. Other examples include left-footedness in parrots (Rogers, 1980) and left-sided control of bird song production (Nottebohm, 1977). Thus, there must be some other reason why populations are systematically asymmetrical. Though the answer is not known, a reasonable speculation is that this asymmetry functions to facilitate interanimal interaction and communication.

If the population is asymmetrical, then it follows that the individuals making up that population are predominantly asymmetrical in one direction. This may be taken as evidence that evolutionary processes were involved, since strong selection pressures must have been at work to compel a particular hemisphere to become specialized in the same manner in more than half the brains in a population. If the population is not skewed, then individual animals may or may not be asymmetrical. If they are, this may or may not reflect an evolutionary process, since the asymmetry of individual animals could be determined by events occurring early in ontogeny as well as by phylogenetic factors. This chapter will deal only with affective behaviors for which there are known population asymmetries on the supposition that these have derived through an evolutionary process and are biologically adaptive to the organism.

EMOTIONAL BEHAVIOR IN ANIMAL POPULATIONS

Strong evidence of population effects for emotional behaviors has been found in chicks and rats.

CHICKS

The newborn chick is a precocial animal, both physically and behaviorally. It is possible to elicit both attack and copulatory behaviors from this animal a few days after hatching. Attack is evoked by holding a hand with the palm facing the chicken, fingers arched over toward the beak, and moving the hand rapidly back and forth. The responses range from an averted gaze to active sparring, pecking, and leaping at the hand. Copulation is measured by placing the hand in a horizontal position with palm facing downward and gently moving it back and forth at chest height. Responses range from ignoring the hand to a full crouch with pecking, tredding, and pelvic thrusting (Howard, Rogers, & Boura, 1980).

Rogers and her colleagues have studied these, and other, behaviors in chicks which have had cycloheximide, an inhibitor of ribosomal protein synthesis, injected into the left or right forebrain on Day 2 of post-hatch life. In comparison with control animals, chicks that received cycloheximide in the left side of the forebrain had an increased likelihood of attacking or copulating (in separate tests) with the experimenter's hand. Those animals that received cycloheximide in the right forebrain did not differ from controls (Howard et al., 1980). Since the suppression or elimination of a hemisphere via cycloheximide caused an increase in these two behaviors, Howard et al. concluded that the left side of the forebrain acted to inhibit the occurrence of attack and copulation, and that the destruction of that side of the brain released the inhibition so the behaviors could be expressed. Thus the brain dynamics appear to be that attack and copulation are under control of the right forebrain, but are actively inhibited by the left side.

Another group in the Howard et al. experiment was one that received testosterone on Day 2 of life. This group also had high attack behavior, similar to that of the group that received cycloheximide in the left forebrain. This raises the possibility that the cycloheximide treatment of the left forebrain released pituitary–gonadal hormones, and this was the cause of the significant increase in attack and copulation. Rogers tested this hypothesis in another experiment (1980a) in which she essentially repeated the experiment described above and then had other groups which received an antiandrogen, cyproterone acetate. The antiandrogen did block the increase in attack behavior seen with testosterone treatment, but it did not have any effect upon the attack scores of chicks with cycloheximide in the left forebrain. Thus there is no androgen involvement related to cycloheximide treatment.

However, testosterone does appear to have an influence upon lateralization, although it is independent of cycloheximide. Rogers (1980a) demonstrated this by injecting testosterone into 2-day-old chicks and later testing them for copulation using the hand-thrust procedure. They were tested both binocularly and monocularly (the visual fibers of the chick crossover completely at the optic chiasm). Animals tested binocularly and those tested with the right eye occluded had very similar copulatory scores, while those whose left eye was occluded had a copulatory score significantly lower than the other two groups. Thus, the chick's forebrain is asymmetrical with respect to the influence of testosterone: The right hemisphere is far more sensitive to this hormone than the left.

Although Rogers used drug treatments in all her studies, it is not necessary to do so to demonstrate a laterality bias for emotional behavior in the chick. Andrew, Mench, and Rainey (1982) showed this by presenting to the bird a stimulus known to evoke marked escape behavior (a brightly colored toy ladder standing against the cage wall). Chicks were placed into the arena so that they were equally likely to fixate the ladder with their right eye or their left. Those birds which fixated initially with the left eye gave peep calls, which are indicative of a frightening or painful situation, while those who initially fixated with the right eye did not give the peep call. Thus, the right hemisphere appears to be dominant for this form of emotional fear behavior.

In summary, the cycloheximide experiments of Rogers demonstrate that in the very young chick copulation and attack behaviors are activated by the right hemisphere while the left acts to suppress these behaviors. Independent of this, a testosterone injection sensitizes the right hemisphere so that it becomes dominant for copulatory behavior. The study of Andrew et al. adds to this by showing that fear is elicited by stimulating the right forebrain, and that it is not necessary to use drugs or hormones to reveal that the chick's brain is lateralized for emotional behaviors.

RATS

Robinson (1979) made localized lesions in the two hemispheres by ligating the right or left middle cerebral artery and then tested them in an open field. The field is a large arena, often square but sometimes round, in which an animal's activity is observed. Previous research has found that high activity scores are associated with increased exploratory behavior and decreased emotional reactivity. In addition, those who have high activity scores have a lower adrenocortical response (Denenberg, 1969b). Robinson started testing his animals immediately after surgery and found that those who had received a sham operation or an infarct in the left hemisphere maintained a low level of constant activity throughout the testing. In contrast, the right-infarct group started with low activity which increased sharply by the 12th day after surgery and then began to decline, returning to baseline by 17 days postsurgery. These findings may be interpreted as indicating that the open-field activity was under control of the left hemisphere with the right side of the brain acting in an inhibitory capacity.

Using a very different paradigm—taste aversion—Denenberg, Hofmann, Garbanati, Sherman, Rosen, and Yutzey (1980) also found evidence for brain laterality of emotional behavior in the rat. This finding was part of a larger and more complex picture involving the effects of early experience upon brain laterality, and a discussion of this experiment will be presented in the next section of this review.

EARLY EXPERIENCES AND BRAIN LATERALITY
FOR EMOTIONAL BEHAVIORS

The studies described above all used "standard" animals reared under usual laboratory conditions. There has been another series of studies in which the early experiences of rats have been varied during the preweaning and/or postweaning interval, and the effects of these manipulations upon later brain laterality have been investigated (for a detailed review of these, see Denenberg, 1981).

Research findings indicate that the addition of extra stimulation in early life acts to facilitate already present laterality differences, or will induce laterality under conditions where it is not normally found.

HANDLING AND ENVIRONMENTAL ENRICHMENT

The two procedures used thus far in these studies involve handling, which is done between birth and weaning, and environmental enrichment, which occurs at the time of weaning. At birth the newborn litter is removed from the nest, sexed, and culled to eight pups. The pups in the nonhandled treatment are then returned to the maternity cage and are not disturbed thereafter until they are weaned at 21 days. If pups are to be handled, they are put singly into 1-gallon cans containing shavings, left there for 3 minutes, and then returned to the maternity cage. This procedure is repeated daily from Day 1 through Day 20 of life (Denenberg, 1977). Handling has a wide variety of effects upon the offspring, involving behavioral, physiological, biochemical, and morphological parameters. A general conclusion is that handling makes the rat less emotional and more exploratory and that it modifies the hypothalamic–pituitary–adrenal axis. For reviews of this material see Denenberg (1969a, 1975, 1981), Denenberg and Zarrow (1971), Levine and Mullins (1966), and Newton and Levine (1968).

When weaned, the pups are placed either into standard laboratory cages or into the experimental condition called the enriched environment. This is a large cage containing food, water, a shelf about halfway up the back wall for the animals to climb upon, and a variety of playthings (Rosenzweig, Bennett, & Diamond, 1972). Typically, 12 animals will be placed in this unit starting at 21 days, and kept there until 50 days of age when they are removed and placed into standard laboratory cages. It has been found that animals reared in such an environment are superior in problem-solving and perceptual tasks; they also show differences in the weight, thickness, and chemistry of their brains (Bennett, 1976; Greenough, 1976; Hebb, 1949; Rosenzweig, 1971; Rosenzweig *et al.*, 1972). We have also found that exposure to this environment reduces the rat's emotional reactivity (Denenberg, 1969a).

OPEN-FIELD ACTIVITY

In our first study we tested the hypothesis that the effects of early experiences are asymmetrically distributed between the two hemispheres (Denenberg, Garbanati, Sherman, Yutzey, & Kaplan, 1978). A number of litters were handled during the infancy period while others were left undisturbed. At weaning these litters were split, half going into laboratory cages and the other half into enriched environments. When 50 days old, all animals were placed into laboratory cages and left undisturbed until adulthood. At that time four males from each litter were randomly assigned to one of four surgical procedures: a left or right neocortical ablation, sham surgery, or no surgery. After recovering, they were tested for 4 days in an open field. In this and subsequent studies the shams and nonoperated animals did not differ and their data were pooled to yield a single intact control group.

The mean activity scores are shown in Table 1. For those animals not handled in infancy, removing a neocortex increased activity, but there were no left–right laterality differences, regardless of the nature of the postweaning environment. However, laterality differences were found within the handled groups. For those who went into laboratory cages after handling, greatest activity was found in animals with an intact left hemisphere. Since this higher activity was not seen in those with an intact brain, we infer that under these rearing conditions activity is controlled by the left hemisphere, but is inhibited by the right side of the brain. The situation is rather different for the group handled in infancy followed by an enriched experience afterwards: There the group with an intact right hemisphere was more active than the one with an intact left hemisphere. Since the same level of activity was seen in the intact-brain group, we conclude that there is right-hemispheric dominance for this combination of rearing conditions.

TASTE AVERSION

As indicated above, the open-field test measures two behavioral dimensions, exploration and emotional reactivity. Therefore, it is difficult to make a theoretical interpretation of the previous find-

TABLE 1. *Summary of experimental findings relating early experiences and brain laterality*

Dependent variable[a]	Independent variables		Intact controls	Right brain intact	Left brain intact
	Days 1–20	Days 21–50			
Open-field activity	Nonhandled	Laboratory cage	8.90[b]	27.64	22.33
	Nonhandled	Enriched environment	9.91[b]	27.08	32.89
	Handled	Laboratory cage	12.51	17.91	36.27[b]
	Handled	Enriched environment	17.52	20.42	3.00[b]
Taste aversion: saline	Nonhandled		28.0	24.3[b]	26.1
	Handled		27.0	22.0[b]	30.5
Taste aversion: lithium	Nonhandled		23.9	23.7	23.8
	Handled		28.7[c]	21.7[c]	25.6[c]
Muricide	Nonhandled	Laboratory cage	96.0[b]	75.0	68.8
	Nonhandled	Enriched environment	79.4	73.7	94.7
	Handled	Laboratory cage	78.0	94.6[b]	67.6
	Handled	Enriched environment	62.9	61.1	57.1

[a]Measurement units: activity—number of squares entered; taste aversion—milliliters of milk ingested; muricide—percentage of animals that killed.
[b]Differs significantly from other values in that row.
[c]All differences are significant.

ings. For that reason, we selected taste aversion as an end-point, since that is an excellent measure of a conditioned aversive response (Garcia, Hankin, & Rusiniak, 1974). In the taste-aversion paradigm, animals associate the taste of a novel food substance with later gastric disturbance. The consequence is that when the novel food is presented on subsequent occasions, either the animals will not eat it or they will taste very small amounts because of the prior association with the stomach upset.

Animals that had been handled or nonhandled in infancy were given, as adults, a sweetened milk solution. After the second day of exposure, they were given an injection of either lithium chloride, which induces a severe gastric disturbance, or physiological saline as a control for the injection. Brain surgery was done 25 days later. Animals had either the right or left neocortex removed, received sham surgery, or were not disturbed. Four weeks later we tested for retention of the taste aversion by presenting the bottle of milk daily for a half-hour and recording the amount consumed over a 13-day interval (Denenberg et al., 1980). Table 1 shows the mean amount of milk consumed during the last 6 days of testing.

Within the saline treatment, there was one significant difference: The groups with the intact right brain consumed less milk than the other groups, regardless of their early experiences. This is the finding referred to in the section above which shows that standard laboratory rats have brains which are lateralized for affective conditioning. The conclusion drawn from this finding is that the right hemisphere is sufficiently sensitive that the injection of saline and the subsequent stomach loading act as unconditioned stimuli and become associated with the ingestion of milk. Since the other groups given the saline injection did not differ, this indicates that the learned fear of the right hemisphere is not expressed in the presence of the left, thereby suggesting that the latter inhibits the former.

A different configuration of findings is seen when we examine the lithium data. There were no differences within the nonhandled treatment. In sharp contrast to this, all differences among the three handled groups were significant.

Note that the average amount consumed by the three non-handled groups given lithium (23.8 ml) does not differ from the amount consumed by nonhandled animals with an intact right brain given saline (24.3 ml). Thus the more powerful lithium treatment could do no more than the simple saline injection in terms of attenuating the extinction of the fear response. In contrast to this, within the handled groups the amount consumed by those with an intact left hemisphere (25.6 ml) and those with intact brains (28.7 ml) is significantly greater than the amount consumed by those with only an intact right hemisphere (21.7 ml). This leads to the conclusion that the effects of handling appear to be acting upon the rat's left hemisphere to reduce its level of emotional reactivity. Since, in the intact handled group, the amount consumed was greater than that of either hemisphere singly, we conclude that each hemisphere acted to inhibit the fear response of the other one. One may speculate as to whether this could be used as a possible model for repression.

MURICIDE

Taste aversion measures emotional behavior by using a conditioning procedure. In order to study a nonlearned emotional behavior we selected muricide, or mouse killing. This is a spontaneous species-specific act that is not dependent upon food deprivation for its occurrence. There were four major groups in the experiment: animals that were handled or not handled in infancy, which were then split with half going into enriched environments at weaning while the others went into laboratory cages. When mature, some had the left or right hemisphere removed while others received sham surgery or no operation. The test for mouse killing was done by placing a single mouse into a cage containing an isolated rat and allowing them to remain together for a maximum of 5 days. The incidence of muricide during that interval is summarized in Table 1 (Garbanati, Sherman, Rosen, Hofmann, Yutzey, & Denenberg, 1983). The brain surgery reduced the killing incidence for nonhandled animals reared in laboratory cages (96.0% vs. 75.0% and 68.8%). These findings suggest that the two hemispheres interact to facilitate killing in the intact-brain group. The differences among the nonhandled enriched environment animals, although they appear large, were found not to be significant. However, within the handled laboratory cage group the differences are significant with those animals having only a right hemisphere killing significantly more than the other two groups, who do not differ between themselves. There were no differences found among the three groups in the handled enriched condition.

Here again we see that handling acts to lateralize the brain. For the handled–laboratory cage condition the handling experience acted to shift predominant control of mouse killing to the right hemisphere. Since the other two groups both had lower killing percentages than the right-intact group, it may be inferred that, in the intact handled animal, the left hemisphere acts to inhibit the killing response of the right hemisphere.

GENERALIZATIONS AND CONCLUSIONS

Table 2 is a summary of the studies described above. There are several important generalizations which may be derived from this table. The first is that brain laterality is not uniquely associated with the human species. Although only the rat and the chick are represented in Table 2, it is clear that there have been sufficient experiments to state that in these species the brain is lateralized for emotional behaviors. Other research with songbirds (Nottebohm, 1970, 1977), nonhuman primates (Dewson, 1977, 1979; Petersen, Beecher, Zoloth, Moody, & Stebbins, 1978), and chicks (Andrew et al., 1982; Rogers, 1980; Rogers & Anson, 1978) have also shown population effects for lateralization of communicative and cognitive functions. Thus, the old belief that laterality, handedness, and speech arose de novo with the advent of the human species may be laid to rest in the graveyard of erroneous scientific concepts. Instead, it is necessary to view brain laterality from an evolutionary perspective, and to be keenly aware that each hemisphere may have its own evolutionary history and in different time periods. In this regard Darwin (1872/1965), in his discussion of emotions in man and animals, drew the interesting conclusion that "the progenitors of man probably uttered musical tones before they had acquired the power of articulate speech; and that consequently, when the voice is used under any strong emotion, it

TABLE 2. *Summary of behavioral laterality effects*

Brain dynamics	"Standard" animal	With added early experience	Ref.
RH activation	Peeps by chicks when viewing stimulus evoking escape behavior		Andrew, Mench, & Rainey (1980)
	Copulatory response in chicks after testosterone injection		Rogers (1980b)
		Greater open-field activity for rats receiving handling and enrichment in early life	Denenberg, Garbanti, Sherman, Yutzey, & Kaplan (1978)
LH activation with RH inhibition	Open-field activity of rats with RH infarct (temporary effect)		Robinson (1979)
		Open-field activity of rats handled in infancy	Denenberg, Garbanti, Sherman, Yutzey, & Kaplan (1978)
		Taste aversion associated with lithium injection for rats handled in infancy	Denenberg, Hofman, Garbanti, Sherman, Rosen, & Yutzey (1980)
RH activation with LH inhibition	Taste aversion associated with saline injection for rats	Taste aversion associated with saline injection for rats handled in infancy	Denenberg, Hofman, Garbanti, Sherman, Rosen, & Yutzey (1980)
		Taste aversion associated with lithium injection for rats handled in infancy	Denenberg, Hofman, Garbanti, Sherman, Rosen, & Yutzey (1980)
	Attack and copulation in chicks		Howard, Rogers, & Boura (1980)
		Mouse killing by rats handled in infancy	Garbanati, Sherman, Rosen, Hofman, Yutzey, & Denenberg (1983)

tends to assume, through the principle of association, a musical character" (p. 87). This linkage of music and emotions is note-worthy because both sets of processes are generally found to be associated with the right hemisphere (see Chapters 1 and 2, this volume). Thus, it follows from Darwin's reasoning that the right hemisphere developed earlier in evolution than the left. Interest-ingly, both Denenberg (1981) and Corballis (1981) have arrived at a similar conclusion, though for different reasons.

The second generalization that comes from Table 2 is that, like the human, the right hemisphere is more involved with emotional behaviors than the left. A general conclusion drawn from the human literature is that damage to the left hemisphere is associated with "strong" emotional responses involving catas-trophic responses or depressive reactions, while the pattern asso-ciated with right-hemisphere damage is much "milder" in nature and has been called an indifference reaction (Gainotti, 1972; Perria, Rosadini, & Rossi, 1961; Rossi & Rosadini, 1967). The data in Table 2 also indicate that strong emotional responses are associated with the right hemisphere (copulation, attack, taste aversion, muricide) while the more mild response of activity in the open field is associated with left-hemisphere activation in combination with right-hemisphere inhibition. The one exception to this con-clusion is that one of the groups in the taste-aversion experiment (handled, lithium treatment, right neocortex ablated) had a brain pattern involving left-hemisphere activation with right-hemisphere inhibition. However, even this group gave a milder reaction than its companion group (handled, lithium treatment, left neocortex ablated) which showed right-hemisphere activation with left-hemisphere inhibition.

The third generalization does not follow directly from Table 2, but is implied by the data listed therein. Note that there is no listing in that table for any finding in which there is left-hemi-sphere activation of an affective process. Yet there are a number of studies involving songbirds, chicks, and monkeys showing that communicative and cognitive processes are associated with activa-tion of the left hemisphere (reviewed in Denenberg, 1981). These observations lead to the conclusion that the brains of animals, if lateralized, will show the same forms of asymmetry as are found in the human brain. That is, the left hemisphere will be primarily involved in communicative and cognitive functions, while the right will be selectively set to respond to spatial and affective information, and both hemispheres will often interact via activation–inhibition mechanisms when affective or emotional processes are involved (Denenberg, 1981).

The final generalization to be drawn from Table 2 is that the brains of rats receiving extra stimulation in early life are more lateralized than the brains of controls. This additional lateralization involves emotional behaviors, of course, and a subset of these findings is that handling, by itself (i.e., without environmental enrichment), acts to reduce the emotional reactivity of the left hemisphere. This was found in the open-field test where handled animals with an intact left hemisphere were more active (36.27 squares) than littermates with only an intact right hemisphere (17.91 squares); in the taste-aversion study where those with a single left hemisphere consumed more milk (i.e., were less fearful) than rats with a single intact right hemisphere (25.6 and 21.7 ml of milk, respectively); and in the investigation of mouse killing where handled animals with an intact left hemisphere had a lower incidence of killing (67.6%) than those with only an intact right hemisphere (94.6%).

The reason why early stimulation makes for a more lateralized brain is not known. However, I have hypothesized "that stimulation in early life acts to enhance the growth and development of the corpus callosum, just as stimulation of sensory systems leads to their growth and development" (Denenberg, 1981, p. 20). I have further argued that the full development of the corpus callosum will result in lateralized brain functions unless one or the other hemisphere is damaged. (Since there is not space to discuss this hypothesis now, the reader is referred to the original article for further details.)

A note of caution needs to be inserted here. The four generalizations listed above have different degrees of certainty associated with each. The first, that animals have lateralized brains, appears quite definite. The others are based upon a relatively narrow data set and should be viewed as hypotheses which are in need of further testing.

THE RECIPROCAL INTERACTION
OF ANIMAL AND HUMAN STUDIES

Animal and human studies of brain laterality reciprocally facilitate each other. For example, the extensive amount of information
we have about the emotional nature of the human brain has aided
considerably in interpreting the findings from the animal studies.
The other side of the coin is that in finding that animals also have
lateralized brains, human researchers are thus compelled to incor-
porate biological and evolutionary principles into their theorizing.

Another area in which findings at different levels are mutually
facilitative is in suggesting new experiments. A case in point has
to do with two sets of human studies concerned with affect and
communication. In one of these Heilman, Scholes, and Watson
(1975) reported that a lesion in the right hemisphere in a region
homologous to Wernicke's area resulted in the inability to comprehend the affective components of language, though the ability
to understand the propositional meaning was not impaired. The
comparison set of findings is that of Ross and Mesulam (1979) in
which two patients, both of whom had lesions in their right
hemisphere in the area homologous to Broca's area, were able to
use propositional speech, although neither had the ability to
impart affective qualities to their speech nor could they use their
limbs, face, or body movements to convey emotions and affect.
Since the vast majority of our statements involve both information
and affect, it is obvious that it is necessary for two sets of homologous brain regions, connected via the corpus callosum, to be
activated. If these findings indeed reflect a general principle, then
our older notion of simple dominance control residing in one
hemisphere independent of the activity of the other hemisphere
will have to be discarded.

The concept of reciprocal interactions of homologous brain
areas can be tested using animals (the monkey and songbird
would be two ideal species) to see whether lesions in the right
hemisphere homologous to the communication area in the left
side would impair the ability to receive and comprehend messages
or to transmit messages to a conspecific. Indeed, there are data
suggesting that this might be the case. In the canary the highest
control station in the brain is called the hyperstriatum ventrale,

pars caudale (HVc). Nottebohm (1970, 1977) has shown that a lesion of the left HVc has a marked effect upon song production, while a lesion to the right HVc has a much smaller effect. Thus, the right side appears to make some contribution to singing, but much less than the left side. This is the basis for the conclusion that there is left dominance for this behavior (Nottebohm, 1977). More recently McCasland and Konishi (1981) have confirmed part of Nottebohm's work by obtaining neuronal recordings from the brains of three species of singing birds. They found electrical activity in the HVc area when birds sang or heard bird calls, while there was no change in activity from electrodes implanted in areas outside of HVc. However, they also found that there was essentially equal activity from the left and right HVc to vocalization. They state that these data eliminate any idea of a simple use–disuse mechanism of dominance at the level of HVc. Although they are correct in their conclusion, their data, as well as Nottebohm's, are compatible with the suggestion made above that the homologous brain regions interact reciprocally.

It is clear from this review that the study of laterality in experimental animals will aid enormously in our understanding of laterality of functions in the human. Experiments which cannot be performed on humans can be carried out with animals, and there is every reason to expect that the finding of behavioral lateralization in animals will open a new era in our understanding of human lateralization.

REFERENCES

Andrew, R. M., Mench, J., & Rainey, C. Right–left asymmetry of response to visual stimuli in the domestic chick. In D. J. Ingle, R. J. W. Mansfield, & M. A. Goodale (Eds.), *Analysis of visual behavior.* Cambridge, Mass.: MIT Press, 1982.

Bennett, E. L. Cerebral effects of differential experience and training. In M. R. Rosenzweig & E. L. Bennett (Eds.), *Neural mechanisms of learning and memory.* Cambridge, Mass.: MIT Press, 1976.

Camp, D. M., Therrien, B. A., & Robinson, T. E. Spatial learning ability is related to an endogenous asymmetry in the nigrostriatal dopamine system in rats. *Society for Neuroscience Abstracts*, 1981, 7, 455.

Collins, R. L. Toward an admissible genetic model for the inheritance of the degree and direction of asymmetry. In S. Harnad, R. W. Doty, L. Goldstein, J. Jaynes, & G. Krauthamer (Eds.), *Lateralization in the nervous system*. New York: Academic, 1977.

Corballis, M. C. On the evolution and growth of lateralization. *Behavioral and Brain Sciences*, 1981, *4*, 24.

Corballis, M. C., & Beale, L. L. Bilateral asymmetry and behavior. *Psychological Review*, 1970, 77, 451–464.

Darwin, C. *The expression of emotions in man and animals*. Chicago: University of Chicago Press, 1965. (Originally published, 1872.)

Denenberg, V. H. The effects of early experience. In E. S. E. Hafex (Ed.), *The behaviour of domestic animals*. London: Bailliere, Tindall & Cassell, 1969. (a)

Denenberg, V. H. Open-field behavior in the rat: What does it mean? *Annals of the New York Academy of Sciences*, 1969, *159*, 852–859. (b)

Denenberg, V. H. Effects of exposure to stressors in early life upon later behavioural and biological processes. In L. Levi (Ed.), *Society, stress and disease: Childhood and adolescence* (Vol. 2). New York: Oxford University Press, 1975.

Denenberg, V. H. Assessing the effects of early experience. In R. D. Myers (Ed.), *Methods in psychobiology* (Vol. 3). New York: Academic, 1977.

Denenberg, V. H. General systems theory, brain organization, and early experiences. *American Journal of Physiology: Regulatory, Integrative and Comparative Physiology*, 1980, *238S*, R3–R13; or *American Journal of Physiology: Regulatory, Integrative and Comparative Physiology*, 1980, 7, R3–R13.

Denenberg, V. H. Hemispheric laterality in animals and the effects of early experience. *Behavioral and Brain Sciences*, 1981, *4*, 1–49.

Denenberg, V. H., Garbanati, J., Sherman, G., Yutzey, D. A., & Kaplan, R. Infantile stimulation induces brain lateralization in rats. *Science*, 1978, *201*, 1150–1152.

Denenberg, V. H., Hofmann, M., Garbanati, J. A., Sherman, G. F., Rosen, G. D., & Yutzey, D. A. Handling in infancy, taste aversion, and brain laterality in rats. *Brain Research*, 1980, *200*, 123–133.

Denenberg, V. H., & Zarrow, M. X. Effects of handling in infancy upon adult behavior and adrenocortical activity: Suggestions for a neuroendocrine mechanism. In D. N. Walcher & D. L. Peters (Eds.), *Early childhood: The development of self-regulatory mechanisms*. New York: Academic, 1971.

Dewson, J. H. Preliminary evidence of hemispheric asymmetry of auditory function in monkeys. In S. Harnad, R. W. Doty, L. Goldstein, J. Jaynes, & G. Krauthamer (Eds.), *Lateralization in the nervous system*. New York: Academic, 1977.

Dewson, J. H. Toward an animal model of auditory cognitive function. In C. L. Ludlow & M. E. Doran-Quine (Eds.), *The neurological bases of language disorders in children: Methods and directions for research* (NINCDS Monograph No. 22). Washington, D.C.: U.S. Government Printing Office, 1979.

Gainotti, G. Emotional behavior and hemispheric side of the lesion. *Cortex*, 1972, *8*, 41–55.

Garbanati, J. A., Sherman, G. F., Rosen, G. D., Hofmann, M., Yutzey, D. A., & Denenberg, V. H. Handling in infancy, brain laterality, and muricide in rats. *Behavioural Brain Research*, 1983, in press.

Garcia, J., Hankin, W. G., & Rusiniak, K. Behavioral regulation of the milieu interne in man and rat. *Science*, 1974, *185*, 227–229.

Glick, S. D., Weaver, L. M., & Miebach, R. C. Amphetamine-induced rotation in normal cats. *Brain Research*, 1981, *208*, 227–229.

Glick, S. D., Zimmerberg, B., & Jerussi, T. P. Adaptive significance of laterality in the rodent. *Annals of the New York Academy of Sciences*, 1977, *299*, 180–185.

Greenough, W. Enduring brain effects of differential experience and training. In M. R. Rosenzweig & E. L. Bennett (Eds.), *Neural mechanisms of learning and memory*. Cambridge, Mass.: MIT Press, 1976.

Hebb, D. O. *The organization of behavior*. New York: Wiley, 1949.

Heilman, K. M., Scholes, R., & Watson, R. T. Auditory affective agnosia. *Journal of Neurology, Neurosurgery and Psychiatry*, 1975, *38*, 9–72.

Howard, K. J., Rogers, L. J., & Boura, A. L. A. Functional lateralization of the chicken forebrain revealed by use of intracranial glutamate. *Brain Research*, 1980, *188*, 369–382.

Jerussi, T. P., & Glick, S. D. Spontaneous and drug-induced rotation (circling behavior) in the Mongolian gerbil (*Meriones unguiculatus*). *Behavioral Biology*, 1976, *16*, 241–244.

Levine, S., & Mullins, R. F., Jr. Hormonal influence on brain organization in infant rats. *Science*, 1966, *152*, 1585–1592.

McCasland, J., & Konishi, M. Central control of avian vocalization: Neuronal recordings from singing birds. *Society of Neuroscience Abstracts*, 1981, *7*, 188.

Newton, G., & Levine, S. (Eds.). *Early experience and behavior*. Springfield, Ill.: Charles C Thomas, 1968.

Nottebohm, F. Ontogeny of bird song. *Science*, 1970, *167*, 950–956.

Nottebohm, F. Asymmetries in neural control of vocalization in the canary. In S. Harnad, R. W. Doty, L. Goldstein, J. Jaynes, & G. Krauthamer (Eds.), *Lateralization in the nervous system*. New York: Academic, 1977.

Perria, L., Rosadini, G., & Rossi, G. F. Determination of side of cerebral dominance with amobarbital. *Archives of Neurology*, 1961, *4*, 173–181.

Petersen, M. R., Beecher, M. D., Zoloth, S. R., Moody, D. B., & Stebbins, W. C. Neural lateralization of species-specific vocalizations by Japanese macaques (*Macaca fuscata*). *Science*, 1978, *202*, 324–327.

Robinson, R. G. Differential behavior and biochemical effects of right and left hemispheric cerebral infarction in the rat. *Science*, 1979, *205*, 707–710.

Rogers, L. J. *Hemispheric specialization in chickens: For attack, copulation, attention switching and hormone control.* Unpublished manuscript, 1980. (a)

Rogers, L. J. Lateralization in the avian brain. *Bird Behaviour*, 1980, *2*, 1–12. (b)

Rogers, L. J. Functional lateralization in the chicken fore-brain revealed by cyclohexamide treatment. *Acta XVII Congress International Ornithology*, 1980, *1*, 653–659.

Rogers, L. J., & Anson, J. M. Cyclohexamide produces attentional persistence and slowed learning in chickens. *Pharmacology, Biochemistry and Behavior*, 1978, *9*, 735–740.

Rosenzweig, M. R. Effects of environment on development of brain and behavior. In E. Tobach, L. R. Aronson, & E. Shaw (Eds.), *The biopsychology of development*. New York: Academic, 1971.

Rosenzweig, M. R., Bennett, E. L., & Diamond, M. C. Brain changes in response to experience. *Scientific American*, 1972, *226*, 22–29.

Ross, E. D., & Mesulam, M. M. Dominant language functions of the right hemisphere. *Archives of Neurology*, 1979, *36*, 144–148.

Rossi, G. F., & Rosadini, G. Experimental analysis of cerebral dominance in man. In C. H. Millikan & F. L. Darley (Eds.), *Brain mechanisms underlying speech and language*. New York: Grune & Stratton, 1967.

Webster, W. G. Territoriality and the evolution of brain asymmetry. In S. J. Dimond & D. A. Blizard (Eds.), *Evolution and lateralization of the brain*. New York: New York Academy of Sciences, 1977.

Zimmerberg, S., Strumpf, A. J., & Glick, S. D. Cerebral asymmetry and left–right discrimination. *Brain Research*, 1978, *140*, 194–196.

CHAPTER

4

EMOTIONAL DISTURBANCES ASSOCIATED WITH FOCAL LESIONS OF THE LIMBIC FRONTAL LOBE

Antonio R. Damasio
G. W. Van Hoesen

The demonstration that some anatomical structures of the frontal lobe are related, in some way, to the control of affect and emotion was made by Egas Moniz when he reported the first results of prefrontal leukotomy (Moniz, 1936, 1937). In his patients, who had either schizophrenic psychosis or severe obsessive neurosis, there was a remarkable improvement of anxiety after surgery, even in those in whom specific symptoms had remained unchanged by the procedure. The link between the frontal lobe and emotional behavior could no longer be doubted. Later, as the notion of the limbic system evolved—a system with a crucial role to play in the control of emotion and affect—it became clear that a large sector of the frontal lobe cortex comprised structures of the limbic system and that, consequently, white matter connections serving those limbic cortices constituted a large sector of the frontal lobe.

Moniz's procedure boldly broke away from tradition and his observations constitute a landmark in the history of brain–behavior relationships. Leukotomy would fetch him the 1949 Nobel Prize, and leave unrecognized his other major contribution —cerebral angiography. But the discovery of leukotomy was pre-

Antonio R. Damasio. Department of Neurology, Division of Behavioral Neurology, University of Iowa College of Medicine, Iowa City, Iowa.
G. W. Van Hoesen. Departments of Anatomy and Neurology, University of Iowa College of Medicine, Iowa City, Iowa.

ceded by some important observations of which Moniz was keenly aware. A patient named Phineas Gage, of the famous "crowbar case," had accidentally injured his frontal lobes and, as a result, exhibited major personality changes. In the words of Harlow, his biographer, "he was no longer Gage." By the time Gage had traveled from New England to California, to die in careless dissipation, there could be little doubt that affect and emotion, more than any other aspect of his behavior, had been modified by his accidental "surgery." The link between the frontal lobe and emotion was further established by the experience of Brickner's patient A (Brickner 1934, 1936). That young man was operated on by Walter Dandy, in order to remove a large frontal meningioma. As a result of the damage produced by the rapidly developing tumor, both frontal lobes had to be ablated extensively—the ablation comprehended mesial, lateral, and orbital frontal cortices and white matter, as far back as the premotor regions, which were spared. Where before the operation there had been discipline, rigid adherence to schedule, concern for completeness of tasks, and, in general, appropriate social inhibition and reserve, there was suddenly, in the postoperative period, a relaxed, boastful, socially uninhibited attitude. Patient A was no longer concerned with his profession, with the planning of a purposeful daily routine, let alone with the design of his future. Yet, his fundamental intellectual ability appeared mostly intact not to mention his perfectly preserved motor, perceptual, and language systems. Moniz cites Brickner's description, and it is possible that the personality changes in patient A provided the major impetus to proceed with the daring prefrontal leukotomy project. But probably no less important was the description of the experimental counterpart, as it were, of Brickner's patient. That became available in Jacobsen's report of two-stage frontal lobe ablations in chimpanzees (Jacobsen, 1935). Following the second ablation, which rendered the intervention bilateral, the traditional nastiness and fussiness of chimpanzees Becky and Lucy had given way to a most gratifying pleasant behavior. The animals could no longer be frustrated, or if they were, they appeared not to care. At the same time their problem-solving ability seemed intact.

More than four decades after these pathbreaking discoveries, the link between frontal lobe structures and emotion, in human and nonhuman primates, is undeniable. Other cortical structures (i.e., the mesial and anterior temporal cortex) and a variety of subcortical structures (i.e., the amygdala, septum, and, naturally, the hypothalamus) have since been associated with emotion and affect. But all of those cortical and subcortical regions are inter-associated in an intricate pattern. They are components of the limbic system. But before we discuss the effects of either focal damage or electrical stimulation of the frontal limbic areas, we will present our current views on the concept of the limbic system and on its structure and function.

STRUCTURE AND FUNCTION OF THE LIMBIC SYSTEM

Dating back to Papez's seminal report (1937) and MacLean's reformulation of it (1949), emotion and affect have been strongly linked to a diverse group of brain structures known collectively as the limbic system. They comprise the so-called "older" cortices that form the medial-most edge of the cerebral hemisphere as well as the subcortical telencephalic areas that partially surround the deep gray matter masses of the basal ganglia. In the three decades that have elapsed since MacLean coined the term "limbic system," it has become clear that multiple complex functions are subserved by key elements of the limbic system. Many of those, such as memory and attention, do not fit that well under the general rubric of emotion. It also appears likely that brain areas which lie outside the most liberal structural definitions of the limbic system have a decisive role to play in affect and emotion. Combined with enduring anatomical arguments over the validity and heuristic value of the limbic system concept (Brodal, 1981), it is somewhat surprising that such opinions have not obliterated that battered term. But although the concept lives on (e.g., in a recent volume, Livingston & Hornykiewicz, 1978, use the bold title *Limbic Mechanisms: The Continuing Evolution of the Limbic System Concept*), there is little evidence to secure the term as a viable part of the neuroscientific lexicon.

Our aim here is not to take sides but to look critically both at new anatomical facts regarding the limbic system as well as at new behavioral observations bearing on this topic. Such an approach has always been a productive strategy with roots well entrenched in the brain sciences.

The cortical structures of the limbic system are well demarcated on the medial surface of the hemisphere by the cingulate sulcus dorsally and the collateral and orbital sulci ventrally. Bridging areas such as the subcallosal gyrus, the posterior orbitofrontal, anterior insular, temporal polar, and perirhinal cortices connect the cingulate and parahippocampal gyri rostrally, while the retrosplenial and retrocalcarine cortices provide a bridge caudally (Figures 1 A and B and 2B).

These areas differ widely in their cytoarchitecture and include Brodmann's areas 23, 24, 25, 27, 28, 29, 35, 36, and 38. None are true isocortical areas, but fall instead into the categories of peri-allocortex and proisocortex of Sanides's (1969) terminology, or the combined mesocortices of Filimonoff's (1947) nomenclature. In short, they are intermediate in structure between the allocortices and the isocortices.

The subcortical structures included in the limbic system vary widely among authors. However, it seems appropriate to include the amygdala, septum, substantia innominata, anterior thalamus, habenula, interpeduncular nucleus, and some additional midbrain areas (Figure 3A). A structural criterion used in justifying this classification centers on the fact that these areas are connected among themselves as well as with the hypothalamus. Additionally, as will be discussed later, many of these nuclei receive direct cortical projections from one or more parts of the limbic lobe.

The final constituents of the limbic system are the interconnecting pathways within the limbic lobe, those that connect limbic lobe areas with subcortical limbic structures, those that connect subcortical limbic structures, and lastly, those that connect elements of the limbic system to the hypothalamus (Figure 3B). These include such pathways as the cingulum, uncinate fasciculus, fimbria-fornix, stria terminalis, ventral amygdalofugal pathway, mammillothalamic tract, mammillotegmental tract, stria medullaris, and habenulointerpeduncular pathway. The medial forebrain bundle, not included in Figure 3B, should be included in this list.

Historically, it has been commonplace to view the limbic system concept in the context of hypothalamic function. There is

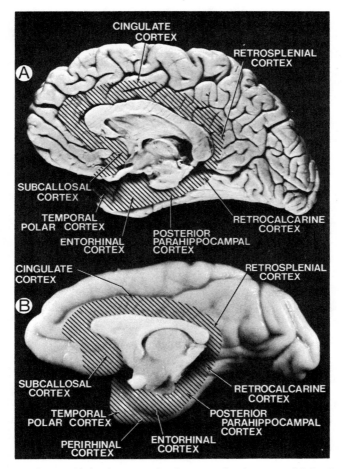

FIGURE 1. (A) *Medial view of the human brain on which the major components of the limbic lobe have been identified.* (B) *Medial view of the rhesus monkey brain on which the major components of the limbic lobe have been identified.*

substantial reason to concur with such a view. The hypothalamus is an important center for controlling the effector activities of both the endocrine system and the autonomic nervous system. Although the structural and vascular basis for the former have been generally understood for nearly three decades, it is only in recent years that the latter have been understood in structural terms. For example, it is now clear that specific nuclei in the hypo-

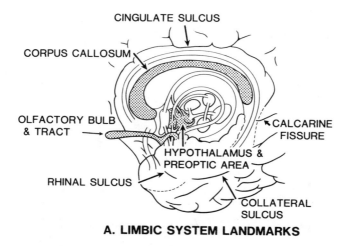

A. LIMBIC SYSTEM LANDMARKS

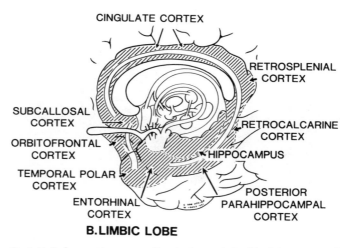

B. LIMBIC LOBE

FIGURE 2. (*A*) *Schematic generalized view of the limbic system depicting important landmarks and sulci.* (*B*) *Location and various components of the limbic lobe.*

thalamus project, as might have been predicted, to sympathetic and parasympathetic centers in both the brainstem and spinal cord (Saper, Loewy, Swanson, & Cowan, 1976). Additionally, there is recent evidence that certain subcortical parts of the limbic system itself, such as the central amygdaloid nucleus, project to

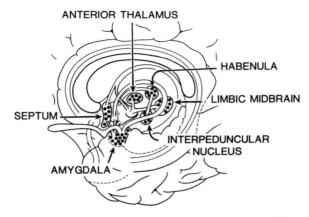

A. SUBCORTICAL LIMBIC STRUCTURES

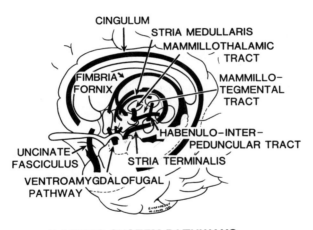

B. LIMBIC SYSTEM PATHWAYS

FIGURE 3. (A) *Various subcortical components of the limbic system.* (B) *Major interconnecting pathways of the limbic lobe.*

brainstem autonomic centers as well (Hopkins & Holstege, 1978). While there is little reason to believe that the hypothalamus itself projects directly to somatic effector areas of the brain, there is good ground to consider that such effects may be mediated via hypothalamic projections to the substantia innominata and amygdala which, in turn, project directly to motor-related areas of the cerebral cortex (Krettek & Price, 1977). It is likely, however, that many parts of the limbic system, and especially the limbic cortices, have rather wide-ranging inroads to key parts of the motor system. For example, the anterior part of the cingulate gyrus projects extensively to the premotor and supplementary motor cortices, and this area receives extensive input from the remainder of the limbic lobe and several subcortical parts of the limbic system (Van Hoesen, Benjamin, & Afifi, 1981). Moreover, there is recent evidence demonstrating that the cortices of the limbic lobe project not only to areas of motor cortex but to major subcortical motor structures such as the caudate nucleus, putamen (Van Hoesen, Yeterian, & Lavizza-Mourey, 1981), and pons (Vilensky & Van Hoesen, 1981). Thus, we view the limbic system and hypothalamus in the context of all major effector activities of the brain, including not only the endocrine and autonomic systems but the motor system as well.

It is pertinent to ask at this point if there are any parts of the brain that are devoid of limbic system influence, and the answer seems decidedly negative. For example, the same parts of the limbic lobe project not only to cortical and subcortical parts of the motor system but to the primary and nonprimary association areas of the cerebral cortex (Mesulam, Van Hoesen, Pandya, & Geschwind, 1977; Pandya, Van Hoesen, & Mesulam, 1981). This was hinted at by Papez himself when he suggested that the radiations of the cingulate gyrus project not only back into his circuit but to cerebral cortex as well, the place where he believed "psychic coloring" of sensations took place. In fact, the demonstration of limbic projections to extensive areas of the cerebral cortex is possibly one of the more surprising discoveries in the modern era of experimental neuroanatomy.

It no doubt has crossed the reader's mind, at this point, that a rather fundamental piece of information is yet lacking in this discussion, that is, the issue of input to the limbic system. Phrased differently, if our understanding of recent findings regarding limbic system anatomy is correct, namely, that it plays a role in widespread endocrine, autonomic, motor, and associative spheres, then it seems only logical that it should receive extensive input from both the internal and external sensoria. Again, this was hinted at by Papez when he implied that the "emotive process" was built up in one part of his circuit as a consequence of input from higher centers, presumably cortical. The structural basis for this has been one of the most poorly understood parts of his circuit, and our lack of knowledge regarding this key question has often been emphasized by MacLean.

New information regarding input to the limbic system has been linked closely to the development of newer and more sensitive anatomical methods that became available in only the past decade, as well as to a renewed interest in the connections of the cerebral cortex (Jones & Powell, 1970; Pandya & Kuypers, 1969). To present an adequate review of that literature would go beyond the aims of this chapter. But suffice it to say that in several higher mammals, limbic system structures receive a large proportion of their input directly from the cerebral cortex, and especially from cortical areas frequently designated as associative (Herzog & Van Hoesen, 1976; Van Hoesen & Pandya, 1975a, 1975b; Van Hoesen, Pandya, & Butters, 1972; Van Hoesen, Pandya, & Butters, 1975). Our interpretation of these findings suggests that key elements of the limbic system are privy to highly integrated sensory information of unimodal, bimodal and multimodal varieties, and thus highly attuned to the complexities of the sensory environment (Van Hoesen et al., 1972).

It should be noted, in this regard, that association cortex input to the limbic system may represent not only a highly sophisticated synthesis of the sensory world as it is happening now, but a record of past events as well. For example, it is reasonable to believe that the record of past experiences, which we lump together under the concept of memory, is stored, in large part, in the cortical association areas. Accordingly, it appears likely that limbic system input reflects not only complex sensory events but a record of how such events interacted with the organism in the past.

In summary, one might conclude that limbic system output is a core element of most activities that take place in the nervous system. As such, one must examine carefully the usefulness of such a pervasive notion and concept, however strong the anatomical support. In this regard, the question is not unlike the older one of where, within the brain, sensation ends and motor activity begins. There is no precise answer to that question and we suspect that likewise the functions of the limbic system have few bounds.

But why should one expect that such would not be the case? Rather than predicting an exact compartmentalization of function within structurally definable discrete systems, why not adopt the attitude that we have developed toward compartmentalized behavior. This should not be construed as an endorsement of holistic viewpoints. On the contrary, limbic system connections are remarkably discrete. They probably exert a specific affect-related influence on functional areas and systems within the brain that are relevant to the larger functions of these areas and systems. Accordingly, there is now abundant structural evidence of remarkable selectivity in limbic system output. Thus, our view can be stated simply: Before we become discouraged with the concept of the limbic system, we should examine closely the question of whether or not affect itself pervades all aspects of behavior. We obviously believe that it does on both the sensory and motor sides of the coin. Thus, we advocate the maintenance and further evolution of the limbic system concept in both behavioral and structural fronts.

FOCAL LESIONS OF THE LIMBIC FRONTAL CORTEX

BILATERAL DAMAGE OF THE CINGULATE GYRUS

The first reports of behavioral disturbances following bilateral damage to the cingulate gyrus came from Nielsen (Nielsen, 1951; Nielsen & Jacobs, 1951). A state of akinesia and mutism was then correlated with a destructive lesion which, at autopsy, was found to involve both anterior cingulate gyri and the nearby corpus callosum. A subsequent report came from Barris and Schuman (1953) who described a patient with akinetic mutism and severe autonomic dysregulation, who had lesions of both anterior cingulate gyri but not of the corpus callosum. That 40-year-old patient presented with mutism, akinesia, indifference to painful stimuli, and incontinence of urine. His stretch reflexes were normal and so were his muscle tone and strength. He had bilateral extensor plantar responses. His temperature rose gradually, pulse and respiration rates accelerated, he became deeply comatose and died 20 days after onset. Postmortem study revealed the presence of bilateral hemorrhagic infarctions of both anterior cingulate gyri.

The extensive damage encroached, but only slightly, into areas 6 and 4, immediately above the cingulate, and into area 32 located anteriorly and inferiorly to the cingulate. The corpus callosum was not involved. No mention was made of the septal region, which may or may not have been involved. It appears the patient suffered bilateral strokes in the territory of the anterior cerebral arteries, in the absence of aneurysm in the anterior communicating artery.

In 1955 Amyes and Nielsen published a large clinical pathologic study of vascular lesions of the anterior cingulate region. The association between bilateral anterior cingulate damage and a syndrome of akinetic mutism and severe autonomic disturbance was emphasized. Damage to the corpus callosum was clearly not responsible for the disturbances, although the issue of whether or not septal damage might contribute to the presentation was not approached. The authors emphasized that all patients died within a few weeks after onset of disease most probably as a result of severe autonomic disturbances and their attending complications. They suggested that complete bilateral destruction of the anterior cingulate cortex and its white matter was incompatible with life. The latter point is still in question since it is possible that the fatal course of those patients may have been the result of hypothalamic lesions. There is no case, to our knowledge, of exclusive bilateral damage to the anterior cingulate gyrus, proven by autopsy, leading to death. Besides we have personally observed patients with extensive bilateral damage of the frontal lobe, inclusive of anterior cingulate gyri, who have recovered from their akinetic mute state and survived. But it is unquestionable that bilateral damage to the cingulate causes a state of disturbed affect, in which expression and experience of emotion are precluded, and any intent to communicate is curtailed.

That the extent of cingulate damage may play a role in the amount of behavioral disturbance is suggested by two additional lines of evidence. First, on the basis of the reports of partial surgical ablation of anterior cingulate or of its connections in humans (starting with the work of LeBeau & Pecker, 1950) it appears that the result of cingulectomy or cingulotomy is, in general, a diminution of anxiety and agitation, while severe and persistent akinesia or mutism are the exception. Clearly, such psychosurgical procedures damage only a small portion of the cingulate and of its connectional outflow. A second line of evidence comes from unilateral vascular lesions of the cingulate in humans. Such lesions generally encompass a sizable portion of the anterior cingulate and of the supplementary motor area which lies immediately above and, occasionally, of the mesial aspect of the motor area. We have observed that those patients present with akinesia and mutism but that recovery is prompt, often starting in the first 2 or 3 days after onset. It is not uncommon for patients to have improved significantly by 2 weeks after onset.

UNILATERAL DAMAGE TO THE CINGULATE GYRUS AND SUPPLEMENTARY MOTOR AREA (SMA)

CASE EXAMPLE

J is a 35-year-old woman with a history of mitral stenosis secondary to rheumatic heart disease for which she was treated with a Beall valve prosthesis. No neurologic complication ever developed in relation to her cardiac condition and she has no history, personal or familial, of neurologic disorder.

On the night of admission she was riding in a car driven by her husband and talking normally, when she suddenly slumped forward, interrupted her conversation, and developed weakness of the right leg and foot. On arrival at the hospital she was alert but speechless, could understand questions and commands, exhibited a paresis of the right lower extremity and had a posture of the right upper extremity characterized by moderate abduction of the arm and flexion of the forearm. It was noted that she was in atrial fibrillation. Further evaluation suggested malfunction of the cardiac prosthesis. A nuclide scan showed a wedge-shaped uptake in the territory of the left anterior cerebral artery. A CT scan showed a unilateral infarction in the mesial aspect of the frontal lobe, encompassing parts of the anterior cingulate, supplementary motor area, and the mesial motor area (where the contralateral lower extremity is represented). The cerebrospinal fluid was clear and revealed no cytological or chemical abnormality. The diagnosis was infarction of the mesial frontal lobe in the territory of a branch of anterior cerebral artery on the basis of embolization from the heart. The patient was treated with heparin, and later, upon stabilization of both the cardiac and neurologic conditions, her valve was replaced.

Special Observations. There was complete absence of spontaneous speech. The patient lay in bed quietly with an alert expression and followed the examiner with the eyes. From the standpoint of affect her facial expression could best be described as neutral. She gave no reply to the questions posed to her, but seemed perplexed by this incapacity. However, the patient did not appear frustrated, and there was no suggestion of impediment in phonation or articulation. She never attempted to mouth words, and no external indication of motion in the phonatory system was discerned. There was no evidence of buccofacial apraxia. She made no attempt to supplement her verbal defect with the use of gesture language. In striking contrast to the lack of spontaneous speech, the patient was able, from the time of admission, to repeat words and sentences slowly, but without delay in initiation. The ease in repetition was not accompanied by echolalia, and the articulation and melody of repeated speech were normal. The patient also gave evidence of good aural comprehension of language by means of nodding behavior. On the third day after onset she was able to produce occasional one-word answers to some questions, but always after a long delay, often of more than 1 minute. Such words were well articulated and melodically intonated. During the delays the facial expression would sometimes be one of perplexity at her defect. Needless to say, the patient could not be engaged in conversation about any given topic. Performance on the Token Test was intact and she performed normally on a test of reading comprehension. After the third day postonset she was able to complete the Visual Naming Test without error, although slowly. She was not able to use the right hand to write and she would not write spontaneously with the left. However, using her left hand, she was able to write single words slowly, from copy and dictation, using capital letters. The patient performed defectively in the Controlled Oral Word Association Test at the level commonly associated with lesions of the frontal lobe.

Spontaneous and syntactically organized utterances to nurses and relatives appeared in the second week postonset, in relation to immediate needs only. She was at this point barely able to carry a telephone conversation using mostly one- and two-word expressions. At 3 weeks she was able to talk in short simple but complete sentences, uttered slowly. But she was still unable to tell the story of her disease (at best the request evoked a simple utterance such as "a stroke" or "mitral stenosis") or to tell us about her family life, interests, or concerns in more than a couple of mere reference words. There is little question that she possessed the information to answer those inquiries. Asked to describe what she saw in pictures and drawings she produced a similar performance, although close questioning revealed that her grasp of both details and overall meaning of the picture was correct. Similarly, she could not generate sentences of more than two or three words on the basis of random stimulus words such as "boy," "car," "health," and "beauty." At no point were paraphasias of phonemic or global nature noted. Entirely normal articulation was observed at all times. Echolalia was never recorded. Her performance on the Controlled Oral World Association test was unchanged. Further assessment of higher nervous function demonstrated her intact performance in constructional praxis (Three-Dimensional Constructional Praxis Test) and the absence of neglect for visual, tactile, and auditory stimulation. There was no evidence of left-sided limb apraxia.

Of further interest, during the period of recovery, was the presence of facial asymmetry noted when the patient attempted to smile. This was not seen when she was repeating sentences for the examiner or when she was specifically evaluated for strength of facial muscles with the usual tests that require volitional use of facial musculature. The phenomenon abated after the second week.

On reevaluation, 1 month later, the patient was remarkably recovered. She had considerable insight into the acute period of the illness and was able to give precious testimony about her experiences then. Asked if she ever suffered anguish for being apparently unable to communicate she answered negatively. There was no anxiety, she reported. She didn't talk because she had "nothing to say." Her mind was "empty." Nothing "mattered." She apparently was able to follow our conversations even during the early period of the illness, but felt no "will" to reply to our questions. In the period after discharge she continued to note a feeling of tranquility and relative lack of concern. This was apparently at some variance with her former personality, but the intensity of the change is difficult to ascertain.

Course. The patient was reevaluated 9 months later. Regarding the motion of her face, she considered it normal and states that nobody ever called her attention to an asymmetry. In fact, whatever was left of her "emotional" facial paralysis was minimal and occurred only occasionally. Strength of the right lower extremity was improved to what has been judged as 90% of her previous ability, and she walked with a barely perceptible defect. However, she reported that, although her "automatic" gait movements were practically normal, the volitional command of her leg and foot was distinctly defective, there being a delay in response to her express wish for movement. On verbal command we were able to confirm that the right leg and foot were less prompt than the left ones. She did not think that the right upper extremity was affected in this manner and this was also our impression. However, the right arm and hand were unable to perform rapid repetitive movements, while the same segments of the left side performed according to expectations. Bilateral simultaneous, rapid, and repetitive movements of the hands were remarkably impaired.

Another area of improvement had been communication. The patient considered herself "almost normal," able to say what she thought most of the time, although she was aware of a need to "prepare" her speech and of talking at a slower rate. She thought that if she did make mistakes they were not noticeable to others. However, she presumed she was unable to write and has not attempted to write a single letter since her illness. Objectively there was an overall reduction in speech output, although we were not able to detect abnormalities of lexicon, syntax, articulation, or melody in any of the utterances she produced. Interestingly there were identifiable "sentence gaps" when the patient, contrary to expectations, did not utter anything; for example, at the end of one testing session, she stood up and left the room without a word, although it appeared that she wanted to comment on her performance or say goodbye. This was in contrast to her habitual courteousness and cooperativeness and was interpreted as a sudden speech inhibition which she had tried to disguise not without embarrassment. Later on the patient confirmed our impression. Formal neuropsychological testing yielded normal performances in all the previously normal tests and, in addition, in the Controlled Oral Word Association test, which had been found to be severely defective during admission. Furthermore she was able to write simple sentences correctly, from dictation and spontaneously, though she took considerable time to create a spontaneous phrase. There were no paragraphs. But the use of language in a creative manner was still severely curtailed, and she had great difficulty in telling us her medical history and in giving an account of the content of pictures.

The preservation of the ability to repeat sentences and, later, the improvement of language without any sign of linguistic defect, suggest that the disturbances involved the "drive" to speak rather than the capacity to formulate speech.

Likewise, the pathological involvement was confined to the phylogenetically older mesolimbic cortex and spared the phylogenetically modern language neocortex of the frontoparietal operculum and superior temporal gyrus. Similarly, the asymmetric involvement of the face in emotionally related movement only, indicates the sparing of the lateral motor neocortex and hallmarks the involvement of mesolimbic structures. The disturbance of movement in the right lower extremity was due to involvement of the nearby motor area (mesial neocortex of Brodmann's area 4), a feature which is occasionally absent when the lesion fails to extend further back.

In short, the results of damage to the cingulate and nearby SMA seem to have been a profound disturbance of behavior which prevented both the normal *expression* and normal *experience* of affect. The patient had a "neutral" facial expression and reported a "neutralized" will to move or communicate. The outer manifestation of these disturbances could best be described as akinesia and mutism, but they might as well be designated as a state of aspontaneity and nonlateralized neglect of most stimuli. At no point did the patient show evidence of impaired social judgment or facetiousness, two signs often associated with disturbances of frontal lobe origin.

Results of Electrical Stimulation
of the Cingulate Cortex

It is interesting and useful to contrast the results of focal damage with those of electrical stimulation. The information from both sets of data is complementary and helps the understanding of the functional role of a given structure.

The cingulate gyrus was first stimulated in monkeys by Smith (1941), Ward (1948), and Kaada, Pribram, and Epstein (1949). Both emotional and autonomic behaviors were seen as a result. Stimulation of the human cingulate gyrus has been carried out by Talairach, Bancaud, Geier, Bordas-Ferrer, Bonis, Szikla, and Rusu (1973) in epileptic patients. By far the most consistent result of stimulation was a "reaction of wakefulness," consisting of a body posture and facial expression suggestive of heightened attention, but in the absence of a stimulus to focus it on. This global modification of the level of vigilance which, in effect, arrested all other activity except the primitive movements to be described below, was practically constant. It is interesting to note that it was not accompanied by autonomic changes such as pupillary dilation or modification of cardiorespiratory rhythm, and it is of note that its opposite, a reaction of somnolence, was never encountered. No complex movement patterns—for example, synergies—were elicited, but a variety of elementary movements were observed instead. These included simple movements of the hand and fingers (repetitive flexion/extension, aimless exploration of surfaces, picking on clothing), simple movements of the mouth (exploratory movement of the tongue, "tasting" movements, swallowing), coordinated movements of finger and mouth (resembling those of an infant sucking), random movements of the eyes, and repetitive, impatient movements of the legs, suggestive of akathisia. When stimulation was combined with the presentation of certain visual stimuli, more complex behaviors appeared, but only while stimulation lasted. For instance, if a banana or orange were shown, the patient would start eating it, often without appropriately peeling it. But if stimulation was interrupted the subject would stop the masticating movements and would abandon the task, even if verbally urged to continue. Most subjects perceived the actions as imposed from the "exterior," without their will interfering on the execution, in spite of attempts at willful control. Some patients rationalized the actions and attributed significance to given movements; for example, a subject declared that his mouth movements were voluntary and in fact required to keep his mouth from "drying."

In addition, many subjects appeared to experience affective changes and behaved in a way suggestive of anguish, sadness, or even fear. Such experiences were rarely expressed verbally and were generally inferred from the subjects' appearance. But more often the affective change was in the direction of euphoria. The subjects appeared relaxed, smiling, jovial, and often became jocular. They reported vague but definitely pleasant reactions, appeared excited, and would exchange pleasantries with the examiner, such as waving or blowing kisses.

The conclusion of the authors was that the cingulate appeared to have a primary and general function of "inciting to action." In addition, it was clear that this area was strongly related to affective behaviors. In other words, electrical stimulation supports the notion that the cingulate is associated with both the experience and expression of affect.

Unilateral Damage to the SMA (Supplementary motor area)

The result of exclusive unilateral destruction of the anterior cingulate in man is not known. However, the result of unilateral destruction of the SMA has been well studied. It differs from the combined cingulate/SMA destruction only in the lesser initial severity. A comprehensive description of such patients can be found in Laplane, Talairach, Meninger, Bancaud, and Orgogozo (1977) who performed unilateral ablations of the SMA in both the left and right hemispheres. The intervention consisted of a circumscribed corticectomy which also involved the mesial portion of area 4, but spared the anterior cingulate and did not involve prefrontal cortex. In the postoperative period the patients developed a state of mutism and akinesia, similar in all respects to the one just described above. Some weeks later, as the patients regained some spontaneity and were able both to produce utterances and to move their bodies purposefully, the authors noted that neither aphasia nor apraxia were present. The patients had a lack of will to speak or move which, though it improved remarkably, persisted in the form of reduced spontaneity of movement, especially that of speech and facial expression. An "emotional," "reversed" facial paralysis was found, similar to that described above in a case of cingulate/SMA damage.

In these unilateral cases it was of particular interest that the clinical picture was similar for lesions of the left or of the right SMA. This apparent independence from cerebral dominance reinforces the notion that the oral communication defect seen in these patients is an impairment of the chance to speak and not of language formulation, a fact which had been suggested by Penfield (Penfield & Welch, 1951) and has recently received additional support (Caplan & Zervas, 1978). Also of special interest was the finding that the degree of akinesia, though present on both sides, was more marked contralaterally. This form of lateralized "neglect" was to be seen in a particularly clear form in what regards facial expression, reduced contralaterally in emotional movements such as smiling.

RESULTS OF ELECTRICAL STIMULATION OF THE SMA

Stimulation of the SMA in man causes a variety of standard responses. The interruption of ongoing voluntary activity by electric stimulation is a functional hallmark of the SMA cortex (Bates, 1951; Penfield & Welch, 1951). If stimulation is applied prior to the execution of an intended movement and during the period for which the movement was expected to last, no action will take place. Both movements of the limbs and movements related to speech have been investigated. Electrical stimulation produces an arrest which lasts for as long as the stimulation is maintained. The patients invariably report that they do not know what precluded them from continuing or initiating the movement which they wanted to perform. The notion that the "will to move" was preempted by an "unknown instance" is commonly referred by the subjects. The phenomenon is suggestively described by Van Buren and Fedio (1976). This response resembles that produced by stimulation of the cingulate and of the head of the caudate or of its vicinity.

Electrical stimulation of the SMA also produces vocalization and complex movement patterns. The movements are never elementary and are not confined to a small group of muscles or to a single segment of the body. They always involve several segments of at least one limb, often two, and commonly the trunk also. Most of those are bilateral, although it is possible to evoke strictly contralateral synergies by stimulation of only one of the SMA. Also, it is possible to produce strictly ipsilateral movements, although these seem to be less frequent.

Sensory responses, generally in the form of nonpainful paresthesias, have been noted with stimulation of the SMA. But a variety of autonomic responses have been evoked by stimulation of the SMA (pupillary changes, modification of respiratory or cardiac rates, sweating). Such responses are generally obtainable from the cingulate cortex too.

Stimulation of the cingulate or SMA produces both distinctive and overlapping results. Stimulation of both areas can preempt ongoing activity and interfere with drive toward action. On the other hand, the reaction of arousal and wakefulness caused by cingulate stimulation has not been seen with stimulation of the SMA. In addition, stimulation of the cingulate appears to modify affect, causing either euphoria or dysphoria or affective neutrality, more so than does stimulation of the SMA. Nor have the vocalizations and complex synergies evoked by SMA stimulation (see Brickner, 1940; Penfield & Welch, 1951) been noted with stimulation of the cingulate. Functionally, the two areas appear to be in a continuum and they form a sort of structural complex related to the drive toward movement. The morphology of both areas supports this notion, both in terms of the cytoarchitecture and of connectivity. The cortex of the cingulate gyrus is a proisocortex or limbic cortex, which gives way to the more differentiated isocortex of the SMA. However, in between, in the depth of the cingulate sulcus, there lies a clearly defined transition zone which shares the characteristics of both limbic and advanced motor cortices. Such an area, described in humans by Braak (1976) using pigment cytoarchitectural techniques, raises the issue of developmental continuity between these cortices. The connectivity of these areas is also most intriguing. The cingulate gyrus projects massively to the SMA and both project strongly to the neostriatum of both sides (Damasio & Van Hoesen, 1980; Van Hoesen, Benjamin, & Afifi, 1981). The SMA is, in addition, strongly interconnected with all other instances of the motor system including the remainder of area 6, area 4, and area 8.

BILATERAL DAMAGE TO THE ORBITOFRONTAL CORTEX

Experimental studies in animals have demonstrated a relation between orbitofrontal lesions and emotional disturbances. Butter and Mishkin (Butter, Mishkin, & Mirsky, 1968; Butter, Mishkin, & Rosvold, 1963; Butter, Snyder, & McDonald 1970), working with rhesus monkeys, showed that orbitofrontal lesions caused marked and consistent reduction in aggressive behaviors. They thought animals with such lesions had lost a regulatory mechanism of aggression, while their capacity to display aggression in specific situations had not been entirely lost. In other words, the animals did look emotionally "blunt" and were more "tame" in many circumstances, but they could still behave aggressively in potentially threatening situations. The lesions crucial for such changes were in the posteromedial region of the orbitofrontal cortex. But the possible relationship between orbitofrontal cortex structures and emotional display had first been hinted at by Kleist, in humans. Kleist (1934) believed that damage to the orbitofrontal cortex caused primarily emotional changes, and that the classical symptoms of "Witzelsucht" and "Moria" were predominantly associated to those lesions. The terms "Witzelsucht" and "Moria" (coined by Oppenheim and by Jastrowitz, respectively, in 1889 and 1888) subsume a large range of manifestations, for example, facetiousness, euphoria, irritability, intolerance, sudden depression, and impaired social judgment. Such symptoms are present, at some point or another, in most patients with bilateral orbitofrontal lesions regardless of the presence of additional lesions in other sectors of the frontal lobe. In most patients such changes are not a permanent feature and a patient who appears facetious and boastful may appear apathetic some time later, or exhibit a sudden temper outburst. Facetiousness often has a sexual content but rarely do patients act according to those verbalized contents. Curiously there is no indication that such verbal play produces any pleasure. Most patients so affected are unable to enjoy pleasurable stimulation especially when the rewards are social, intellectual, or esthetic. This parallels, or explains, their lack of appreciation for social rules, their shallow affect, and their limited response to and experience of pain. They rarely exhibit true depression or elation, nor do they have the organization of the psychopathic personality even if they may appear psychopathic.

A detailed correlation between these manifestations and restricted portions of the orbitofrontal cortex, in humans, is not possible yet. That is due to the special nature of lesions in this part of the brain. Exclusive bilateral ablation of those structures has never been performed in humans and their exclusive bilateral involvement due to vascular causes is unlikely (bilateral orbitofrontal damage can be seen in the setting of ruptured anterior communicating aneurysms, but only along with other lesions). Information regarding dysfunction of the orbitofrontal cortex has been gleaned from cases of severe closed head injury, in which extensive additional pathological changes preclude unequivocal anatomical–clinical correlations, and from cases of cerebral tumor, with all the problems of functional correlation related to that type of pathological material. Possibly the best way of enquiring into the results of orbitofrontal damage has been the analysis of behaviors in survivors of herpes simplex encephalitis. The reasons are as follows. Herpes simplex encephalitis selectively affects all cortical structures of the limbic system, bilaterally. The mesial and polar temporal cortices, the orbitofrontal cortices, and the anterior cingulate cortices are generally destroyed in such cases. A good example of the distribution of lesions can be found in the postmortem study by Barbizet, Duizabo, and Poirier (1978). In our own study of such patients, we have found that they share some clinical features with those who have (1) exclusive cingulate damage, and (2) exclusive mesial temporal damage. In common with the former they go through a period of severe akinesia and mutism, from which they recover with a considerable degree of aspontaneity—they regain normal verbal communication and generally exhibit a grossly intact motor system. In common with the latter they have a severe amnesic syndrome—encoding of any new material is practically precluded and there is a variable retrograde memory defect which can span many years. But in addition to those manifestations, the encephalitic patients exhibit a form of social disinhibition, lack of appropriate judgment and lack of concern for previously acquired rules of personal behavior, which has not been observed in patients with exclusively cingulate or exclusively mesial temporal lesions. We are inclined to believe that those additional features of behavior are associated with extension of the lesions into the orbitofrontal cortex.

UNILATERAL DAMAGE TO THE ORBITOFRONTAL CORTEX

Exclusive unilateral damage to the orbitofrontal cortex is just as rare as bilateral damage. Cerebral tumors, especially meningiomas, can affect this region unilaterally but, whatever the extent of real damage, the lesions are not exclusively in the orbitofrontal cortex. Ruptured aneurysms will often damage one side only of the orbitofrontal cortex, but, just as often, the damage will extend to the septal region and the anterior hypothalamus. It is noteworthy that in the latter instance patients will exhibit most of the signs characteristic of bilateral orbitofrontal lesions although with lesser intensity. In addition, they present with a variant of amnesic syndrome characterized by a profound defect of retrieval of remote as well as recent memories, in the face of remarkably preserved encoding ability (Damasio & Eslinger, 1983).

SUMMARY

In conclusion, it appears that a variety of focal lesions of the frontal lobe cortex are associated with disturbances of either the experience or the expression of emotion. Those disturbances do not appear in isolation and are variably associated with (1) defects in general drive toward movement, or with (2) memory disturbances, or with (3) impaired social behavior. Both unilateral and bilateral lesions can be associated with the disturbances, the latter tending to cause the more severe and lasting syndromes. All of the critical lesions, however, have been found in "limbic" cortices of the frontal lobe, either in its mesial or orbitofrontal surfaces. In contrast, focal lesions of the lateral frontal lobe cortices, notably the cortices of the motor, premotor and lateral prefrontal regions, have not been associated with the type of disturbances described above.

ACKNOWLEDGMENTS

The preparation of this chapter was supported in part by NIH Grant NS 14944 and by a University of Iowa Scholar Award.

REFERENCES

Amyes, E. W., & Nielsen, J. M. Clinicopathologic study of vascular lesions of the anterior cingulate region. *Bulletin of the Los Angeles Neurological Societies*, 1955, *20*, 112–130.

Barbizet, J., Duizabo, P. H., & Poirier, J. Étude anatomo-clinique d'un cas d'encéphalite amnésiante d'origine herpétique. *Revue Neurologique*, 1978, *134*, 241–253.

Barris, R. W., & Schuman, H. R. Bilateral anterior cingulate gyrus lesions: Syndrome of the anterior cingulate gyri. *Neurology*, 1953, *3*, 44–52.

Bates, J. Stimulation of the mesial surface of the human cerebral hemisphere after hemispherectomy. *Brain*, 1951, *76*, 405–437.

Braak, H. A primitive giganto pyramidal field buried in the depth of the cingulate sulcus of the human brain. *Brain Research*, 1976, *109*, 219–233.

Brodal, A. *Neurological anatomy* (3rd ed.). New York: Oxford Press, 1981.

Brickner, R. M. An interpretation of frontal lobe function based upon the study of a case of partial bilateral frontal lobectomy. *Research Publication of the Association for Research in Nervous and Mental Disease*, 1934, *13*, 259–351.

Brickner, R. M. *The intellectual functions of the frontal lobes: Study based upon observation of a man after partial bilteral frontal lobectomy.* New York: Macmillan, 1936.

Brickner, R. M. A human cortical area producing repetitive phenomena when stimulated. *Journal of Neurophysiology*, 1940, *3*, 128–130.

Butter, C. M., Mishkin, M., & Mirsky, A. F. Emotional responses toward humans in monkeys with selective frontal lesions. *Physiology and Behavior*, 1968, *3*, 213–215.

Butter, C. M., Mishkin, M., & Rosvold, H. E. Conditioning and extinction of a food rewarded response after selective ablations of frontal cortex in rhesus monkeys. *Experimental Neurology*, 1963, *7*, 65–75.

Butter, C. M., Snyder, D. R., & McDonald, J. A. Effects of orbital frontal lesions on aversive and aggressive behaviors in rhesus monkeys. *Journal of Comparative and Physiological Psychology*, 1970, *72*, 132–144.

Caplan, L. R., & Zervas, N. T. Speech arrest in a dextral with right mesial astrocytoma. *Archives of Neurology*, 1978, *35*, 252–253.

Damasio, A. R., & Eslinger, P. J. *Amnesic syndrome and personality disorder following bilateral frontal and temporal lobe damage.* In preparation, 1983.

Damasio, A. R., & Van Hoesen, G. W. Structure and function of the supplementary motor area. *Neurology*, 1980, *30*, 359.

Filimonoff, I. N. A rational subdivision of the cerebral cortex. *Archives of Neurology and Psychiatry*, 1947, *58*, 296–311.

Herzog, A. G., & Van Hoesen, G. W. Temporal neocortical afferent connections to the amygdala in the rhesus monkey. *Brain Research*, 1976, *115*, 57–69.

Hopkins, D. A., & Holstege, G. Amygdaloid projections to the mesencephalon, pons and medulla oblongata in the cat. *Experimental Brain Research*, 1978, *32*, 529–547.

Jacobsen, C. F. Functions of the frontal association area in primates. *Archives of Neurology and Psychiatry*, 1935, *33*, 558–569.

Jones, E. G., & Powell, T. P. S. An anatomical study of converging sensory pathways within the cerebral cortex of the monkey. *Brain*, 1970, *93*, 793–820.

Kaada, B. R., Pribram, K. H., & Epstein, J. A. Respiratory and vascular responses in monkeys from temporal lobe, insula orbital surface and cingulate gyrus. *Journal of Neurophysiology*, 1949, *12*, 347–356.

Kleist, K. *Gehirnpathologie*. Leipzig: Barth, 1936.

Krettek, J. E., & Price, J. L. Projections from the amygdaloid complex to the cerebral cortex and thalamus in the rat and cat. *Journal of Comparative Neurology*, 1977, *172*, 687–722.

Laplane, D., Talairach, J., Meininger, V., Bancaud, J., & Orgogozo, J. M. Clinical consequences of corticectomies involving the supplementary motor area in man. *Journal of the Neurological Sciences*, 1977, *34*, 301–314.

LeBeau, J., & Pecker, J. Étude de certaines formes d'agitation psychomotrice en cours de l'épilepsie et de l'arriération mentale, traités par la topecomie péricalleuse antérieure bilateral. *Semaine des Hôpitaux de Paris*, 1950, *26*, 1.

Livingston, K. E., & Hornykiewicz, O. (Eds.). *Limbic mechanisms: The continuing evolution of the limbic system concept*. New York: Plenum, 1978.

MacLean, P. D. Psychosomatic disease and the "visceral brain": Recent developments bearing on the Papez theory of emotion. *Psychosomatic Medicine*, 1949, *11*, 338–353.

Mesulam, M. M., Van Hoesen, G. W., Pandya, D. N., & Geschwind, N. Limbic and sensory connections of the inferior parietal lobule (area PG) in the rhesus monkey. *Brain Research*, 1977, *136*, 393–414.

Moniz, E. *Tentatives opératoires dans le traitement de certaines psychoses*. Paris: Masson, 1936.

Moniz, E. Prefrontal leucotomy in the treatment of mental disorders. *American Journal of Psychiatry*, 1937, *93*, 1379–1385.

Nielsen, J. M. Anterior cingulate gyrus and corpus callosum. *Bulletin of the Los Angeles Neurological Societies*, 1951, *16*, 235.

Nielsen, J. M., & Jacobs, L. L. Bilateral lesions of the anterior cingulate gyri. *Bulletin of the Los Angeles Neurological Societies*, 1951, *16*, 230.

Pandya, D. N., & Kuypers, H. G. J. M. Corticocortical connections in the rhesus monkey. *Brain Research*, 1969, *13*, 13–36.

Pandya, D. N., Van Hoesen, G. W., & Mesulam, M. M. The corticocortical projections of the cingulate cortex in the rhesus monkey. *Experimental Brain Research*, 1981, *42*, 319–330.

Papez, J. W. A proposed mechanism of emotion. *Archives of Neurology and Psychiatry*, 1937, *38*, 725–744.

Penfield, W., & Welch, K. Supplementary motor area of cerebral cortex; clinical and experimental study. *Archives of Neurology and Psychiatry*, 1951, *66*, 289–317.

Sanides, F. Comparative architectonics of the neocortex of mammals and their evolutionary interpretation. *Annals of the New York Academy of Sciences*, 1969, *167*, 404–423.

Saper, C. B., Loewy, A. D., Swanson, L. W., & Cowan, W. M. Direct hypothalamo-autonomic connections. *Brain Research*, 1976, *117*, 305–312.

Smith, W. K. Vocalization and other responses elicited by excitation of the regio singularis in the monkey. *American Journal of Physiology*, 1941, *133*, 451–452.

Talairach, J., Bancaud, J., Geier, S., Bordas-Ferrer, M., Bonis, A., Szikla, G., & Rusu, M. The cingulate gyrus and human behaviour. *Electroencephalography and Clinical Neurophysiology*, 1973, *34*, 45–52.

Van Buren, J. M., & Fedio, P. Functional representation on the medial aspect of the frontal lobes in man. *Journal of Neurosurgery*, 1976, *44*, 275–289.

Van Hoesen, G. W., Benjamin, D., & Afifi, A. K. Limbic cortical input to area 6 in the monkey. *Anatomical Record*, 1981, *199*, 262–263.

Van Hoesen, G. W., & Pandya, D. N. Some connections of the entorhinal (area 28) and perirhinal (area 35) cortices of the rhesus monkey: I. Temporal lobe afferents. *Brain Research*, 1975, *95*, 1–24. (a)

Van Hoesen, G. W., & Pandya, D. N. Some connections of the entorhinal (area 28) and perirhinal (area 35) cortices of the rhesus monkey: III. Efferent connections. *Brain Research*, 1975, *95*, 39–59. (b)

Van Hoesen, G. W., Pandya, D. N., & Butters, N. Cortical afferents to the entorhinal cortex of the rhesus monkey. *Science*, 1972, *175*, 1471–1473.

Van Hoesen, G. W., Pandya, D. N., & Butters, N. Some connections of the entorhinal (area 28) and perirhinal (area 35) cortices of the rhesus monkey: II. Frontal lobe afferents. *Brain Research*, 1975, *95*, 25–38.

Van Hoesen, G. W., Yeterian, E. H., & Lavizza-Mourey, R. Widespread corticostriate projections from temporal cortex in the monkey. *Journal of Comparative Neurology*, 1981, *199*, 205–219.

Vilensky, J. A., & Van Hoesen, G. W. Corticopontine projections from the cingulate cortex in the rhesus monkey. *Brain Research*, 1981, *205*, 391–395.

Ward, A. A. The cingular gyrus, area 24. *Journal of Neurophysiology*, 1948, *1*, 13–24.

EMOTIONAL CONCOMITANTS
OF PSYCHOSURGERY

Donald T. Stuss
D. Frank Benson

INTRODUCTION

A strong association between the frontal lobes and human emotion
has been recognized since the masterful descriptions of Phineas
Gage (Harlow, 1868). This efficient and capable foreman of a
railroad construction crew had suffered a severe injury to the
frontal lobes when an iron tamping bar was blown upward into
his left maxilla, exiting through the vertex of the skull (see Figure 1). The patient survived, and 2½ months postinjury Harlow
described:

> His physical health is good, and I am inclined to say that he has
> recovered. . . . The equilibrium or balance, so to speak, between
> his intellectual faculty and animal propensities, seems to have been
> destroyed. He is fitful, irreverent, indulging at times in the grossest
> profanity (which was not previously his custom), manifesting but
> little deference for his fellows, impatient of restraint or advice when
> it conflicts with his desires, at times pertinaciously obstinate, yet
> capricious and vacillating, devising many plans of future operation,
> which are no sooner arranged than they are abandoned in turn for
> others appearing more feasible. A child in his intellectual capacity
> and manifestations, he has the animal passions of a strong man.
> Previous to his injury, though untrained in the schools, he possessed
> a well-balanced mind, and was looked upon by those who knew

Donald T. Stuss. Schools of Medicine (Neurology) and Psychology, University
of Ottawa, Ottawa General Hospital, Ottawa, Ontario, Canada.
D. Frank Benson. Department of Neurology, UCLA School of Medicine, Los
Angeles, California.

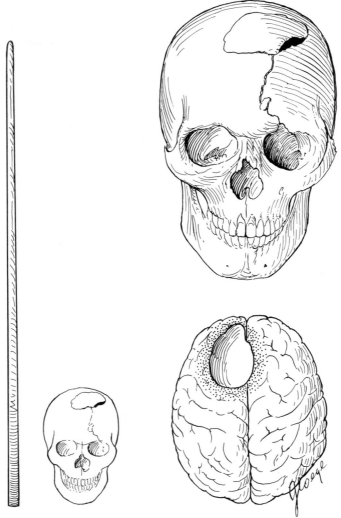

FIGURE 1. *Phineas Gage. On the left, this composite figure depicts the size and location of the frontal skull lesion in relation to the size of the iron tamping bar. On the right are an enlarged depiction of the skull defect and an artistic rendering of the probable location of brain destruction.*

him as a shrewd, smart business man, very energetic and persistent in executing all his plans of operation. In this regard, his mind was radically changed, so decidedly that his friends and acquaintances said he was "no longer Gage." (pp. 339–340)

This brilliant beginning, strongly implying frontal lobe participation in emotion, was followed by many additional observations and studies in patients with frontal lobe damage of various etiologies, but correlation of the frontal lobe damage with specific emotional disorder has proved difficult. Orderly discussion of emotional disorders has been hindered by lack of consistent terminology and, in addition, there is a lack of clearcut focal pathology involving the frontal lobes. The frontal lobes are vast, encompass almost 40% of the total cortical area of the human brain, are infrequently injured unilaterally, and are in such immediate juxtaposition that truly unilateral or focal pathology is uncommon. Also, the effects of pathology involving human prefrontal cortex tend to become widespread with involvement of other areas. Moreover, the human prefrontal cortex is sufficiently unique that animal experiments provide little insight to human frontal lobe activities. Finally, few human studies have investigated the possible confounding influence of premorbid states.

Clarification of some terms defining emotion is essential. Literally thousands of words are currently used to describe various emotions. Thus, Conte (1975), from a number of sources, selected 223 terms that represented emotion. Davitz (1970) asked a group of students to write brief descriptions of emotional experiences and from these descriptions compiled a list of 556 words and phrases that had been used to describe emotion. Formal studies have linked emotion with ethnologic, psychoanalytic, psychophysiological, evolutionary, sociobiologic, information processing, and innumerable psychologic theories, each producing their own vocabulary so that thousands of imprecise, overlapping terms are currently used to define emotion. The following definitions will serve for this chapter:

Mood is defined as a frame of mind or emotional state of a person (*Oxford English Dictionary*, 1979; *Stedman's Medical Dictionary*, 1979), the internal expression of the subjective feeling tone (Hinsie & Campbell, 1970; *Oxford English Dictionary*, 1979). Mood may be specific (e.g., anger, joy) and may oscillate or swing

(Hinsie & Campbell, 1970; *Oxford English Dictionary*, 1979; *Stedman's Medical Dictionary*, 1979). In summary, mood is a relatively pervasive internal disposition, defined by the internal state of mind, not the external behavioral manifestations.

Affect appears to have a biphasic meaning. To some, it can reflect purely the inward disposition, the mental state, in which the term affect represents the mood, feelings, desires, and emotional tones in contrast to reason (*Oxford English Dictionary*, 1979). More commonly, however, a physical aspect is meant by this term, reflecting the external manifestations of the feeling tone (*Oxford English Dictionary*, 1979; *Stedman's Medical Dictionary*, 1979; *New Webster's Dictionary*, 1975). Affect is then distinguished from mood in that it refers both to the mood (in terms of the inner subjective feeling tone) and to the external manifestations of this feeling (Hinsie & Campbell, 1970). One dictionary of psychology (Harriman, 1947) defines affect as "a broad term subserving emotion, feeling, mood and (usually) temperamental characteristics. Affects are more pervasive and enduring than momentary emotional states, and they are identified with drives and propensities. Their ideational contents are vague and generalized." In general, the characteristics ascribed to affect emphasize the outward appearance of the inward feeling, with comparatively little association to reason or ideation and a relatively stable and enduring status. That an observed affect may not coincide with an individual's mood is well recognized in neurobehavior, most strikingly in the wild overflow of emotional expression that may occur in pseudobulbar palsy (Lieberman & Benson, 1977) and the unreal euphoria of multiple sclerosis.

Emotion is a far more difficult term to define and, as suggested above, is broadly and vaguely used at present. To some, the term suggests only a connotation of agitated, excited mental states (emotional). Emotion is often given more cognitive connotation than either mood or affect, although emotion is also thought to include both of the latter. Emotion is "the affective state of consciousness in which joy, sorrow, fear, fate, and the like is experienced" (*New Webster's Dictionary*, 1975). "In current usage, emotion and affect are used interchangeably, although some use emotion to refer primarily to the consciously perceived feelings and their objective manifestations, and affect to include also the drive and energies that are presumed to generate both conscious and unconscious feelings" (Hinsie & Campbell, 1970). Emotion, thus, is a broader term that brings together a sizeable number of behavioral responses linking bodily and mental activities with the underlying feeling tone.

Personality, on the other hand, is the sum of characteristics or qualities that make an individual a unique self and intelligent being (*Oxford English Dictionary*, 1979; *Stedman's Medical Dictionary*, 1979; *New Webster's Dictionary*, 1975). Personality, as such, may be affected by all behavioral aspects including attention, memory, self-reflection, mood, affect, and emotion. It is the

> characteristic, and to some extent predictable, behavior–response patterns that each person evolves, both consciously and unconsciously, as his style of life. The personality represents a compromise between inner drives and needs, and the controls that limit or regulate their expression. Such controls are both internal (e.g., conscience, superego) and external (reality demands). The personality functions to maintain a stable, reciprocal relationship between the person and his environment. (Hinsie & Campbell, 1970, p. 556)

The terms mood, affect, emotion, and personality have often been used interchangeably in describing the effects of damage to the frontal lobes on human behavior. Many common defining characteristics exist for these terms, and the definitions must be sufficiently indefinite to allow some interchangeable use. It is within this broad operational definition, used in conjunction with other variables such as the location of a brain lesion or the premorbid personality, that studies to clarify the specific emotional concomitants of frontal system dysfunction can be defined.

BACKGROUND

Theories of emotion abound. These range from the early physiologic theories (Cannon, 1927; James, 1890) to complex attempts to correlate psychoanalytic, ethnological, cultural, and other theories with emotional behavior. There is a tendency to seek simplifications such as pain–pleasure dichotomy (agonistic–hedonistic), the four F's of MacLean (1949), the circular definitions of Plutchik (1980) and Conte (1975), and the linear, polar models of other

investigators. Many of the postulated schemes are limited; a theory
is hypothesized, supporting data gathered, and the theory then
proposed as an explanation of emotion. Many deal only with the
emotional state of normal individuals, focusing on external
modifying factors while totally ignoring the potential variations
of brain function among normals. Others utilize animal behavior,
modified physically or environmentally, and attempt interpola-
tions to human emotion. Yet others look for consistent behavior
aberrations among brain-injured humans (usually with inadequate localization) and attempt to dissect emotional behavior
from these observations. All prove inadequate to encompass the
rich variation of emotional life so consistently observed. In summary, the multiple studies of emotional behavior currently in the
literature appear as confounding as helpful and provide little
foundation upon which to study the emotional disturbances secondary to frontal lobe damage.

DESCRIPTIONS

Observations of patients with frontal pathology suggest certain
characteristic changes. The most commonly reported primary
neurologic diseases that involve the frontal lobe and produce
behavioral changes are mass lesions, tumors, hemorrhages, and
the like. Luria (1966, 1973) has reported extensively on the effects
of mass lesions on frontal lobe function including emotional
behavior, and there is a long history of such descriptions. Starr
(1884) reported 23 cases of frontal lobe lesions, describing a lack of
self-control and decreased ability to fix attention. Kolodny (1929)
described two frontal lobe behavior alterations with frontal tumor,
the first was a "psychic" change which could be called a mood
alteration, either exaltation or depression, and the second was
an alteration in "behavior," the social aspects of personality.
Holmes (1931) described three personality changes in frontal
disease: (1) apathy and indifference; (2) depression, automaticity,
and incontinence; (3) restlessness, exuberance, euphoria, and
"Witzelsucht." Stookey, Scarff, and Teitelbaum (1941) confirmed
Holmes's finding but added that stupor and vesical incontinence
could also occur, although not consistently. Belyi (1979) suggested
that the major personality alteration in individuals with frontal

lobe tumor was "despontaneity." He described a sharp decrease of initiative and spontaneous volition, crude changes in the emotional sphere, and peculiar disorders of thinking. The alterations in behavior were said to depend primarily upon whether the tumor was unilateral or bilateral.

A far more voluminous group of reports concerning abnormal emotional status following frontal lobe injury concerns individuals who suffered injury, particularly gunshot wounds, to the frontal lobe (Faust, 1960; Feuchtwanger, 1923; Kleist, 1934b; Kretschmer, 1956; Lishman, 1966, 1968; Walch, 1956). Lishman (1968) summarized this vast array of offerings and suggested a behavioral syndrome based on frontal damage that he described as "including one or more of the following symptoms in severe degrees: lack of judgment, reliability or foresight; facetiousness, childish behavior, disinhibition, and euphoria."

Somewhat similar personality changes following closed-head injury has been described. Levin, Grossman, Rose, and Teasdale (1979) described depression, anxiety, and withdrawal in their patients. Other authors (Roberts, 1976; Stuss & Richard, 1982) describe socially inappropriate behavior, outbursts of irritability, changes in attitude toward social mores, and a general lack of inhibition in closed-head injury patients. These observations must be tempered somewhat, however, by the probability that the injury involves more than the frontal lobe. Ommaya and Gennarelli (1976) note that the temporal poles, frontal poles, and the orbitofrontal cortex are the areas involved most severely in closed-head injuries, and Alexander (1982) has emphasized the high frequency of frontal damage following head injury and correlated this with characteristic behavioral changes.

While many studies have suggested that specific behavioral abnormalities follow frontal lobe damage, many are now realized to be based on subcortical and/or widespread damage so that the specificity of the alteration as a function of frontal lobe abnormality must be suspect. For instance, one classic "frontal lobe" disorder, Huntington disease, primarily, if not exclusively, involves subcortical structures, and the behavioral abnormalities so prominent in this disorder should not be considered "frontal." Similarly, multiple sclerosis is often said to produce significant frontal behavioral abnormalities, but this disease is so inconsistent in location of pathology that the behavior disturbances seen cannot be considered exclusively frontal. Vascular accident producing infarction of one portion of the frontal lobe only is rare, and is most often associated with other evidence of vascular disease affecting other brain areas, particularly deep structures. Few purely frontal cardiovascular accidents (CVAs) have been reported.

As the primary diseases of the central nervous system and the head injury cases do not provide good localizing information, studies of patients who had undergone prefrontal psychosurgery have been looked upon to provide more specific information. Over 100,000 patients had psychiatric disturbances treated with destructive lesions in the frontal lobe during the 1940s and 1950s and many studies of psychiatric outcome were performed. All are descriptions of emotional behavior and most suffer from two serious defects. First, there was little or no formal testing of emotional status on a before and after surgery basis. While many patients were described before and after surgery, with few exceptions, the follow-up studies were limited in time and strongly focused on recovery from premorbid psychiatric symptomatology. The duration of follow-up was often surprisingly short and there are almost no long-term studies of the effects of frontal destructive lesions on emotional behavior over the years. A second important problem was that most patients had a serious personality defect as the major defect leading to surgery. Postsurgical observations are contaminated by the presurgical behavioral aberrations.

The earliest reports of psychosurgery (Freeman, Watts, & Hunt, 1942) suggested that the major postlobectomy signs were inertia, lack of ambition, decrease in consecutive thinking, indifference to the opinions of others, satisfaction with the results of inferior quality, and poor judgment. Reitman (1946) described a triad of symptoms similar to Rylander's (1939) observation: extraversion (lack of restraint), increased motor activity (restlessness), and euphoria. Greenblatt, Arnot, and Solomon (1950) described the following major postleukotomy personality alterations: a lack of inhibition, euphoria including restlessness and purposelessness, and a slowness of thinking and acting, producing a dullness, a lack of emotional expression and display, and decreased interest and drive. In 1966 Greenblatt and Solomon modified this into four major outcomes of total bilateral frontal lobotomy: (1) decreased drive; (2) decreased self-concern; (3) depression of outwardly directed behavior and social sense; and (4) shallower affective life.

Other authors have discussed personality changes following leukotomy in more psychological terms. They suggested a decrease in neuroticism, depression, and intropunitiveness, while extroversion significantly increased (Meyer, 1960; Petrie, 1952; Smith, Kiloh, Cochrane, & Kljajic, 1976). Many considered that the presence and severity of personality changes were a reflection of the type of psychosurgery (Rees, 1973; Ström-Olsen & Carlisle, 1970; Tan, Marks, & Marset, 1971). Thus, many have considered the postleukotomy frontal lobe personality to display emotional changes characterized by a lack of sensitivity and appreciation, more concrete thinking, more immediate reaction, a simpler and slower intellectual life, and impoverishment of imagination. In summary, multiple observations from many vantage points indicate distinct alterations of emotional response in patients who have sustained frontal damage.

PROBLEMS

While there is general acceptance that emotional changes can follow frontal lobe pathology, such changes cannot always be clearly documented. For instance, Hebb (1939, 1945) was unable to note any of the three mental changes suggested by Holmes (1931) in four patients who had undergone surgical excision of frontal lobe tissue, and he found no defect of social adjustment on a 6-year follow-up of a man following partial bilateral frontal lobectomy. Hebb (1945) suggested that psychosurgery had not yielded any interpretable evidence concerning normal frontal lobe functioning.

One problem stems from variation in assessment techniques. Most reports have been limited to clinical observations of personality in patients with frontal lobe abnormality with few reports of psychometric tests. Projective testing done after leukotomy demonstrates a variety of alterations, most of a mild degree. Scoville and Bettis (1977) found no significant alteration in personality or emotion when using the Thematic Apperception Test; Rorschach inkblot interpretations demonstrated increased fantasy activity in the postleukotomy patients but adequate evaluation of reality was present. When the Minnesota Multiphasic Personality

Inventory (MMPI) has been given to postleukotomy patients, the results have not been conclusive. The inconclusiveness of the commonly used personality evaluations reflects a number of factors including differences in sites of lesion location, differences in premorbid personality, and that most personality tests are quite possibly misleading for brain-damaged subjects. Tests such as the MMPI were devised and validated on normal subjects or patients with clinically defined psychiatric syndromes. Their use in brain-damaged patients presupposes that the personality changes demonstrated after brain damage are the same as those occurring in functional psychiatric disorder, a supposition that has been proved incorrect (Bear & Fedio, 1977).

Localization within the frontal lobes was not available for most of the studies discussed above. Some observations indicate that behavioral alterations may be specific for particular locations. Welt (1888) provided an early correlation of personality changes with lesion location. A furrier, premorbidly a good-natured, sociable person, fell 100 feet from a window; upon recovery, he was cantankerous and nasty. Postmortem examination revealed bilateral orbital scarring with greater involvement of the right hemisphere. The importance of orbitofrontal cortical areas for personality–emotional change was reaffirmed by Kleist (1934a, 1934b), who suggested that orbitofrontal cortical areas and connections were important to a unified and self-determined personality. Pathology in this area resulted in deviant behavior, peurile and facetious attitude, and euphoria. This emphasis on the medial orbital and/or basal frontal areas in connection with emotional and mood aspects has been reported frequently (Earp, 1979; Goldstein, 1944; Meyer & Beck, 1954; Rees, 1973; Reitman, 1946; Rylander, 1939), and was a primary reason that psychosurgeons emphasized this area for treatment of psychopathology (Freeman & Watts, 1950; Greenblatt & Solomon, 1953).

In parallel to the emphasis on orbitobasalar areas in emotion, a distinction between dorsolateral convexity and orbitofrontal pathology has been noted. Kleist (1934b) stated that, in comparison to orbitofrontal damage, frontal convexity damage resulted in decreased psychic and motor initiation and in deficiencies in thought formation. In an attempt to categorize the personality alterations seen with localized frontal disturbance, Blumer and

Benson (1975) suggested two distinct syndromes. The first, called pseudodepressed, described a distinct retardation of activity including apathy, unconcern, lack of drive, and lack of emotional reactivity, and was most often correlated with pathology involving the lateral convexity of the frontal lobes on one or both sides. In the second syndrome, called pseudopsychopathic, the strongest findings were those of disinhibition including facetiousness, sexual and personal hedonism, and a lack of concern for others. The latter syndrome was most often associated with orbitofrontal pathology.

Research on the effects of selective frontal lobe damage on emotional behavioral aspects in animals has gradually led to more specific concepts of localization in frontal lobes. Early formulations (Butter & Snyder, 1972) stated that orbitofrontal cortical lesions resulted in a profound effect on emotional reactions in the monkey where dorsolateral lesions had little or no effect. Sato (1971; Sato, Onishi, & Otsuki, 1971) reported that orbital and lateral surfaces of cats were differentially involved in emotional adaptation to changes in environment. A more recent study (Rosenkilde, 1979) describes five subregions of prefrontal cortex in the monkey. In general, the medial orbital area appears to be most relevant for autonomic emotional reactions, but lesions in other areas resulted in disturbances of behavior frequently associated with the frontal lobe personality.

While traditionally considered fundamental, the role of premorbid factors such as sex, age of onset or age of treatment, and premorbid personality on the effect of frontal lobe damage on behavior has been difficult to demonstrate. Scoville and Ryan (1955), for example, indicate that leukotomy in older patients led to better improvement. Stookey *et al.* (1941) suggested that the three personality types secondary to frontal lobe disease reported by Holmes were determined, at least partially, by individual personality. Reitman (1946) noted that outcome following orbital leukotomy was dependent on premorbid personality, the best outcome occurring in patients with preoperative symptoms of blockage of thought, depersonalization, and indecision, while the poorest outcome occurred in restless, excited, aggressive patients.

Probably the most consistent report from both the human and animal literature suggests that frontal lobe damage does not change but accentuates the premorbid personality. Jarvie (1954) reviewed past personality traits and reported that the disinhibition secondary to frontal lobe damage did not cause anything new in the personality, but altered self–environment relationships such that previous hidden tendencies were now more overt. In the animal literature, regardless of the species (cat, rat, monkey), the emotional behavior following frontal ablation does not drastically change from premorbid behavior but becomes accentuated (Langworthy & Richter, 1939; Richter & Hawkes, 1939; Messimy, 1948; Sato, 1971). Finally, Pollitt (1960) and Tan *et al.* (1971) suggest that premorbid personality, sex, and age may not be important factors in the emotional behavior following frontal brain injury in the human.

The influence of premorbid states is particularly relevant in the assessment of emotional concomitants after psychosurgery, since there is evidence suggesting underlying CNS structural and/or biochemical alteration in apparently purely functional disorders (Franzen & Ingvar, 1975; Halstead, 1947; Lassen, Ingvar, & Skinhøj, 1978; Luchins, Weinberger, & Wyatt, 1979; Naeser, Levine, Benson, Stuss, & Weir, 1981; Pontius, 1972; Pontius & Yudowitz, 1980; Stamm & Kreder, 1979; Tucker, Stenslie, Roth, & Shearer, 1981). Effects of premorbid pathology must be controlled in order to isolate the effect of the localized brain pathology.

CURRENT STUDIES OF EMOTIONAL DISORDER IN FRONTAL-DAMAGED PATIENTS

CLINICAL STUDIES

In addition to personality alterations, two clinical syndromes appear to illuminate specific aspects of frontal behavioral abnormality. Recent studies suggest that confabulation and reduplication are dependent upon frontal system dysfunction.

CONFABULATION

Confabulation may be defined simply as the production of incorrect information; this may be in response to a standard question or it may be information presented spontaneously by the patient. Confabulation ranges from a mild elaboration to a totally fantastic and wildly bizarre fabrication. While recognized and recorded for many years (Berlyne, 1972), particularly as a major and distinctive feature of the Korsakoff syndrome (Victor, Adams, & Collins, 1971), only in recent years have formal studies probed the mechanisms of confabulation. Mercer, Wapner, Gardner, and Benson (1977) demonstrated that the degree of confabulation in amnesic patients was not closely correlated with either severity of memory disturbance or with suggestibility. They did find a close correlation between confabulation and the subjects' ability to self-correct. As self-correction improved, the amount of confabulation decreased, even though the amnesia remained profound. This inability to self-correct suggested an abnormality of awareness, an inattention to the meaning of the words being produced.

Several subsequent studies (Stuss, Alexander, Lieberman, & Levine, 1978; Kapur & Coughlan, 1980) reported patients who demonstrated a related but different problem, a severe, fantastic, and spontaneous confabulation. Each of these patients had documented frontal lobe structural pathology of considerable extent. Kapur and Coughlan (1980) demonstrated that the amount of confabulation presented by their patient decreased concomitantly with improvement in the patient's performance on frontal lobe tests. A recent experimental project on confabulation (Shapiro, Alexander, Gardner, & Mercer, 1981) has verified the presence of mild confabulation in patients with frontal lobe disease, and formal studies demonstrate great difficulty provoking such patients to examine the incongruities of their verbalizations.

The studies on confabulation suggest that the disorder, regardless of degree, is a cognitive disorder of awareness, directly related to an inability to be self-corrective. Correlation of confabulation with bifrontal structural pathology is suggested but not proved by the studies to date. Confabulation appears to be a disturbance of the personality; not only is there an abnormal relationship of the individual with the environment but a superimposed apathy, an abulic, unconcerned attitude is frequently present.

REDUPLICATION

Reduplication is a disorder that appears to be related to confabulation. Reduplicative paramnesia is a term used in the neurologic literature primarily in reference to the reduplication of a known environment (Benson, Gardner, & Meadows, 1976; Paterson &

Zangwill, 1944; Ruff & Volpe, 1981), a disturbance also known as reduplication of place (Weinstein & Kahn, 1955). In contrast, the Capgras syndrome is usually listed as an unusual psychiatric disorder (Freedman & Kaplan, 1975) and features reduplication of close relatives or well-known acquaintances. The patient with Capgras syndrome is convinced that this person is actually an imposter who closely resembles the real person. In reduplicative paramnesia the patient, who knows the name of the hospital and the current situation, nonetheless places the hospital (or other living unit) in a considerably different location, almost always one that is important in the patient's past. In both instances the patient demonstrates awareness of correct data, such as the name of the hospital or the name and appearance of the family member, but is unable to accept this data as real. These delusions are firmly held, even in the face of absolute evidence of their falseness.

Several recent studies on these subjects (Benson *et al.*, 1976; Alexander, Stuss, & Benson, 1979) correlated the presence of reduplicative paramnesia and the Capgras syndrome with structural brain damage. In both instances severe bifrontal structural pathology was present. Each of the individuals reported in these studies showed a notable alteration of emotional behavior including an unconcerned attitude, apathy, and euphoria, displaying a remarkably inappropriate contentment with their situation. It was postulated that the cognitive disorder of decreased awareness plus the inability to be self-corrective was a key to the two syndromes and that these deficits were products of frontal lobe malfunction. A recent report suggests that unilateral right-hemisphere (frontal plus parietal) pathology is sufficient to produce reduplication of environment (Ruff & Volpe, 1981). Most reports in the literature, and two of the four cases reported by Ruff and Volpe, have clear evidence of bilateral pathology, but the possibility that only one frontal area need be involved deserves consideration.

PSYCHOSURGERY

PROJECT DESCRIPTION

While very little controlled research on emotional response has been performed on patients who have undergone prefrontal leukotomy, the placement of specifically placed lesions in the frontal lóbes should provide data for the study of the effect of frontal defect on emotion/personality. In a recently performed neuropsychological investigation of the long-term effects of prefrontal leukotomy (Stuss, Kaplan, Benson, Weir, Naeser, & Levine, 1981), several studies of emotional competency were included. While the results are not conclusive, these studies are worthy of discussion.

In cooperation with other investigators, the authors had the opportunity to thoroughly assess 16 patients who had undergone prefrontal leukotomy between the years 1947 and 1954. In each case the surgery was performed as treatment for severe schizophrenia. Based on the degree of psychiatric recovery following the surgery, three groups of patients were outlined: I, good recovery; II, moderate recovery; III, no recovery. Detailed description of the patient population, the type of surgery, the size and location of the lesions, the degree of psychiatric recovery, and the results on extensive neuropsychologic testing have been presented in a series of papers (Benson, Stuss, Naeser, Weir, Kaplan, & Levine, 1981; Naeser et al., 1981; Stuss, Kaplan, & Benson, 1982; Stuss et al., 1981). For comparison purposes, two control groups were organized: IV, a nonleukotomized schizophrenic group of the same age, duration of symptoms, and treatment program except for the leukotomy; and V, age- and education-matched normal subjects.

Investigation of emotion in these groups was based on four techniques. Observation and assessment of the emotional state of each individual during the prolonged and demanding test situation was the first technique. In addition, three formal tests were presented to probe emotional responses. In one standardly used test, the Thematic Apperception Test (Murray, 1943), only three cards, numbers 2, 13MF, and 8M, were selected. The Thematic Apperception Test is a projective technique in which drawings of unstructured situations that theoretically elicit emotional responses are presented. The subjects are instructed to make up a story based on their perception of what the picture demonstrates. The responses were recorded verbatim and scored for the presence of main motives or feelings as well as for strength of emotion, measured on a scale of 1 to 5, based on intensity, duration, frequency, and importance of the emotion in the patient's plot.

The second psychological test is a newly reported technique that requests matching of facial expressions (Cicone, Wapner, & Gardner, 1980). In a 24-item test two positive expressions (happy and surprise/glee), four negative expressions (sad, disgust, fear, and anger), and one neutral expression are used. One of the emotional faces (target) and four other faces were presented; the patient was instructed to pick the face showing an emotional expression similar to the target face. For each trial the three incorrect choices consist of one expression from the same pole (positive or negative), one from the opposite pole, and one neutral. As a control, facial recognition was formally assessed (Cicone et al., 1980). The leukotomized subjects showed only minimal difficulty with the facial recognition testing, suggesting that any difference found in their score on the emotional expression matching test cannot be attributed to problems in facial recognition.

The third psychological test, an Emotional Situations Test, was specifically designed for this project to probe the responses of patients to drawings of emotional situations. Nine target stimuli made up the test (see Figure 2). Three portrayed sad scenes, three depicted happy or fun scenes, and the final three represented neutral scenes. The nine target stimuli were presented individually and in random order. Three response stimuli were presented, facial expressions depicting either a happy, sad, or a neutral expression. The subject was required to choose the facial reaction card thought to go best with the target stimulus. Following selection, the patient was requested to describe why the selected facial response went with the specific target stimulus and why the other facial expressions were not appropriate with that picture.

RESULTS

In the clinical observations on the patients who had undergone prefrontal leukotomy, three major factors were noted. First, the outward emotional reaction (affect) proved difficult to assess and the underlying mood could only be guessed. There was no evidence that suggested a "pseudodepression"—no expressions of depression nor significant degree of retardation were noted, although most of the patients showed some degree of apathy. It would be more accurate to state that the patients were, almost without exception, passive, and most also showed a rather easy

FIGURE 2. *Emotional Situations Test. In this example, a sad situation was presented pictorially to the subject. The facial expressions presented for matching to the emotional situation are shown in the lower half of the figure.*

irritability. Despite this, few mood swings were noted, even through a period of intense and demanding testing. The second point of note is that the patients were poor at verbalizing their emotional state and, even more pertinent, showed almost no relationship between the verbal response and the outward manifestations as observed by the examiner. Almost invariably, verbal responses were noncommital (e.g., "I am O.K."), and irritability and anger were seldom verbalized even though obvious to the observer. Whether this type of response should be considered an asynchrony of mood and affect or represents a separation of language and action could not be determined from observation alone. However, experience with these patients in many other neuropsychological tests strongly supported a divorce of language and action. The third major observation concerns the residual psychiatric symptomatology. Each of the subjects in Groups I–IV had a severe and intractable psychosis originally and most were still under treatment for schizophrenia. Some of the observed behavior clearly reflects underlying psychiatric problems. For instance, some patients carried on conversations with nonexistent companions and others responded to visual hallucinations during the period of testing.

Just as in most earlier reports on the behavior of postleukotomy patients, the premorbid psychiatric state proved to be an insurmountable unknown and, in final consideration, the clinical observations on our subjects were too complex to be accepted for correlation of the emotional behavior with the site of leukotomy.

The Thematic Apperception Test was presented to all subjects in all five groups and no significant differences were found. The nonleukotomized schizophrenic group (IV) produced more responses that were not logically associated with the presented picture, a finding in keeping with their responses to other neuropsychological tests. On the other hand, the leukotomized schizophrenics, even those too psychotic to be out of the hospital (Group III) or those with large bifrontal destructive lesions (Group I), gave responses that were not significantly different from the control subjects. The TAT, which uses unstructured situations and demands projection of emotional responses, as used, proved insufficiently sensitive to elicit the effect of the localized prefrontal damage.

On a purely logistical basis, some of the patients could not be tested for the Matching of Facial Expressions. Most particularly, several patients in Group III and Group IV, those with the most severe schizophrenic symptomatology, were not given this test. Those subjects from these groups who did complete the task performed the most poorly. Nonetheless, for statistical purposes, only three groups (I, II, V) could be analyzed and they showed no statistically significant differences. There was some indication that the group with the largest orbitofrontal lesions (Group I) were not as good as the normals in matching the facial expressions, but subjects in Group II, all of whom also had sizeable bilateral orbitofrontal lesions, performed at the same limits as the normal control subjects. We cannot state, at least as determined by this test, that the presence of sizeable bifrontal leukotomy lesions produced any defect in the matching of emotional facial expressions.

One study in the literature (Cicone et al., 1980) states that this test was done poorly by patients with frontal damage. This study, utilizing some of the leukotomized subjects reported here and comparing them to normal control subjects, demonstrated a significant difference. Two factors deserve consideration. First, the leukotomy patients were considered as a single group, ignoring the presence of psychiatric recovery or the size of the lesion. Secondly, the control subjects were not matched for age and education. The possibility that the differences were on the basis of the ongoing schizophrenia, the long-term use of psychiatric medication, or the long-term institutionalization rather than frontal damage deserves consideration.

All five groups completed the entire Emotional Situations Test and, in contrast to the Matching of Facial Expressions Test, significant group differences ($F(4,19) = 8.5$) were demonstrated for the total number of correct responses. The normal control subjects performed considerably better than any of the other four groups (see Figure 3). The normal subjects analyzed the target stimulus and chose the correct face to represent the emotional reaction. It had been hypothesized that Group III and Group IV would have difficulties, based on the degree of schizophrenic symptomatology, whereas Group I would perform normally, as this group had performed normally on many other neuropsychologic tests. Actually, all four patient groups were inferior to the normal group regardless of IQ, memory, or attention levels, suggesting that the presence of the orbitofrontal pathology interfered with analysis of the emotional aspects of the pictured situation. Moreover, only the normal control group consistently gave abstract interpretations, whether the choices were correct or incorrect, when asked to explain why a particular response face had been chosen, but only the nonleukotomized group produced illogical, nonassociated responses.

This finding, the presentation of nonrelated responses, was demonstrated across many neuropsychological tests given to the nonleukotomized group, in striking contrast to the rare occurrence in the leukotomized schizophrenics (Stuss et al., 1982). As examples, when a nonleukotomized schizophrenic was asked why

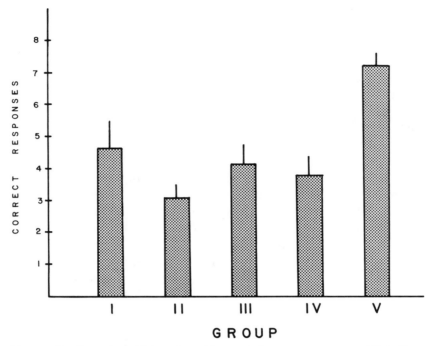

FIGURE 3. *Emotional Situations Test, total correct responses. This figure shows the number of correct matchings of facial responses with the emotional states for the five experimental groups. The response is independent of the quality of the verbalized explanation. Group I, good-recovery leukotomized subjects; Group II, moderate-recovery leukotomized subjects; Group III, no-recovery leukotomized subjects; Group IV, nonleukotomized schizophrenics; Group V, normal control subjects.*

a particular expression was chosen to match the emotional situation, such unrelated responses as these were presented: "That's what the pillar looks like unwrapped"; "Guilty of murder with a salad bowl" (for a neutral face chosen for a boy standing by a tree); "It's an electric chair"; "That's Bing Crosby, I think"; "I don't like it."

On the other hand, leukotomized schizophrenics tended to note similarities ("Both are blue") or nonemotional relationships between the face and the target stimulus ("A boy would sit in a chair like that"). Their answers often showed awareness of a relationship, even though in error. Thus, for the coffin picture one subject chose the happy face, with the following explanation: "It is a sad affair and he is happy. When a person dies he is dressed up and a smile sometimes appears on his face. . . . Tears don't happen during death . . . since there are no tear glands." Another subject correctly matched the sad face with the sad hanging scene and said, "He is crying because they executed the person." A third chose the happy face with the sad scene of a man in a coffin and when asked why, explained that he was happy that it was not he "personally" in the coffin.

Analysis of the last two tests suggests that the emotional disturbances in the leukotomized (frontally damaged) schizophrenics can be differentiated from those of the nonleukotomized schizophrenics even though both perform poorly. The leukotomized subjects' perception of emotion as demonstrated in the Matching Facial Expressions Test were more often correct, even though the Emotional Situations Test demonstrated that they often failed to associate their perceptions with a situation. This dissociation of perceptual and cognitive awareness can be considered a cognitive defect of emotion. One aspect of the reported personality disturbance following prefrontal damage appears to be an inability to translate mood or emotion into appropriate behavior. The personality thus appears to be a disconnected phenomenon with the emotional behavior separated from the environment.

In summary, clinical observation showed abnormalities but these could not systematically differentiate groups. The Thematic Apperception Test, a test devised to elicit emotional responses, appeared insensitive to the effects of prefrontal leukotomy. Two additional tests, specifically devised to test the effect of brain damage on emotion and behavior, were only partially helpful, but indicate the importance of further investigations of the separation of the verbal and physical responses of emotional behavior.

INTEGRATION AND INTERPRETATION

It appears possible to use formal neuropsychological testing techniques in patients with well-localized frontal lobe pathology to demonstrate abnormalities of emotional response. Two important facets are clear; first, studies of emotion in brain-damaged patients are highly dependent upon the definition of an emotion, and most current approaches obfuscate investigation by failing to define precisely the topic of study. A second crucial facet concerns premorbid emotional behavior. In the research presented here, the presence of schizophrenic symptomatology and long-term institutionalization were of major significance. Against this background we can attempt an integration of our findings with neuroanatomy.

The broad variation of emotions affected is compatible with the known neuroanatomical connections and the current theories of the function of the frontal lobes. As outlined by Nauta (1971, 1972, 1973), the frontal cortical–cortical connections appear significant for planning, initiating, and executing behavior and, in addition, for monitoring the effect of an action on the external environment. Frontal–RAS and frontothalamic connections affect selective arousal and selective gating of information (Luria, 1973; Scheibel, 1980); damage to these systems results in apathy and inappropriate behavior. Most important for emotional control is involvement of the frontal–limbic system. Livingston (1969, 1977) has described two separate but parallel circuits of frontal–limbic–hypothalamic–midbrain pathways; a medial frontal–cingulate–hippocampus circuit and an orbital–frontal–temporal–amygdala circuit both exert modulating effects on mood and behavior.

Nauta (1973) has proposed that the major neocortical representation of the limbic system occurs in the prefrontal cortex. The limbic system receives and modulates the internal milieu of a person including the visceral–endocrine relationship with the environment. Nauta states, "The failure of the affective and motivational responses of the frontal lobe patient to match environmental situations that he nonetheless can describe accurately could thus be tentatively interpreted as the consequence of a loss of a modulatory influence normally exerted by the neocortex upon the limbic mechanisms by the frontal lobe" (Nauta, 1971, p. 182). This interpretation accurately depicts a state compatible with the behavioral defects of the leukotomized schizophrenics described in this study.

A second interpretation (not exclusive of the first) concerns the fact that information from the external environment gathered through all modalities, both extroceptive and introceptive, converge only in the frontal lobe. Testing of the affective consequences of a chosen behavior and choosing between alternative modes of thought and action would thus appear to be frontal functions. Damage to this "anticipatory selection process" may underlie some of the behavioral changes of frontal impairment such as flatness of affect, instability of intent, loss of ability to foresee the outcome of an action, and socially inappropriate behavior (Nauta, 1971). Moreover, Nauta hypothesizes a presetting similar to Teuber's (1964) corollary discharge mechanism so that successive interoceptive information acts as navigational markers and provides "temporal stability of complex goal-directed forms of behavior" (1971, p. 183).

From these considerations the effect of frontal psychosurgery on emotional behavior appears obvious. Most of the procedures used for psychosurgery interrupted one of the two major connections between the frontal lobe and the limbic–subcortical structures (Nauta, 1973). Therefore, the effects of frontal lobe damage on emotional behavior must be considered not only in terms of premorbid personality and the specific test items used but also on the specific localization of the pathology within the frontal lobes that determines which of the frontal systems has been affected. Different surgical procedures would appear to affect different components of the frontal–limbic circuits and, theoretically, should result in different alterations of the emotional state.

In addition, emotional changes that are related to the alterations following frontal lobe pathology may follow damage to other areas of the brain. For example, emotional disturbances that are somewhat similar to those following frontal lobe damage have been described after right inferior parietal lobe pathology (Mesulam & Geschwind, 1978). Massive interconnections exist between the parietal lobes, the frontal lobes, and the cingulate gyri. Similar connections between the frontal and prefrontal cortices with other portions of the central nervous system are also recognized. Future studies of emotional behavior following frontal lobe pathology should carefully document the specific cerebral areas disconnected from the prefrontal integrating region. The variety of neuroanatomical connections to the frontal lobes is immensely complex, and the possibility that emotional behavior changes may vary dependent upon the exact combinations of neuroanatomical loss appears probable.

The concept of a "frontal lobe personality" is woefully inadequate, and any study of emotion following frontal damage limited to a single factor (e.g., premorbid personality, response to specific testing, clinical syndromes, neuroanatomical locus) will not only be limited but misleading. Understanding of the effect of the frontal lobes on emotional life demands integration of multiple studies over a broad spectrum of interests.

SUMMARY

In this chapter the effect of frontal lobe damage on emotional behavior has been studied through careful definition of the terms mood, affect, emotion, and personality, through an abbreviated review of pertinent clinical observations in the past, through review of some recent studies of confabulation and reduplicative paramnesia implicating frontal pathology, and through both clinical observations and formal studies of emotion on a small group of patients who had undergone prefrontal leukotomy. While a great variety of emotional alterations can be seen in patients with frontal lobe damage, two of the most specific include a lack of inhibition and a dissociation between the patient's verbalization and the observed response. The emphasis was on the multiple factors which are present in any individual's emotional behavior including premorbid personality, type of stress situation, and the specific localization of the anatomic damage in the frontal lobes.

ACKNOWLEDGMENTS

Preparation of this chapter was supported in part by Grant No. NSO6209, National Institutes of Health, to Boston University School of Medicine; the Research Service of the Veterans Administration; University of Ottawa Faculty of Social Sciences Grant; the National Research Council of Canada; the Ontario Mental Health Foundation; and the Augustus S. Rose Endowment Fund. The library search assistance of Ms. Francine Sarazin in gratefully acknowledged. D. Ferrill assisted in the scoring of the leukotomy data. Sheila Statlander is thanked for the preparation of the stimuli in the Emotional Situations Test.

REFERENCES

Alexander, M. P. Traumatic brain injury. In D. F. Benson & D. Blumer (Eds.), *Psychiatric aspects of neurologic disease* (Vol. 2). New York: Grune & Stratton, 1982.

Alexander, M. P., Stuss, D. T., & Benson, D. F. Capgras syndrome: A reduplicative phenomenon. *Neurology*, 1979, *29*, 334–339.

Bear, D. M., & Fedio, P. Quantitative analysis of interictal behavior in temporal lobe epilepsy. *Archives of Neurology*, 1977, *34*, 454–467.

Belyi, B. I. [Syndrome of aspontaneity in frontal lobe tumours] (Russian). *Zhurnal Nevropatologii i Psikhiatrii*, 1979, *79*, 901–907.

Benson, D. F., Gardner, H., & Meadows, J. C. Reduplicative paramnesia. *Neurology*, 1976, *26*, 147–151.

Benson, D. F., Stuss, D. T., Naeser, M. A., Weir, W. S., Kaplan, E. F., & Levine, H. The long-term effects of prefrontal leukotomy. *Archives of Neurology*, 1981, *38*, 165–169.

Berlyne, N. Confabulation. *British Journal of Psychiatry*, 1972, *120*, 31–39.

Blumer, D., & Benson, D. F. Personality changes with frontal and temporal lobe lesions. In D. F. Benson & D. Blumer (Eds.), *Psychiatric aspects of neurologic disease*. New York: Grune & Stratton, 1975.

Butter, C. M., & Snyder, D. R. Alterations in aversive and aggressive behaviors following orbital frontal lesions in rhesus monkeys. *Acta Neurobiologiae Experimentalis*, 1972, *32*, 525–566.

Cannon, W. B. The James–Lange Theory of emotions: A critical examination and an alternative theory. *American Journal of Psychology*, 1927, *34*, 106–124.

Cicone, M., Wapner, W., & Gardner, H. Sensitivity to emotional expressions and situations in organic patients. *Cortex*, 1980, *16*, 145–158.

Conte, H. R. *A circumplex model for personality traits*. PhD dissertation, New York University, 1975.

Davitz, J. R. A dictionary and grammar of emotion. In M. Arnold (Ed.), *Feelings and emotions: The Loyola Symposium*. New York: Academic, 1970.

Earp, J. D. Psychosurgery: The position of the Canadian Psychiatric Association. *Canadian Journal of Psychiatry*, 1979, *24*, 353–365.

Faust, C. Die psychischen störungen nach Hirntraumen. In H. W. Grunle (Ed.), *Psychiatrie der Gegenwart* (Vol. II). Berlin: Springer, 1960.

Feuchtwanger, E. *Die Funktionen des Stirnhirns ihre Pathologie und Psychologie*. Berlin: Springer, 1923.

Franzen, G., & Ingvar, D. H. Absence of activation in frontal structures during psychological testing of chronic schizophrenics. *Journal of Neurology, Neurosurgery and Psychiatry*, 1975, *38*(10), 1027–1032.

Freedman, A. M., & Kaplan, H. I. *Comprehensive textbook of psychiatry.* Baltimore: Williams & Wilkins, 1975.

Freeman, W., & Watts, J. W. *Psychosurgery in the treatment of mental disorders and intractable pain* (2nd ed.). Springfield, Ill.: Charles C Thomas, 1950.

Freeman, W., Watts, J. W., & Hunt, T. *Psychosurgery.* Baltimore: Thomas, 1942.

Goldstein, K. The mental changes due to frontal lobe damage. *Journal of Psychology,* 1944, *17,* 187–208.

Greenblatt, M., Arnot, R., & Solomon, H. *Studies in lobotomy.* New York: Grune & Stratton, 1950.

Greenblatt, M., & Solomon, H. C. *Frontal lobes and schizophrenia.* New York: Springer, 1953.

Greenblatt, M., & Solomon, H. C. Studies of lobotomy. In *The brain and human behavior: Proceedings of the Association for Research in Nervous and Mental Disease,* 1966, *36,* 19–34.

Halstead, W. C. Specialization of behavioral functions and the frontal lobes. *Research Publication of the Association for Research in Nervous and Mental Disease,* 1947, *27,* 59–66.

Harlow, J. M. Recovery after severe injury to the head. *Publication of the Massachusetts Medical Society (Boston),* 1868, *2,* 327–346.

Harriman, P. L. *Dictionary of psychology.* New York: Philosophical Library, 1947.

Hebb, D. O. Intelligence in man after large removals of cerebral tissue: Report of four left frontal cases. *Journal of General Psychology,* 1939, *21,* 73–87.

Hebb, D. O. Man's frontal lobes: A critical review. *Archives of Neurology and Psychiatry,* 1945, *54,* 10–24.

Hinsie, L. E., & Campbell, R. J. *Psychiatric dictionary* (4th ed.). Toronto: Oxford University Press, 1970.

Holmes, G. Discussion on the mental symptoms associated with cerebral tumors. *Proceedings of the Royal Society of Medicine,* 1931, *24,* 997–1000.

James, W. *Principles of psychology* (Vols. I & II). New York: Dover, 1890.

Jarvie, H. F. Frontal lobe wounds causing disinhibition: A study of six cases. *Journal of Neurology, Neurosurgery and Psychiatry,* 1954, *17,* 14–32.

Kapur, N., & Coughlan, A. K. Confabulation and frontal lobe dysfunction. *Journal of Neurology, Neurosurgery and Psychiatry,* 1980, *43*(5), 461–463.

Kleist, K. *Gehirnpathologie.* Leipzig: Barth, 1934. (a)

Kleist, K. *Kriegsverletzungen des Gehirns.* Leipzig: Barth, 1934. (b)

Kolodny, A. Symptomatology of tumor of the frontal lobe. *Archives of Neurology and Psychiatry,* 1929, *21,* 1107–1127.

Kretschmer, E. Lokalisation und Beurteilung psychophysischer syndrome bei Hirnverletzten. In E. Rehwald (Ed.), *Das Hirntrauma.* Stuttgart: Thieme, 1956.

Langworthy, O. R., & Richter, C. P. Increased spontaneous activity produced by frontal lobe lesions in cats. *American Journal of Physiology*, 1939, *126*, 158–161.

Lassen, N. A., Ingvar, D. H., & Skinhøj, E. Brain function and blood flow. *Scientific American*, 1978, *October*, 62–71.

Levin, H. S., Grossman, R. G., Rose, J. E., & Teasdale, G. Long-term neuropsychological outcome of closed head injury. *Journal of Neurosurgery*, 1979, *50*, 412–422.

Lieberman, A., & Benson, D. F. Pseudobulbar palsy. *Archives of Neurology*, 1977, *34*, 717–719.

Lishman, W. A. Psychiatric disability after head injury: The significance of brain damage. *Proceedings of the Royal Society of Medicine*, 1966, *59*, 261–266.

Lishman, W. A. Brain damage in relation to psychiatric disability after head injury. *British Journal of Psychiatry*, 1968, *114*, 373–410.

Livingston, K. E. The frontal lobes revisited: The case for a second look. *Archives of Neurology*, 1969, *20*, 90–95.

Livingston, K. E. Limbic system dysfunction induced by "kindling": Its significance for psychiatry. In W. H. Sweet, S. Obrador, & J. G. Martín-Rodríguez (Eds.), *Neurosurgical treatment in psychiatry, pain and epilepsy*. Baltimore: University Park Press, 1977.

Luchins, D. J., Weinberger, D. R., & Wyatt, R. J. Schizophrenia: Evidence of a subgroup with reversed cerebral asymmetry. *Archives of General Psychiatry*, 1979, *36*, 1309–1311.

Luria, A. R. *Human brain and psychological processes*. New York: Harper & Row, 1966.

Luria, A. R. [*The working brain*] (B. Haigh, trans.). New York: Basic Books, 1973.

MacLean, P. D. Psychosomatic disease and the "visceral brain": Recent developments bearing on the Papez Theory of emotion. *Psychosomatic Medicine*, 1949, *44*, 338–353.

Mercer, B., Wapner, W., Gardner, H., & Benson, D. F. A study of confabulation. *Archives of Neurology*, 1977, *34*, 429–433.

Messimy, M. R. A propos des troubles psychiques au cours des lobectomies préfrontales. *Revue Neurologie*, 1948, *79*, 537–539.

Mesulam, M. M., & Geschwind, N. On the possible role of neocortex and its limbic connections in attention and schizophrenia. In L. C. Wynne, R. L. Cromwell, & S. Matthysse (Eds.), *The nature of schizophrenia: New approaches to research and treatment*. New York: Wiley, 1978.

Meyer, A., & Beck, E. *Prefrontal leucotomy and related operations: Anatomical aspects of success or failure*. Springfield, Ill.: Charles C Thomas, 1954.

Meyer, V. Psychological effects of brain damage. In H. J. Eysenck (Ed.), *Handbook of abnormal psychology: An experimental approach*. New York: Basic Books, 1960.

Murray, H. A. *Thematic Apperception Test*. Cambridge: Harvard University Press, 1943.

Naeser, M. A., Levine, H. L., Benson, D. F., Stuss, D. T., & Weir, W. S. Frontal leukotomy size and hemispheric asymmetries on computerized tomographic scans of schizophrenics with variable recovery. *Archives of Neurology*, 1981, *38*, 30–37.

Nauta, W. J. H. The problem of the frontal lobe: A reinterpretation. *Journal of Psychiatric Research*, 1971, *8*, 167–187.

Nauta, W. J. H. Neural associations of the frontal cortex. *Acta Neurobiologiae Experimentalis*, 1972, *32*, 125–140.

Nauta, W. J. H. Connections of the frontal lobe with the limbic system. In L. V. Laitinen & R. E. Livingston (Eds.), *Surgical approaches in psychiatry*. Baltimore: University Park Press, 1973.

New Webster's dictionary. New York: Consolidated Book Publishers, 1975.

Ommaya, A. K., & Gennarelli, T. A. A physiopathological basis for noninvasive diagnosis and prognosis of head injury severity. In R. McLaurin (Ed.), *Head injuries: Second Chicago Symposium on Neural Trauma*. New York: Grune & Stratton, 1976.

Oxford English dictionary; compacted edition. Oxford and London: Oxford University Press, 1979.

Paterson, A., & Zangwill, O. L. Disorders of visual space perception associated with lesions of the right cerebral hemisphere. *Brain*, 1944, *67*, 331–358.

Petrie, A. A comparison of the psychological effects of different types of operations on the frontal lobes. *Journal of Mental Science*, 1952, *98*, 326–329.

Plutchik, R. A general psychoevolutionary theory of emotion. In R. Plutchik & H. Kellerman (Eds.), *Emotion: Theory, research and experience*. New York: Academic, 1980.

Pollitt, J. D. Natural history studies in mental illness. A discussion based on a pilot study of obsessional states. *Journal of Mental Science*, 1960, *106*, 93–112.

Pontius, A. Neurological aspects in some type of delinquency especially among juveniles. *Adolescence*, 1972, *7*, 289–308.

Pontius, A., & Yudowitz, B. S. Frontal lobe system dysfunction in some criminal actions as shown in the narratives test. *Journal of Nervous and Mental Disease*, 1980, *168*, 111–117.

Rees, W. L. The value and limitations of psychosurgery in the treatment of psychiatric illness. *Psychiatrie, Neurologie und Neurochirurgie (Amsterdam)*, 1973, *76*, 323–334.

Reitman, F. Orbital cortex syndrome following leucotomy. *American Journal of Psychiatry*, 1946, *103*, 238–241.

Richter, C. P., & Hawkes, C. D. Augmentation spontanée d'activité et de nourriture chez les rates après ablation des pôles frontaux du cerveau. *Journal of Neurology and Psychiatry*, 1939, *II*, 231–242.

Roberts, A. H. Sequelae of closed head injuries. *Proceedings of the Royal Society of Medicine*, 1976, *69*, 137–140.

Rosenkilde, C. E. Functional heterogeneity of the prefrontal cortex in the monkey: A review. *Behavioral and Neural Biology*, 1979, 25(3), 301–345.

Ruff, R. L., & Volpe, B. T. Environmental reduplication associated with right frontal and parietal lobe injury. *Journal of Neurology, Neurosurgery and Psychiatry*, 1981, 44, 382–386.

Rylander, G. *Personality changes after operations on the frontal lobes: A clinical study of 32 cases.* Copenhagen: Munksgaard, 1939.

Sato, M. Prefrontal cortex and emotional behaviors. *Folia Psychiatrica et Neurologica Japonica*, 1971, 25, 69–78.

Sato, M., Onishi, T., & Otsuki, S. Integrating functions of the prefrontal cortex on emotional behaviors. *Folia Psychiatrica et Neurologica Japonica*, 1971, 25, 283–293.

Scheibel, A. B. Anatomical and physiological substrates of arousal: A view from the bridge. In J. A. Hobson & M. A. B. Brazier (Eds.), *The reticular formation revisited.* New York: Raven, 1980.

Scoville, W. B., & Bettis, D. B. Results on orbital undercutting today: A personal series. In W. H. Sweet, S. Obrador, & J. G. Martín-Rodríguez, *Neurosurgical treatment in psychiatry, pain and epilepsy.* Baltimore: University Park Press, 1977.

Scoville, W. B., & Ryan, V. G. Orbital undercutting in the aged. Limited lobotomy in the treatment of psychoneuroses and depressions in elderly persons. *Geriatrics*, 1955, 9–10 (July), 311–317.

Shapiro, B. E., Alexander, M. P., Gardner, H., & Mercer, B. Mechanisms of confabulation. *Neurology*, 1981, 31, 1070–1076.

Smith, J. S., Kiloh, L. G., Cochrane, N., & Kljajic, I. A prospective evaluation of open prefrontal leucotomy. *Medical Journal of Australia*, 1976, 1, 731–735.

Stamm, J. S., & Kreder, S. V. Minimal brain dysfunction: Psychological and neurophysiological disorders in hyperkinetic children. In M. Gazzaniga (Ed.), *Handbook of behavioral neurobiology* (Vol. 2: *Neuropsychology*). New York: Plenum, 1979.

Starr, M. A. Cortical lesions of the brain: A collection and analysis of the American cases of localized cerebral disease. *American Journal of Medical Science New Series*, 1884, 87, 366.

Stedman's medical dictionary illustrated. Baltimore: Waverly, 1979.

Stookey, B., Scarff, J., & Teitelbaum, M. Frontal lobectomy in the treatment of brain tumors. *Annals of Surgery*, 1941, 113, 161–169.

Ström-Olsen, R., & Carlisle, S. Bi-frontal stereotactic tractotomy: A follow-up study of its effects on 210 patients. *British Journal of Psychiatry*, 1970, 118, 141–154.

Stuss, D. T., Alexander, M. P., Lieberman, A., & Levine, H. An extraordinary form of confabulation. *Neurology*, 1978, 28, 1166–1172.

Stuss, D. T., Kaplan, E. F., & Benson, D. F. Long-term effects of prefrontal leucotomy: Cognitive functions. In R. N. Malatesha & L. Hartlage (Eds.), *Neuropsychology and cognition* (Vol. II). The Hague: Martinus Nijhoff, 1982.

Stuss, D. T., Kaplan, E. F., Benson, D. F., Weir, W. S., Naeser, M. A.,

& Levine, H. Long-term effects of prefrontal leucotomy: An overview of neuropsychologic residuals. *Journal of Clinical Neuropsychology*, 1981, *3*, 13–32.

Stuss, D. T., & Richard, M. T. Neuropsychological sequelae of coma after head injury. In L. P. Ivan & D. Bruce (Eds.), *Coma: Physiopathology, diagnosis and management*. Springfield, Ill.: Charles C Thomas, 1982.

Tan, E., Marks, I. M., & Marset, P. Bimedial leucotomy in obsessive-compulsive neurosis: A controlled serial enquiry. *British Journal of Psychiatry*, 1971, *118*, 155–164.

Teuber, H.-L. The riddle of frontal lobe function in man. In J. M. Warren & K. Akert (Eds.), *The frontal granular cortex and behavior*. New York: McGraw-Hill, 1964.

Tucker, D. M., Stenslie, C. E., Roth, R. S., & Shearer, S. L. Right frontal lobe activation and right hemisphere performance: Decrement during a depressed mood. *Archives of General Psychiatry*, 1981, *38*, 169–174.

Victor, M., Adams, R. D., & Collins, G. H. *The Wernicke-Korsakoff syndrome*. Philadelphia: F. A. Davis, 1971.

Walch, R. Uber die Aufgaben der Hirnverzetetenheime nach dem Bundesversorgungsgesetz. In E. Rehwald (Ed.), *Das Hirntrauma*. Stuttgart: Thieme, 1956.

Welt, L. Ueber charakterveränderüngen des Menschen infolge von Läsionen des Stirnhirns. *Deutsche Archiv der Klinishe Medizin*, 1888, 42.

Weinstein, E. A., & Kahn, R. L. *Denial of illness: Symbolic and physiologic aspects*. Springfield, Ill.: Charles C Thomas, 1955.

EMOTIONAL CHANGES ASSOCIATED WITH BASAL GANGLIA DISORDERS

Richard Mayeux

INTRODUCTION

Basal ganglia diseases are disorders usually associated with involuntary movements, alterations in muscle tone, and posture. These clinical manifestations are generally specific enough to enable the clinician to establish an accurate diagnosis. Advances in neurotransmitter biochemistry and pharmacology have resulted in amelioration or improvement of symptoms in this group of otherwise disabling diseases. Nearly every patient with a basal ganglia disease has some type of emotional disturbance. This may be primary to the disease or a secondary manifestation such as a reactive depression or drug-induced psychosis. In spite of the high frequency of psychopathology associated with these diseases, the emotional symptoms are poorly characterized and divergent views exist regarding their etiology.

In this review five diseases of the basal ganglia will be discussed: Parkinson disease, Huntington disease, Wilson disease, progressive supranuclear palsy, and Sydenham chorea. These were chosen because they represent the spectrum of basal ganglia diseases; the neuropathology and clinical features of these disorders are also well established. Other diseases, such as dystonia or Gilles de la Tourette syndrome, are not discussed because of their less precise relationship to altered basal ganglia function.

Richard Mayeux. Department of Neurology, Columbia University College of Physicians and Surgeons, The Neurological Institute of New York, New York, New York.

PARKINSON DISEASE

James Parkinson began his description of "the shaking palsy" with a statement alluding that "the senses and intellect remain uninjured" (Parkinson, 1938). However, throughout the monograph he refers to the patients he describes as "melancholy" and "unhappy." He further commented on a "wished-for release" or a desire for death's release from their illness. A state of delirium in the final stages was also mentioned. These comments probably constitute the first account of the two most frequently observed emotional changes in parkinsonian patients: depression and psychosis.

Although the reported incidence is quite variable, depression has been frequently reported in patients with Parkinson disease. At the turn of the century European investigators began to comment on this association. Patrick and Levy (1922) reported that 33% of the parkinsonian population they had examined were depressed before the onset of the illness, and that another 20% became depressed during the course of the disease. Mjones (1949), who studied many of the clinical aspects of "paralysis agitans," was also struck by the high frequency of associated depression. He described a continuum from dysphoria to severe affective change accompanied by lack of insight and poor impulse control. He further subdivided depression into "reactive type," in which the patient failed to realize the extent of his or her illness as a burden to his or her environment, and the "organic type," distinguished by the fact that intellectual functions began to suffer. Both forms were observed in approximately 40% of his patients. Later studies only confirmed this association, and subsequent investigators began to characterize the symptoms of depression in parkinsonian patients.

Warburton (1967) evaluated 140 patients referred for thalamotomy. Using the Maudsley Personality Inventory he classified depressive symptoms into three types: fleeting unsustained symptoms, sustained depressive symptoms preventing adjustment to the illness, and sustained depression with suicidal ideation. Over one-half of the parkinsonian patients he evaluated had significant depression (71% females, 56% males). He further commented that many patients described vivid suicidal thoughts. Mindham (1970) used standard psychiatric diagnostic criteria and retrospectively determined the presence of various types of psychopathology in 89 parkinsonian patients admitted specifically to the hospital for "mental illness." Ninety percent of these patients displayed evidence of a depressive affect. In most instances depression was not the primary psychopathology, and the incidence of depression was no different in the control group. This may have been a falsely elevated figure, however, because the parkinsonian population was drawn primarily from a psychiatric facility. Another retrospective study (Brown & Wilson, 1972) determined the presence of depression using the Hamilton Depression Scale. Charts of 111 patients were reviewed and 52% of the parkinsonians were deemed significantly depressed. Celesia and Wanamaker (1972) found depression among 45% of 170 parkinsonian patients, using similar criteria to that of Warburton (1967). A control group was not examined in these two investigations, and most of the subjects were hospitalized. Mayeux, Stern, Rosen, and Leventhal (1981) evaluated 55 consecutive well-functioning outpatients, reported to be independent and free of dementia. Using the Beck Depression Index, 47% of this group was depressed compared with 4% of the control group of spouses.

The reported severity of depression has been mild to moderate (Celesia & Wanamaker, 1972; Mayeux, Stern, Rosen, & Leventhal, 1981; Warburton, 1967), and suicide is rarely encountered (Mjones, 1949). In spite of this, when parkinsonian patients are compared with similarly disabled patients, such as general medical or surgical patients (Warburton, 1967), paraplegics (Horn, 1974), patients with multiple sclerosis (Riklan, Levita, & Diller, 1961), or other chronic diseases (Robins, 1976), they have always emerged as more significantly depressed.

Depression has been observed to occur before the overt onset of other signs of parkinsonism. Mindham (1970) noted this in 12% of his patients. A similar figure was reported by Brown and Wilson (1972), and others have noted even a higher figure (Mayeux, Stern, Rosen, & Leventhal, 1981; Patrick & Levy, 1922).

Depression has been inconsistently related to various aspects of the disease. Some have found that depressed parkinsonian patients were more often women (Celesia & Wanamaker, 1972; Warburton, 1967). Brown and Wilson (1972) found a slight relationship to the degree of rigidity, and other investigators have found slight, yet significant correlations between the degree of depression and the disability associated with parkinsonism (Mayeux, Stern, Rosen, & Leventhal, 1981; Mindham, 1970, 1974). Other investigators have not observed this association (Celesia & Wanamaker, 1972; Warburton, 1967). Some have speculated that depression in parkinsonian patients may be related to alterations in central amines other than dopamine (Brown & Wilson, 1972; Mayeux, Stern, Rosen, & Leventhal, 1981); however, this remains an unproven hypothesis.

Levodopa therapy has had a curious relationship to depression. It has been implicated as a cause (Cherrington, 1970; Goodwin, 1971; Jenkins & Groh, 1970), and as a form of treatment for depression (Barbeau, 1969; Celesia & Wanamaker, 1972; Yahr, Duvoisin, Schear, Barrett, & Hoehn, 1969). Mindham, Marsden, and Parkes (1976) found that levodopa could exacerbate depression in some patients, but was a poor antidepressant. Others have concluded that levodopa has no specific relationship to the presence of depression in parkinsonian patients (Marsh & Markham, 1973; Mayeux, Stern, Rosen, & Leventhal, 1981).

Antidepressant therapy, particularly imipramine (Strang, 1965), desipramine (Laitinen, 1969), and nortriptyline (Anderson, Aabro, Gulmann, Hjelmsted, & Pedersen, 1980), has been found to be effective in controlled investigations in depressed parkinsonian patients. When this has failed in some severely depressed parkinsonians, electroconvulsive therapy has been reported to be effective (Asnis, 1977; Lebensohn & Jenkens, 1975; Yudofsky, 1979).

Intellectual impairment of a mild degree may be associated with depression. Mjones (1949) first noted this association and in recent studies Mayeux, Stern, Rosen, and Leventhal (1981) and Mayeux and Stern (in press) have noted a pattern of intellectual dysfunction that includes inattention along with impaired memory and calculations.

Table 1 summarizes the literature covering the clinical characteristics of depression in Parkinson disease. It is reasonable to conclude that Parkinson disease may predispose patients to depression. In some, this may represent a reaction to the disability inherent to the disease, while in others altered monoamine metabolism or medications may be a contributing or causal factor.

Many parkinsonian patients become passive and lose their initiative and motivation. In some instances the degree of result-

TABLE 1. *Depression in Parkinson disease*

Prevalence: 37–50%
Premorbid symptom: 10–15%
Severity: mild to moderate (rare suicide)
No consistent relationship to age, sex, degree of disability, or type of
   therapy
Associated symptoms
   Inattention
   Impairment of memory and calculations
Treatment
   Tricyclic antidepresssant
   ECT?

---

ing apathy can be so great as to cause a loss of interest in daily activities and social interactions. This apathetic state may be associated with depression; however, it may also occur independently. Excessive dependency, fearfulness, anxiety, and emotional lability have been observed in parkinsonian patients (Lishman, 1979), but the prevalence of these symptoms in any given population is unknown.

Psychosis in Parkinson disease is usually a drug-related phenomenon. Celesia and Wanamaker (1972) found psychosis, defined as episodes of hallucinations or delusions that were usually reversible, among 13% of 153 patients with Parkinson disease. In all but three patients this was attributed to the administration of drugs, particularly levodopa and anticholinergics. In the majority of these patients intellectual impairment was also noted. Other investigators have noted a high frequency of psychosis among parkinsonian patients with any degree of intellectual impairment (Boller, Mizutani, Roessmann, & Gambetti, 1980; Sacks, Krohl, Messeloff, & Schwartz, 1972). Other dopaminergic agents such as bromocriptine, lergotrile (Serby, Angrist, & Lieberman, 1978), and pergolide (Ilson, Fahn, Mayeux, Cote, & Snider, in press) have been found to induce psychosis. Anticholinergic therapy has also been associated with confusion, delusions, and hallucinations (Porteous & Ross, 1956).

Non-drug-related psychosis or a schizophreniform-like illness has been rarely noted in Parkinson disease (Davison & Bagley, 1969). Mindham (1970) found that only two of 89 patients whose records he reviewed had symptoms suggestive of schizophrenia.

Crow, Johnstone, and McClelland (1976) reported the coincidence of schizophrenia and parkinsonism in four patients. Each of these patients had signs and symptoms of Parkinson disease before the onset of delusions or hallucinations. In each case the psychosis was not considered drug related, although three of the four patients described were on anticholinergic therapy. No evidence of intellectual impairment was found in these patients and the episodes were brief in duration. An additional feature in each case was a reactive depression that resolved as the psychosis improved. Table 2 summarizes the characteristics of psychosis in Parkinson disease.

Sands (1942) referred to the "masked personality" of people who would eventually develop Parkinson disease. He described their premorbid personality as one in which constant anxiety, aggressiveness, and anger were suppressed, and later, chronically repressed. Similarly Booth (1948) found that parkinsonian patients were industrious, independent, rigid, and moralistic before the onset of their illness. These investigators included subjects with postencephalitic, "arteriosclerotic," and idiopathic Parkinson disease, and relied upon subjective evaluation. In a prospective evaluation of 118 patients referred for stereotactic surgery, Diller

TABLE 2. *Psychosis in Parkinson disease*

Drug-induced (10–15% of all patients)
Anticholinergic
  Trihexyphenidyl (benzhexol)
  Amantadine
  Benztropine
Dopaminergic
  Levodopa
  Bromocriptine
  Lergotrile
  Pergolide
Usually associated with some degree of intellectual impairment
Non-drug-related (*rare*)
Brief in duration
Associated depression
No change in intellectual ability

---

and Riklan (1956) objectively assessed personality and background concluding that their patients were too diverse to conceive of a "parkinsonian personality." Obviously a large, well-controlled study would be required to determine if any particular personality trait occurs in patients who eventually develop Parkinson disease.

HUNTINGTON DISEASE

Involuntary movements and intellectual decline are usually the predominant features of this disease. "Insanity with a tendency to suicide," was also a manifestation described by Huntington (1872). Nearly every patient who develops Huntington disease can be expected to have a significant emotional disorder (Bear, 1977; Bruyn, 1968), and at times a primary psychiatric diagnosis may be made before motor or intellectual symptoms develop (Dewhurst, Oliver, Trick, & McKnight, 1969; Heathfield, 1967). Family members, especially those at risk, are particularly fearful of the prospect of developing serious psychopathology (Stern & Eldridge, 1975; Wexler, 1979). No particular evolution or sequence of emotional symptomatology has ever been described. Brothers (1964) reported that "personality and character changes" were the initial symptoms in 28% of 237 patients (see Table 3). In these patients Brothers (1964) described a variety of nonspecific emotional symptoms such as irritability, aggressiveness, irresponsibility, promiscuity, alcoholism, and "schizoid" behavior. He cautioned that the mental symptoms might be so subtle in the early stages that they would be apparent only to close family members. Subsequent

TABLE 3. *First symptoms recorded in Huntington chorea patients in Victoria*

Mode of onset	Males	Females	Total
Chorea	81	59	140
Personality and character change	29	37	66
Unknown	16	15	31

Note. From "Huntington's Chorea in Victoria and Tasmania" by C. Brothers, *Journal of Neurological Sciences*, 1964, *1*, 405–420. Copyright 1964 by Elsevier Biomedical Press B. V. Reprinted by permission.

investigators, however, have also noted these as early symptoms of psychopathology in Huntington disease (Bruyn, 1968; Dewhurst *et al.*, 1969; Dewhurst, Oliver, & McKnight, 1970; Hans & Gilmore, 1968; Oliver & Dewhurst, 1969).

Bear (1977) suggested that a possible sequence of emotional changes might occur (see Table 4): an early prodrome of irritability, aggression, promiscuity, and antisocial behavior followed by mood changes such as depression or, less frequently, mania; later, apathy, psychosis, self-neglect, and abulia might occur in association with profound dementia. Bear emphasized that there has never been a longitudinal investigation of emotional changes in Huntington disease, and this might represent only a theoretical model.

There is an enormous variability in the reported types of psychiatric disturbances in patients with Huntington disease. Some have attributed this to the sex of the individual patient (Tamir, Whittier, & Korenyi, 1969), or to individual family characteristics (Dewhurst *et al.*, 1970; Garan, 1973; Hans & Gilmore, 1968; Oliver & Dewhurst, 1969). More likely, this variability is related to the sensitivity of the examiners and to their documentation of psychiatric symptoms (Bruyn, 1968; Dewhurst *et al.*, 1970). Standard measures of psychopathology, such as the Minnesota Multiphasic Personality Inventory, have been used, but have not reliably distinguished Huntington disease patients from patients with other neurological disorders (Boll, Heaton, & Reitan, 1974; Norton, 1975). Clinical descriptions of individual cases and epidemiological surveys point to a wide range of emotional changes associated with Huntington disease. In the large survey by Brothers

TABLE 4. *Possible sequence of emotional symptoms in Huntington disease*

Early	Middle	Late
Irritability	Depression	Apathy
Aggressiveness	Mania	Abulia
Promiscuity	Psychosis	Dementia
Antisocial behavior		

Note. Adapted from "Emotional and Behavioral Changes in Huntington's Disease" by D. Bear, *Report to the Commission to Combat Huntington's Disease,* 1977.

(1964) psychosis, mania, depression, and dementia were as noted in Table 5.

Depression and suicide have frequently been observed in patients with Huntington disease (Chandler, Reed, & Dejoung, 1960; Dewhurst *et al.*, 1970). McHugh and Folstein (1975) reported a mood disturbance resembling a manic–depressive disorder. Episodes of depression accompanied by hopelessness, guilt, and delusions of "sinfulness" often accompanied by suicidal thoughts were described. Psychomotor retardation and intellectual decline have also been associated with depression. In many instances the depression lasted months to years before resolving. Episodes of mania were found to alternate with depression. Recently Folstein, Folstein, and McHugh (1979) reported their experience with affective disorders in Huntington patients. Using established research criteria they were able to document bipolar illness in five of ten patients (see Table 6).

Apathy, a want of feeling or affect, or a loss of interest and emotional involvement, occurs frequently in Huntington disease. It may be an early (Brothers, 1964; McHugh & Folstein, 1975) or a late symptom (Bear, 1977; McHugh & Folstein, 1975). It often results in a severe loss of initiative and motivation. McHugh and Folstein (1975) have observed that apathy may be subtle initially, but tends to progress with the other features of the disease leaving the patient reduced to a state of inertia, abulia, and mutism. Patients gradually lose interest in work, household affairs, and even in the progression of their disease state. Although careful documentation of this symptom is lacking, some authors have

TABLE 5. *Psychiatric diagnosis of 155 Huntington disease patients*

Schizophrenic reaction:	20
Paranoid state:	15
Depressive state:	13
Manic state:	4
"Organic dementia":	103
	155

Note. From "Huntington's Chorea in Victoria and Tasmania," by C. Brothers, *Journal of Neurological Sciences*, 1964, *1*, 405–420. Copyright 1964 by Elsevier Biomedical Press B.V. Reprinted by permission.

TABLE 6. *Huntington disease: Types of psychiatric disorder*

	n
Manic–depressive disorder, manic or bipolar	2
Manic–depressive disorder, depressed	3
Auditory hallucinatory state	2
Demoralization	2
Irritability, social withdrawal	2

Note. From "Psychiatric Syndromes in Huntington's Disease" by S. E. Folstein, M. F. Folstein, and P. R. McHugh, *Advances in Neurology*, 1979, *23*, 281–289. Copyright 1979 by Raven Press. Reprinted by permission.

suggested that apathy heralds the onset of intellectual decline in patients with Huntington disease (Bruyn, 1968; Caine, Hunt, Weingartner, & Ebert, 1978; McHugh & Folstein, 1975). Apathy, a negative or passive symptom, is one to which the patient has little insight, thus creating problems in the immediate home environment. The spouse often has to "nag" the patient to shower, to socialize, or to tend to other family matters. Physicians may be unaware of the degree of apathy unless directly involved with the family. This has partially been explained by the nature of the patient–physician relationship, in that it is a structured setting in which the patient is passive or receiving of attention. Caine *et al.* (1978) noted apathy in their description of the dementia of Huntington disease. Their patients rarely initiated independent activity; however, they did participate in structured ward activities. They suggested that this may be a manifestation of their difficulty in organizing and planning activities. In addition, it may well represent a link between intellectual and behavioral dysfunction. Mayeux, Stern, Rosen, and Benson (1981) found apathy to be the most common emotional symptom in huntingtonian patients using the Brief Psychiatric Rating Scale as an objective measure of psychopathology. Table 7 lists the other emotional changes found to be associated with Huntington disease in that investigation. In addition, using a brief but quantitative neuropsychological measure, a significant correlation between the appearance of apathy and intellectual decline was found. Many investigators have observed the apathetic state to be periodically interrupted for

TABLE 7. *Emotional changes in Huntington disease (n = 20)*

Depression:	6	(4 with associated thought disorder)
Mania:	1	
Psychosis:	4	
Apathy:	9	(correlation with intellectual impairment and episodic irritability)

minutes to even days by episodes of irritability, aggression, and restlessness (Caine *et al.*, 1978; McHugh & Folstein, 1975).

Psychosis has been infrequently encountered as an initial symptom of Huntington disease, and may appear at any time during the illness (Bruyn, 1968; Folstein *et al.*, 1979; Mayeux, Stern, Rosen, & Benson, 1981; Rosenbaum, 1941). In the three patients reported by Mayeux, Stern, Rosen, and Benson (1981), hallucinations and delusions were often more difficult to manage than the involuntary movements or dementia. The thought disorders reported in Huntington disease range from bizarre somatic delusions to delusions of persecution involving mind and body control.

Treatment of emotional disorders in Huntington disease has met with variable results. Pharmacotherapy for apathy has never been addressed formally. Caine *et al.* (1978) and Folstein *et al.* (1979) found that by structuring the hospital environment the degree of apathy was somewhat lessened. Dextroamphetamines and methylphenidate have been used in other diseases that are accompanied by apathy, such as Alzheimer disease; however, there is no convincing evidence of their effectiveness (*Medical Letter*, 1978). Episodic irritability, associated with apathy, has been successfully treated by combinations of lithium carbonate and butyrophenones (Leonard, Kitzen, Shannon, & Brown, 1974). Depression may respond to tricyclic antidepressants (Caine *et al.*, 1978; McHugh & Folstein, 1975; Whittier, Haydu, & Crawford, 1961). Unfortunately this does not affect the progression of the illness and may offer only transient benefit. Regular psychological and support systems are usually needed for the patient and family to help in the management of depression. Shoulson (1980) reported that tricyclic antidepressants do not appear to have an effect on the progression of psychiatric symptoms. Similarly, phenothia-

TABLE 8. *Treatment of psychiatric symptoms in Huntington disease*

Depression	Tricyclic antidepressant (temporary improvement)
Psychosis	Butyrophenes
Apathy	Structure
	CNS stimulants
Episodic irritability	Lithium in combination with butyrophenone

zines have only a temporary benefit in the psychosis of Huntington disease (Shoulson, 1980). Table 8 summarizes the treatment strategies used for psychiatric symptoms in Huntington patients.

PROGRESSIVE SUPRANUCLEAR PALSY (STEELE–RICHARDSON–OLSVEWSKI SYNDROME)

Steele, Richardson, and Olsvewski (1964) described a peculiar basal ganglia disorder that was manifest by supranuclear paralysis of external ocular movements, dysarthria, axial dystonia, and mild dementia. The pathological substrate of this disorder was neurofibrillary tangles, gliosis, and demyelination particularly in the basal ganglia, brainstem, and cerebellar nuclei. In some patients, symptoms included an insidious onset of vague changes in personality. In three of the nine patients they described, irritability with fits of aggressive behavior was the most obvious emotional change.

Albert, Feldman, and Willis (1974) made a careful and timely description of the pattern of intellectual impairment noted in progressive supranuclear palsy. They referred to this as "subcortical dementia." Characteristically, the combination of forgetfulness, slowing of thought processes, and inability to manipulate acquired knowledge was present in association with a particular pattern of emotional change that fell into one of two categories: apathy with intermittent irritability or euphoria, and depression. The most striking change was a gradual onset of indifference (apathy) in most of these patients. This led to poor bodily hygiene and loss of interest in household affairs. In their review of 42 other patients from the literature, these same characteristics were present in over half of the patients. The appearance of the apathetic state or a mood disorder is considered by some to be one of the characteristic features of subcortical dementia (Mayeux, Stern, Rosen, & Benson, 1981). Inappropriate and even forced laughing or crying, suggesting lability of affect associated with pseudobulbar palsy, was seen in 14 of the 42 patients reported (Albert *et al.*, 1974). In nearly every case, personality change occurred in conjunction with the onset of cognitive impairment; however, in three cases it was the initial symptom. Albert *et al.* (1974) concluded that apathy and depression were the most frequently encountered emotional changes of progressive supranuclear palsy.

Pharmacotherapy for this disease in general has been quite limited. Attempts to employ antiparkinson medication such as levodopa or anticholinergics have met with limited success. Similarly, attempts to treat the apathetic or depressed state of these patients have not been successful.

WILSON DISEASE
(HEPATOLENTICULAR DEGENERATION)

"The clinical syndrome comprises involuntary movements, mostly tremulous but sometimes athetoid or spasmodic, rigidity, dysarthria, emotional overaction (spastic smiling, etc.) and at times a mental disorder of an unspecified and mostly transient kind" (Wilson, 1940). Earlier, Wilson (1912) had described four patients with a peculiar constellation of extrapyramidal signs and symptoms in association with a mental disorder. He had also reviewed the literature and described eight other similar patients.

Emotional changes remain an enigma in Wilson disease primarily because of their extreme variability. In the original monograph, Wilson (1912) described an emotional overaction with involuntary laughing. He stated that he thought there was a dissociation between the affect and the emotional expression. Later, he referred to the emotional disturbances in a similar manner, but included instability of mood, irritable outbursts, and psychosis in his discussion (Wilson, 1940). He concluded that the emotional symptomatology did not persist and therefore might not be related to the pathological changes in the basal ganglia.

Emotional disturbances may occur early or late in the disease. Sternlieb and Scheinberg (1964) noted psychiatric disturbances as the first manifestations of Wilson disease in 15% of their patients. In an additional 24%, emotional disturbances appeared simultaneous with or just after the first neurological or hepatic manifestastions of the disorder. In general, Scheinberg, Sternlieb, and Richmond (1968) have noted that the majority of patients develop some form of psychiatric disturbance during the course of their illness. Walker (1969) noted the onset of a diverse group of psychiatric symptoms prior to any neurologic or hepatic manifestations in all of the patients he encountered (see Table 9). In each case, patients were often treated by a psychiatrist or given a descriptive psychiatric diagnosis before the actual diagnosis of Wilson disease was established.

Three major categories of emotional disturbance have emerged consistently in Wilson disease: personality disorder, affective disorder, and psychosis. A variety of behavioral traits or personality disorders are reported including hysteria, increased sexuality, aggression, hostility, school phobia, irritability, excitability, poor impulse control, and antisocial behavior. These tend to be intermittent and may not require psychiatric intervention. The most consistent reported personality change, however, is that first noted by Wilson (1912), emotional lability.

Affective disturbance, usually manifest by depression, may be associated with a delusional state or even fleeting episodes of uncontrollable weeping (Lishman, 1979). Psychosis may occur in the late stages of the illness (Scheinberg & Sternlieb, 1965; Wilson, 1940). It is usually of a paranoid type and may be associated with delusions or hallucinations resembling schizophrenia. Beard

TABLE 9. *Presenting psychiatric symptoms in Wilson disease (n = 12)*

Thought disorder:	3
Depression:	2
Character disorder:	1
Phobias:	2
"Hysteria":	3
Mental retardation:	1

Note. From "The Psychiatric Presentation of Wilson's Disease (Hepatolenticular Degeneration) with an Etiologic Explanation" by S. Walker, *Behavioral Neuropsychiatry*, 1969, *1*, 38–43.

(1959) cautioned that the diagnosis of schizophrenia in association with Wilson disease was incorrect, and attributed the thought disorder to disorders of consciousness associated with hepatic dysfunction. As with other emotional disturbances, the psychosis of Wilson disease appears to be episodic in nature, although there are reports of patients with sustained thought disorder (Sternlieb & Scheinberg, 1964). Standard treatment for Wilson disease has resulted in improvement of most emotional symptoms. In the series by Sternlieb and Scheinberg (1964), 40% of the patients improved significantly following the administration of penicillamine. Other symptomatic therapies for depression and/or psychosis are less predictable.

SYDENHAM CHOREA

Sydenham chorea or chorea minor is a disorder of childhood associated with irregular involuntary movements of the face, trunk, and extremities. The terms "Sydenham chorea," "St. Vitus's dance," and "chorea minor" are used interchangeably to refer to chorea of presumed rheumatic origin. The etiology of this disorder is still uncertain, but it is considered to be a manifestation of rheumatic fever (Aron & Carter, 1977). The usual onset is between the ages of 5 and 15. Chorea gravidarum may be related to Sydenham chorea and to a rheumatic etiology; however, this relationship remains uncertain.

Typically, the chorea is associated with involuntary movements, incoordination, weakness, and psychiatric phenomena. The severity of all of these features is variable. Emotional lability appears to be the most consistently encountered psychiatric problem. Apathy may also occur in some patients with intermittent or episodic irritability. In its most severe form, a confusional state with hallucinations or delusions may be present. Gatti and Rosenheim (1969) described a girl who presented with a psychiatric disturbance. Her affect was bland and she showed surprisingly little insight into her medical problem. Moderate to severe intellectual impairment, in addition to her apathetic state, was noted. Most of her symptoms cleared within a 1-year period. Bender (1945) suggested that intellectual or cognitive impairment occurred only during the acute phase of the disease, as did all psychiatric phenomena. Sacks, Feinstein, and Taranta (1962) also found that children in the acute stages of rheumatic chorea tended to be withdrawn, unassertive, and irritable, but they concluded that this was more likely to be a reaction to the illness rather than a result of central nervous system disease.

Emotional sequelae of Syndenham chorea were studied by Freeman, Aron, Collard, and McKay (1965). Forty patients and an equal number of controls were reevaluated on an average of 29 years after their illness. All subjects were grouped by an independent psychiatrist's examination into one of three categories: no psychopathology, personality or character disorder, and psychoneurosis. Most of the choreic patients still had some degree of psychiatric illness (75%), while only a quarter of the control medical group displayed such symptoms. In the chorea group, 16.7% had significant manifestations of psychoneurosis such as excessive phobias, obsessive–compulsive behavior, conversion reactions, and anxiety. None of the control group displayed this type of emotional change. A high incidence of premorbid emotional symptoms existed in the chorea group. Aron, Freeman, and Carter (1965) found that half of their group of choreic patients had had preexisting emotional disorders before the onset of Sydenham chorea. Some authors (Stehbens & MacQueen, 1972) have argued that the effect of a major illness such as rheumatic fever could explain the high incidence of emotional changes during the postillness period. This was verified in a group of patients with rheumatic fever with and without Sydenham chorea; the postillness adjustment period and the degree of psychopathology was similar in both groups (Stehbens & MacQueen, 1972).

While it appears that emotional changes are present in patients with Sydenham chorea, the degree of severity and the sequelae remain a controversial issue. There is a striking consistency, however, in that this is a disorder of basal ganglia associated with emotional lability, apathy with intermittent irritability, and less frequently, thought disorder. Not all patients manifested these symptoms, but the vast majority of children with Sydenham chorea did have this particular constellation of signs and symptoms which are possibly related to changes reported in the basal ganglia.

CONCLUSIONS

The neurological phenomenology of disorders of basal ganglia are quite clear. Generally they fall into four categories, as seen in Table 10. Postural changes range from the stooped, simian posture of Parkinson disease to the hyperextended dystonic posture of progressive supranuclear palsy. Involuntary movements of the trunk may be seen in Huntington or Sydenham chorea. Some degree of postural instability may be present in all patients with these disorders. Gait disturbance is almost always encountered and may range from a shuffling, unstable, bradykinetic one to a choreic or dancing gait. Involuntary movements are generally the hallmark of basal ganglia disease, and tremor, dystonia, and a variety of dyskinesias are observed. Articulatory disturbances are frequently seen and may range from dysarthria and hypophonia to near mutism.

In many of these disorders a characteristic dementia is present and has been referred to as "subcortical dementia." Characteristically, forgetfulness without true amnesia and a mild degree of cognitive impairment is noted. Emotional disorders are similarly consistent and tend to fall into four classes (see Table 11). Affective disturbance, primarily depression and less frequently mania, is the most frequently encountered symptom. Apathy, characterized by loss of initiative and motivation, interrupted by episodes of irritability or aggression also occurs in these patients. Lability of emotion and psychosis are less frequently encountered, although they are seen regularly. There are obvious variations in the clinical expression of these emotional disturbances in each disorder, and within each type of disorder there may be a broad range of symptomatology.

These disorders share neuropathological changes within the basal ganglia. Each is probably a related manifestation of disturbed neurotransmitter biochemistry. Certain pharmacological agents with known effects on central amines can produce similar mood disorders and psychosis. In addition, some primary psychiatric disorders have been thought to be linked to an alteration in monoamine metabolism. Although indirect and unproven, it is intriguing to consider that alterations in catechol or indolamine

TABLE 10. *Neurological phenomenology of basal ganglia disease*

Postural change	Stooped, kyphotic	PD
	Hyperextended, dystonic	PSP, WD, HD
	Truncal involuntary movements	HD, SC
Gait disturbance	Shuffling, unsteady, bradykinetic	PD, PSP, WD
	Choreic	HD, SC
Involuntary movements	Tremor	PD
	Dystonia	PD, PSP, WD, HD
	Dyskinesia	HD, SC
Language (speech) disturbance	Dysarthric	PD, HD, WD, PSP
	Hypophonic	PD, HD, WD, PSP
	Mutism	PD, HD, WD, PSP

Note. Explanation of abbreviations: Parkinson disease (PD); Huntington disease (HD); Wilson disease (WD); progressive supranuclear palsy (PSP); Sydenham chorea (SC).

TABLE 11. *Emotional disorders associated with basal ganglia disease*[a]

	PD	HD	PSP	WD	SC
Affective disorder (depression)	++	+++ (Rare mania)	++	+	++
Apathy with episodic irritability or aggression	++	+++	++	−	+
Lability of emotion	−	+	+++	++	++
Thought disorder		+	−	+	+

Note. Explanation of abbreviations: Parkinson disease (PD); Huntington disease (HD); progressive supranuclear palsy (PSP); Wilson disease (WD); Sydenham chorea (SC).
[a]Excluding all medication-related phenomena.

159

metabolism may underlie the emotional changes as well as the motoric features of basal ganglia diseases.

REFERENCES

Albert, M. L., Feldman, R. G., & Willis, A. L. The "subcortical dementia" of progressive supranuclear palsy. *Journal of Neurology, Neurosurgery and Psychiatry*, 1974, *37*, 121–130.

Andersen, J., Aabro, E., Gulmann, N., Hjelmsted, A., & Pedersen, H. E. Antidepressive treatment in Parkinson's disease. *Acta Neurologica Scandinavica*, 1980, *62*, 210–219.

Aron, A. M., & Carter, S. Sydenham's chorea. In E. S. Goldensohn & S. H. Appel (Eds.), *Scientific approaches to clinical neurology*. Philadelphia: Lea & Febiger, 1977.

Aron, A. M., Freeman, J. M., & Carter, S. The natural history of Sydenham's chorea. *American Journal of Medicine*, 1965, *38*, 83–95.

Asnis, G. Parkinson's disease, depression and ECT: A review and case study. *American Journal of Psychiatry*, 1977, *134*(2), 191–195.

Barbeau, A. L-Dopa therapy in Parkinson's disease: A critical review of nine years' experience. *Canadian Medical Association Journal*, 1969, *101*, 791–800.

Bear, D. Emotional and behavioral changes in Huntington's disease. *Report to the Commission to Combat Huntington's Disease*, 1977.

Beard, A. W. The association of hepatolenticular degeneration with schizophrenia. *Acta Psychiatrica et Neurologica Scandinavica*, 1959, *34*, 411–428.

Bender, L. Organic brain conditions producing behavioral disturbances. In N. D. C. Lewis & B. Pacella (Eds.), *Modern trends in child psychology*. New York: International Universities Press, 1945.

Boll, T., Heaton, R., & Reitan, R. Neuropsychological and emotional correlates of Huntington's chorea. *Journal of Nervous and Mental Diseases*, 1974, *158*, 61–69.

Boller, F., Mizutani, T., Roessmann, U., & Gambetti, P. Parkinson disease, dementia, and Alzheimer disease: Clinicopathological correlations. *Annals of Neurology*, 1980, *7*, 329–335.

Booth, G. Psychodynamics in parkinsonism. *Psychosomatic Medicine*, 1948, *10*, 1–14.

Brothers, C. Huntington's chorea in Victoria and Tasmania. *Journal of Neurological Sciences*, 1964, *1*, 405–420.

Brown, G. L., & Wilson, W. P. Parkinsonism and depression. *Southern Medical Journal*, 1972, *65*, 540–545.

Bruyn, T. W. Huntington's chorea: Historical, clinical and laboratory synopsis. In P. J. Vinken & G. W. Bruyn (Eds.), *Handbook of clinical neurology*. Amsterdam: North Holland, 1968.

Caine, E. D., Hunt, R. D., Weingartner, H., & Ebert, M. J. Huntington's dementia. *Archives of General Psychiatry*, 1978, *35*, 377–384.

Celesia, G. G., & Wanamaker, W. M. Psychiatric disturbances in Parkinson's disease. *Diseases of the Nervous System*, 1972, *33*, 577–583.

Chandler, J., Reed, T., & Dejoung, R. Huntington's chorea in Michigan: III. Clinical observations. *Neurology*, 1960, *10*, 148–153.

Cherrington, M. Parkinsonism, L-dopa and mental depression. *Journal of the American Geriatric Society*, 1970, *18*, 513–516.

Crow, J. J., Johnstone, E. D., & McClelland, H. A. The coincidence of schizophrenia and parkinsonism: Some neurochemical implications. *Psychological Medicine*, 1976, *6*, 227–233.

Davison, K., & Bagley, C. R. Schizophrenia-like psychoses associated with organic disorders of the nervous system: A review of the literature. In R. N. Herrington (Ed.), *Current problems in neuropsychiatry, British Journal of Psychiatry*, Special Publication No. 4, 1969, 113–184.

Dewhurst, K., Oliver, J., & McKnight, A. L. Socio-psychiatric consequences of Huntington's disease. *British Journal of Psychiatry*, 1970, *116*, 255–258.

Dewhurst, K., Oliver, J., Trick, L., & McKnight, A. Neuro-psychiatric aspects of Huntington's chorea. *Continua Neurologica*, 1969, *31*, 258–268.

Diller, L., & Riklan, M. Psychosocial factors in Parkinson's disease. *Journal of the American Geriatric Society*, 1956, *4*, 1291–1300.

Folstein, S. E., Folstein, M. F., & McHugh, P. R. Psychiatric syndromes in Huntington's disease. *Advances in Neurology*, 1979, *23*, 281–289.

Freeman, J. M., Aron, A. M., Collard, J. E., & McKay, M. C. The emotional correlates of Sydenham's chorea. *Pediatrics*, 1965, *35*, 42–49.

Garan, D. Huntington's chorea and schizophrenia. *Advances in Neurology*, 1973, *1*, 729–734.

Gatti, F. M., & Rosenheim, E. Sydenham's chorea associated with transient intellectual impairment. *American Journal of Diseases of Children*, 1969, *118*, 915–918.

Goodwin, F. K. Psychiatric side effects of levodopa in man. *Journal of the American Medical Association*, 1971, *218*, 1915–1920.

Hans, M. B., & Gilmore, T. H. Social aspects of Huntington's chorea. *British Journal of Psychiatry*, 1968, *114*, 93–98.

Heathfield, K. W. G. Huntington's chorea. *Brain*, 1967, *90*, 203–232.

Horn, S. Some psychological factors in parkinsonism. *Journal of Neurology, Neurosurgery and Psychiatry*, 1974, *37*, 27–31.

Huntington, G. W. On chorea. *Medical and Surgical Reports*, 1872, *26*, 317–321.

Ilson, J., Fahn, S., Mayeux, R., Cote, L., & Snider, S. Pergolide treatment of parkinsonism. In S. Fahn, D. Calne, & I. Shoulson (Eds.), *Experimental therapeutics of movement disorders*. New York: Raven Press, in press.

Jenkins, R. B., & Groh, R. H. Mental symptoms in parkinsonian patients treated with L-dopa. *Lancet*, 1970, *2*, 177–180.

Laitinen, L. Desipramine in the treatment of Parkinson's disease. *Acta Neurologica Scandinavica*, 1969, *45*, 109–113.

Lebensohn, Z., & Jenkins, R. B. Improvement of parkinsonism in depressed patients treated with ECT. *American Journal of Psychiatry*, 1975, *132*, 283–285.

Leonard, D., Kitzen, M., Shannon, P., & Brown, J. Double blind trial of lithium carbonate and haloperidol in Huntington's chorea. *Lancet*, 1974, *2*, 1208–1209.

Lishman, W. A. *Organic psychiatry*. London: Blackwell, 1979.

Marsh, G. G., & Markham, C. H. Does levodopa alter depression and psychopathology in parkinsonism patients? *Journal of Neurology, Neurosurgery and Psychiatry*, 1973, *36*, 925–935.

Mayeux, R., & Stern, Y. Intellectual impairment and dementia in Parkinson disease. In R. Mayeux & W. Rosen (Eds.), *The dementias*. New York: Raven Press, in press.

Mayeux, R., Stern, Y., Rosen, J., & Benson, D. F. Subcortical dementia: A recognizable clinical entity. *Transactions of the American Neurological Association*, 1981, *106*, 313–316.

Mayeux, R., Stern, Y., Rosen, J., & Leventhal, J. Depression, intellectual impairment, and Parkinson disease. *Neurology*, 1981, *31*, 645–650.

McHugh, P. R., & Folstein, M. F. Psychiatric symptoms of Huntington's chorea: A clinical and phenomenologic study. In D. Blumer & D. F. Benson (Eds.), *Psychiatric aspects of neurologic disease*. New York: Grune & Stratton, 1975.

Medical Letter, 1978, *20*, 75.

Mindham, H. S. Psychiatric syndromes in parkinsonism. *Journal of Neurology, Neurosurgery and Psychiatry*, 1970, *30*, 188–191.

Mindham, H. S. Psychiatric aspects of Parkinson disease. *British Journal of Hospital Medicine*, 1974, *11*, 411–414.

Mindham, R. H. S., Marsden, C. D., & Parkes, J. D. Psychiatric symptoms during L-dopa therapy for Parkinson's disease and their relationship to physical disability. *Psychological Medicine*, 1976, *6*, 23–33.

Mjones, H. Paralysis agitans. *Acta Psychiatrica et Neurologica (Supplement)*, 1949, *54*, 1–195.

Norton, J. C. Patterns of neuropsychological test performance in Huntington's disease. *Journal of Nervous and Mental Disease*, 1975, *161*, 276–279.

Oliver, J., & Dewhurst, K. Six generations of ill-used children in a Huntington pedigree. *Postgraduate Medicine*, 1969, *45*, 757–760.

Parkinson, J. An essay of the shaking palsy, 1817. *Medical Classics*, 1938, *2*, 964–997.

Patrick, H. T., & Levy, D. M. Parkinson's disease: A clinical study of 146 cases. *Archives of Neurology and Psychiatry*, 1922, *7*, 711–720.

Porteous, H. B., & Ross, D. N. Mental symptoms in parkinsonism following benzhexol hydrochloride therapy. *British Medical Journal*, 1956, *2*, 138–140.

Ricklan, M., Levita, E., & Diller, L. Psychologic studies in neurological diseases—A review: Parkinson's disease and multiple sclerosis. *Journal of the American Geriatric Society*, 1961, *9*, 857–867.

Robins, A. H. Depression in patients with parkinsonism. *British Journal of Psychiatry*, 1976, *128*, 141–145.

Rosenbaum, D. Psychosis with Huntington's chorea. *Psychiatric Quarterly*, 1941, *15*, 93–99.

Sacks, L., Feinstein, A. R., & Taranta, A. A controlled psychologic study of Sydenham's chorea. *Journal of Pediatrics*, 1962, *61*, 714–722.

Sacks, O. W., Krohl, M. S., Messeloff, C. R., & Schwartz, W. F. Effects of levodopa in Parkinsonian patients with dementia. *Neurology*, 1972, *22*, 615–619.

Sands, I. J. The type of personality susceptible to Parkinson disease. *Journal of the Mount Sinai Hospital (New York)*, 1942, *9*, 792–794.

Scheinberg, I. H., & Sternlieb, I. Wilson's disease. *Annual Review of Medicine*, 1965, *16*, 119–134.

Scheinberg, I. H., Sternlieb, I., & Richmond, J. Psychiatric manifestations in patients with Wilson's disease. *Birth Defects*, 1968, *4*, 85–87.

Serby, M., Angrist, B., & Lieberman, A. Mental disturbances during bromocriptine and lergotrile treatment of Parkinson's disease. *American Journal of Psychiatry*, 1978, *135*, 1227–1229.

Shoulson, I. Huntington disease: A prospective evaluation of functional capacities in patients treated with neuroleptics and antidepressants. *Neurology*, 1980, *30*, 393. (Abstract)

Steele, J. C., Richardson, J. C., & Olsvewski, J. Progressive supranuclear palsy. *Archives of Neurology*, 1964, *10*, 333–359.

Stehbens, J. A., & MacQueen, J. C. The psychological adjustment of rheumatic fever patients with and without chorea. *Clinical Pediatrics*, 1972, *11*, 638–640.

Stern, R., & Eldridge, R. Attitudes of patients and their relatives to Huntington's disease. *Journal of Medical Genetics*, 1975, *12*, 217–223.

Sternlieb, I., & Scheinberg, I. H. Penicillamine therapy for hepatolenticular degeneration. *Journal of the American Medical Association*, 1964, *189*, 748–754.

Strang, R. R. Imipramine in treatment of parkinsonism: A double-blind placebo study. *British Journal of Medicine*, 1965, *2*, 33–34.

Tamir, A., Whittier, J., & Korenyi, C. Huntington's chorea: A sex difference in psychopathological symptoms. *Diseases of the Nervous System*, 1969, *30*, 130.

Walker, S. The psychiatric presentation of Wilson's disease (hepatolenticular degeneration) with an etiologic explanation. *Behavioral Neuropsychiatry*, 1969, *1*, 38–43.

Warburton, J. W. Depressive symptoms in Parkinson patients referred for thalamotomy. *Journal of Neurology, Neurosurgery and Psychiatry*, 1967, *30*, 368–370.

Wexler, N. S. Genetic "Russian roulette": The experience of being at risk for Huntington's disease. In S. Kessler (Ed.), *Genetic counselling: Psychological dimensions*. New York: Academic, 1979.

Whittier, J., Haydu, G., & Crawford, J. Effect of imipramine on depression and hyperkinesia in Huntington's disease. *American Journal of Psychiatry*, 1961, *118*, 79.

Wilson, S. A. K. Progressive lenticular degeneration. *Brain*, 1912, *34*, 295–509.

Wilson, S. A. K. *Neurology* (Vol. II). Baltimore: Williams & Wilkins, 1940.

Yahr, M. D., Duvoisin, R. S., Schear, M. J., Barrett, R. E., & Hoehn, M. M. Treatment of parkinsonism with levodopa. *Archives of Neurology*, 1969, *21*, 343–354.

Yudofsky, S. C. Parkinson's disease, depression, and electroconvulsive therapy: A clinical and neurobiologic synthesis. *Comprehensive Psychiatry*, 1979, *20*, 579–581.

PERSONALITY AND EMOTIONAL COMPLICATIONS OF EPILEPSY

Paul B. Pritchard, III

PERSONALITY CHANGES

INTRODUCTION

Personality disorder has been attributed to epileptic patients for well over 100 years. The concept of "the epileptic personality" evolved, but the attributes thereof were often more pejorative than supported by systematic evaluation. Possible influences such as responses from society, family dynamics, underlying brain pathology, seizure type and etiology, age at onset of seizures, and antiepileptic drugs must be considered in investigation of the epileptic patient. Furthermore, recognition of and control for special population groups of epileptic patients may be critical.

Tizard (1962) outlined basic theories concerning possible aberrations of personality in epileptic patients:

1. Most epileptics share a characteristic personality ("the epileptic personality").
2. The same range of personality traits are found among epileptics as in nonepileptics, and there is no characteristic epileptic personality.
3. Although there is no characteristic epileptic personality,

Paul B. Pritchard, III. Neurology Service, Veterans Administration Medical Center, Charleston, and Department of Neurology, Medical University of South Carolina, Charleston, South Carolina.

there is a higher proportion of neurotic behavior among epileptics.
4. Epileptics have personality abnormalities based on the nature of the causative brain lesion.
5. Different types of epilepsy are associated with different personality types.

Tizard (1962) went on to criticize the methodology of previous studies of personality in epileptics. She noted that many studies had focused on highly selected patient populations. Previous studies had used a variety of selection criteria, whether clinical, electroencephalographic, or otherwise. In addition, the methods of personality assessment were often incomplete. The limitations of such tests as the Rorschach were self-evident. Many studies had not been controlled for intelligence, education, and social background.

Assessment of Personality and Neuropsychological Function

Personality and neuropsychological evaluation of epileptic patients must take into account the vagaries of hemispheric specialization following brain injury (Milner, 1971, 1974). In addition to hemispheric specialization for cognitive function, the emotive specialization of the cerebral hemispheres must be considered. Reliance on personality tests alone, such as the Minnesota Multiphasic Personality Inventory (MMPI), is not sufficient for assessment of psychological functions.

Dodrill (1978) has devised a neuropsychological test battery designed to aid investigation in this area. The battery includes tests of intellectual functioning, emotional status, and lateral dominance. The Wonderlic Personnel Test, which may be given and scored rapidly, provides a reasonable and rapid assessment of intellectual function comparable to Wechsler Adult Intelligence Scale (WAIS) Full-Scale IQ results (Dodrill, 1980). Workers from the University of Washington have formulated the Washington Psychosocial Seizure Inventory, which develops a profile in such areas as family background, financial status, vocational adjustment, medical management, and interpersonal adjustment (Dodrill, Batzel, Queisser, & Temkin, 1980).

FACTORS INVOLVED IN PSYCHOLOGICAL
AND PERSONALITY OUTCOME

The responses of society in general and family in particular are relevant to social adjustment by the epileptic. So long as the diagnosis of epilepsy is stigmatized, societal reactions will influence social adjustment. Ziegler (1979) emphasized the importance of control (of and by the epileptic and his family) in psychological adaptation. He discussed the related concepts of autonomy ("degree of control over personal relationships") and competence ("degree of control over physical environment"). There is significant interaction between the patient and his family in relation to autonomy and competence. For instance, the patient may use seizures and compliance with treatment to exert control. Ziegler warned against the "malignant intrafamilial spiral" which often occurs in early adulthood when the question of independent living by the epileptic is raised. He advised collaborative goals and guidelines between the epileptic and his family to avoid this outcome.

Hodgman, McAnarney, Myers, Iker, McKinney, Parmelee, Schuster, and Tutihasi (1979) investigated the issues of communication, self-image, and school performance in adolescent epileptics. Surprisingly, there was an inverse relationship between the degree of seizure control and open communication about the seizure disorder. The authors found that more disabled patients were unexpectedly optimistic about future prospects, such that they tended to have a better self-image than those patients who were more nearly normal. They also found that better seizure control and less neurologic disability did not correlate positively with better school performance. Rather, the best index of good overall function was whether the patient was attending the school grade appropriate to his age.

Stores (1978) demonstrated a correlation between reading skills in epileptic schoolchildren and the type of epilepsy. Children with generalized epilepsy performed as well as a control population of nonepileptics. Children with temporal lobe epilepsy had poorer scores of reading accuracy, and those with left temporal lobe foci on EEG performed less well than those with right-sided temporal lobe foci. Epileptic males performed less well than epileptic females in reading skills in both generalized epilepsy and temporal lobe epilepsy groups. Epileptic males had difficulty in sustaining attention to a task for long periods of time. There was a tendency toward social isolation for all epileptic school-children, but this was especially so for those with left temporal lobe epilepsy.

Antiepileptic drugs may have an effect on personality and psychological test performance (Reynolds, 1981). Wolf and Forsythe (1978) demonstrated an increased incidence of behavior disorder in children with febrile convulsions who were treated with phenobarbital. The likelihood of behavior disorder did not correlate with antiepileptic drug levels. Further inquiry into the effect of antiepileptic drugs was done by Dodrill and Wilkus (1978a), using a broad range of neuropsychological tests. They made comparisons in a double-blind crossover study of phenytoin, carbamazepine, and sulfthiame. Test results were compared for patients with lower or higher serum levels of phenytoin. The "low group" performed significantly better than the "high group," with the primary differences in relation to tasks requiring a strong motor component. Compared with sulfthiame, the group on phenytoin performed significantly better on most subtests, particularly those requiring concentration, attention to task, and general intelligence. There were fewer differences between phenytoin and carbamazepine administration, but test results always favored carbamazepine. In a previous study (Dodrill & Troupin, 1977) patients on carbamazepine made fewer errors in tests requiring attention and problem solving. There was also slight improvement in emotional status as shown by MMPI scores.

Seizure etiology also has a significant effect on performance on personality and neuropsychological tests. Matthews and Klove (1968) demonstrated more nearly normal MMPI scores for patients in whom the etiology for seizures was unknown. Dikmen and Reitan (1978) found successively lower performances on neuropsychological tests among a control group with no brain disease, a group with posttraumatic epilepsy without neurological abnormality, and those with posttraumatic epilepsy with focal neurological signs, using the Wechsler–Bellevue Intelligence Scale, Halstead's Neuropsychological Test Battery, and the Trail-Making Test. They stressed that there was marked impairment even in posttraumatic epileptics without abnormal neurological signs, so that the neurological exam and neuropsychological testing complement rather than replicate each other.

Lindsay, Ounsted, and Richards (1979a) made a follow-up survey on a group of 100 patients with temporal lobe epilepsy whom they had initially coded in 1964. They classified the social outcome at follow-up, and there was a significant relationship to seizure etiology. The best outcome was in patients in whom the seizure etiology was not known. Five other biological variables assessed at the beginning of the study were relevant to outcome. An IQ less than 90 was associated with poor outcome. If seizures began before the median age of 2 years, 4 months, the outcome was likely to be worse. Both severity of grand mal seizures and maximum frequency of temporal lobe seizures were inversely related to social outcome. Laterality of the discharge focus on EEG was important in that the patients with right temporal lobe epilepsy fared better than those with discharge foci in the left temporal lobe. Two behavioral disorders in childhood, the hyperkinetic syndrome and catastrophic rage, also predicted poor social outcome.

Several investigators have correlated neuropsychological testing with EEG abnormalities (Dodrill & Wilkus, 1978b). Using the neuropsychological test battery of Halstead and Reitan, the authors showed an orderly decrease in test performance with increasing slow-wave abnormality on EEG. They also demonstrated a relationship in test performance to the type and distribution of epileptiform discharges, finding the best performance with no discharges, intermediate performance with focal discharges, and worst performance with generalized discharges. The degree of slow-wave abnormality was a more potent predictor of test performance.

Hermann, Schwartz, Karnes, and Vahdat (1980) used the MMPI to evaluate the relationships of psychopathology to seizure type and age at onset. There were no overall differences in MMPI scores between temporal lobe and generalized epilepsy. However,

analyses of individual MMPI measures showed significant interactions between seizure type and age at onset. Patients with
adolescent-onset temporal lobe epilepsy were considered at higher
risk for developing psychological dysfunction. In a related study,
Hermann, Schwartz, Whitman, and Karnes (1980) used a measure
of aggression derived from the MMPI, the sum of t scores for
validity scale F and clinical scales 4 (psychopathic deviate) and 9
(hypomania). The study was limited to the use of the MMPI-
derived scales, but they could not support the contention that
temporal lobe epilepsy is preferentially associated with aggressiveness.

McIntyre, Pritchard, and Lombroso (1976) used the Kagan
Matching Familiar Figures Test and the Davitz–Mattis Metaphor
Test to measure cognitive style and ability to decipher verbal-
affective messages in a group of temporal lobe epileptics and
matched controls. Left temporal lobe epileptics demonstrated a
reflective conceptual approach, while the right temporal lobe epileptics were more impulsive. In an earlier study (Zern, Kenney, &
Kvaraceus, 1974) there had been an association between impulsive
conceptual tempo and a tendency to engage in outwardly directed
aggressive behavior. McIntyre *et al.* (1976) also demonstrated an
increased nonconsensuality score with the Davitz–Mattis Metaphor Test for left temporal lobe epileptics, who had difficulty in
assigning affect labels and presumably would be predisposed to
interpersonal difficulties.

Waxman and Geschwind (1975) described a characteristic
clinical syndrome of interictal behavior in temporal lobe epileptics
consisting of changes in sexual behavior (usually hypoactive),
religiosity and deepened philosophical interests, and hypergraphia
with compulsive writing or drawing. Bear and Fedio (1977) used
dual questionnaires to systematically investigate 18 personality
traits which have been attributed to temporal lobe epilepsy. They
were able to differentiate right and left temporal lobe groups from
controls with both the rater evaluations and self-description questionnaires. Patients with right temporal lobe epilepsy were typi-
fied by changes in affective drive or behavior, consistent with the
emotive function of the right cerebral hemisphere. In keeping
with the ideative function of the left cerebral hemisphere, patients
with left temporal lobe epilepsy identified with intellectual con-

templation. There was no correlation between scores and seizure frequency, but the duration of epilepsy was important, suggesting that personality changes may reflect progressive changes in limbic structures secondary to temporal lobe discharges, producing a consistent profile of changes in behavior. Bear (1979a, 1979b) hypothesized the formation of neuronal circuits and synaptic connections ("sensory–limbic hyperconnection") as the anatomical basis for the personality changes in temporal lobe epilepsy. Hermann and Chhabria (1980) offered support for Bear's theory.

SEXUAL DYSFUNCTION

CASE HISTORY

A 39-year-old married man suffered a blow to the left hemicranium, resulting in skull fracture and laceration of the underlying cerebral cortex. He lost consciousness for 4 days and was dysphasic when he regained consciousness. His language function recovered over the next year and one-half. Eight months after the injury he had the onset of "blackout spells," each preceded by a feeling of depersonalization and *déjà vu*: "I am not myself and I don't know where I am or what I am doing." Witnesses reported that he would adopt a blank stare, with loss of contact and automatisms, usually continuing some preictal activity.

Fourteen years after cerebral injury, he had been free of complex partial seizures for 1 year, and there had never been any generalized seizures. He was in excellent physical health, but he complained bitterly of impotence, first noticed 1 year earlier. He insisted that his libido was preserved, and he denied any other stigmata of endocrinopathy. Physical examination showed no gynecomastia or abnormality of body hair. Examination of the external genitalia and prostate were normal. Serum levels of phenytoin, carbamazepine, and phenobarbital were within the usual therapeutic range.

Sexual dysfunction has been linked with temporal lobe epilepsy in most reports. Personality disorder and nonavailability of consort because of the social stigma of epilepsy are possible contributing factors, but the role of underlying brain lesions and the chronic effects of antiepileptic drugs must be considered.

Marriage, Fertility, and Reproductive Function

Although most of the literature concerning sexual dysfunction in epileptics relates to complex partial (temporal lobe or psychomotor) epilepsy, several surveys have examined reproductive function and marriage in relation to general epileptic populations. Dansky, Andermann, and Andermann (1980) surveyed 200 epileptic patients from the Montreal Neurological Institute. They studied an equal number of each gender, but seizure types, EEG abnormalities, and neurological status were not addressed. The authors did observe that their series contained a disproportionate number of temporal lobe epileptics because of the local interest in temporal lobectomy. They demonstrated that only 38% of the males had married, whereas 61% of the women had done so ($p < .001$). They noted some variation in the likelihood of marriage by age at seizure onset. For males, an earlier onset of epilepsy diminished the chances of marriage. They compared results with a similar earlier study from the same clinic which had demonstrated a marked decrease in marriage rates for epileptic men and women. There had been considerable improvement in marriage rates for women. A positive reproductive history was also more common for women (58%) than for men (33%) in the entire series. However, married epileptic men attained the expected fertility rate, but the rate for married epileptic women was less than expected.

In a surgical series (Cogen, Antunes, & Correll, 1979), 25 temporal lobe epileptics underwent temporal lobectomy for intractable seizures. The authors noted a potpourri of sexual dysfunction in their patients preoperatively, including both increased and decreased libido in men. A small minority of women in the series reported decreased libido prior to operation. There was improvement in seizure control in 76% following temporal lobectomy, and 3 patients also had improved libido.

Parody of Sexual Function

Some cases in the literature which have purported to describe "sexual seizures" have actually described episodic somatosensory symptoms of genital distribution. However, three women who had ictal events resembling sexual intercourse were described by

Currier, Little, Suess, and Andy (1971). Two women with temporal lobe spikes on EEG exhibited nonorgasmic sexual performance, abating with the use of antiepileptic drugs. A third woman reported episodic "sexual feelings"; a basal tumor indenting the hypothalamus was subsequently identified in her case. The authors emphasized that the ictal sexual activity was not appropriate or purposeful: "They are as different from appropriate sexual functions as running epilepsy is from the 100 yard dash" (p. 264).

Disrobing is commonly held to be a component of complex partial seizures, but systematic analysis of seizure components has demonstrated that this is a rather infrequent accompaniment (Rodin, 1973). Hooshmand and Brawley (1969) documented outright exhibitionism as a part of temporal lobe seizures and provided some guidelines for medicolegal interpretation of such events.

HYPOSEXUALITY

Hyposexuality has been considered a complication of temporal lobe epilepsy for many years. Gastaut and Colomb (1954) attributed "global hyposexuality" to temporal lobe epilepsy. A decrease in sexual drive in these patients may be considered an epileptic inversion of the Kluver–Bucy syndrome associated with bilateral temporal lobe damage. In a long-term follow-up study of temporal lobe epilepsy (Lindsay, Ounsted, & Richards, 1979b), the findings of Dansky et al. (1980) were corroborated in that women met the expected marriage rates, but less than half of the eligible men were married. The prognosis for marriage was best in those patients for whom the seizure etiology was not apparent.

Taylor (1969) considered 100 patients with intractable temporal lobe seizures who had undergone temporal lobectomy by Falconer at the Maudsley Hospital. Hyposexuality was evident in 72% (no significant difference by gender), usually as decreased sexual drive. One should note that many of Taylor's patients required institutional care because of mental deficiency or psychiatric disorder, however. Temporal lobectomy improved sexual function in 22 patients. Normal sexual adjustment was noted to be proportional to overall social adjustment, and sexual dysfunction was more likely when epilepsy was of early onset, when psychomotor attacks included a fall or slump, or when concomitant psychosis was involved.

Two other studies restricted to male epileptics (Saunders & Rawson, 1970; Pritchard, 1980) compared the incidence of hyposexuality in temporal lobe epileptics with nontemporal epileptics. Sexual dysfunction was significantly more likely in temporal lobe epileptics, and both of these studies stressed the prevalence of erectile dysfunction. We found an overall incidence of hyposexuality in 48% of temporal lobe epileptics in an outpatient clinic. There was absolute or relative impotence in most hyposexual subjects, occasionally associated with decreased libido. We found no relationship between hyposexuality and laterality of the discharge focus, degree of seizure control, or antiepileptic drugs (type, number, or serum level). Temporal lobe epileptics with abnormal computed tomography or mesiobasal location of temporal lobe spike foci were at increased risk for sexual dysfunction. Endocrine evaluation of our patients included interictal assessment of plasma testosterone and serum gonadotrophins and prolactin. Serial serum gonadotrophins following intravenous luteotrophic hormone-releasing factor (LH-RH), showed examples of eugonadotrophic, hypogonadotrophic, and hypergonadotrophic hypogonadism.

Several reports concerning the effects of temporal lobectomy on hyposexuality have indicated improvement in some cases. In the series from Johns Hopkins, Walker (1972) described global hyposexuality in 32 out of 47 cases. He noted that diminished interest in sexuality extends to lack of sexual fantasies and sexual discussion. He also noticed an association between hyposexuality and aggressive behavior. Temporal lobectomy was followed by improvement in sexual function in about one-third of his cases, and improvement was correlated with decreased frequency of seizures. Similar studies (Jensen & Larsen, 1979; Taylor, 1971) concur with Walker's report.

ENDOCRINOPATHY

Although there is general agreement that some form of hyposexuality is common among temporal lobe epileptics, the pathogenetic mechanisms are not established. The possible role of antiepileptic drugs has been considered (Timiras & Hill, 1980; Toone, Wheeler, & Fenwick, 1980). The latter study compared epileptic patients with nonepileptic controls. They noted significant elevation of serum gonadotrophins, prolactin, testosterone, and sex-hormone binding globulin in the epileptics. They also found a positive correlation between serum phenytoin and primidone levels and serum prolactin, in addition to a similar relationship between serum phenytoin levels and serum testosterone. They found no direct correlation between the endocrine data and degree of sexual dysfunction. In a small series of complex partial epileptics examined postictally (Pritchard, Wannamaker, Sagel, & de Villier, 1981), we found a significant elevation (up to tenfold) of serum prolactin following electroencephalographically monitored complex partial seizures, peak elevations occuring within 15 minutes of the seizures. Simultaneous determinations of gonadotrophins showed no change in relation to seizures. In view of the known association between hyperprolactinemia and impotence in males (Franks, Jacobs, Martin, & Nabarro, 1978), it is tempting to postulate that episodic hyperprolactinemia associated with complex partial epilepsy is involved in the pathogenesis of impotence in temporal lobe epilepsy.

GELASTIC AND DACRYSTIC EPILEPSY

Affective symptomatology is an established ictal component, particularly in reference to complex partial seizures. Affective symptoms in this context run the gamut of affective experience, including anger, fear, and depression, as well as more pleasurable feelings (Daly, 1975). Hermann, Dikmen, Schwartz, and Karnes (1982) consider ictal fear an important determinant in the pathogenesis of interictal psychopathology associated with temporal lobe epilepsy. Daly (1975) classified ictal laughter and weeping as affective automatisms.

Occasionally, laughter is the prominent or sole manifestation of an epileptic seizure. Daly and Mulder (1957) coined the term "gelastic" (Greek, *gelas* = joy) epilepsy for these cases. Loiseau, Cohadon, and Cohadon (1971) emphasized that laughter is merely a symptom of epilepsy, preferring the term "epileptic laughter" to gelastic epilepsy. Epileptic laughter must be distinguished from the pathological outbursts of laughter (and weeping) of pseudo-bulbar palsy, the "Witzelsucht" of frontal lobe disease, and inappropriate laughter associated with anxiety or psychosis.

Gascon and Lombroso (1971) outlined criteria for epileptic laughter: lack of external precipitants, association with other epileptic manifestations, ictal and/or interictal discharges on EEG, and stereotyped recurrence of symptoms. They collected ten cases of gelastic epilepsy. Half of their cases had pathology in the diencephalon, and the remaining five had unilateral lesions of the temporal lobe. They characterized the epileptic laughter of the diencephalic cases as "mainly its motor aspects without its affective component," whereas there was more affective, infectious laughter from those with temporal lobe lesions. Interestingly, all of their temporal lobe cases were on the right.

Chen and Forster (1973) confirmed the association of epileptic laughter with interictal temporal lobe discharges on EEG in their report of ten additional cases. In contrast to Gascon and Lombroso (1971), they noted a preponderance of left temporal lobe involvement (seven of nine temporal cases). Two of their patients also had cursive seizures. The combined incidence of cursive and gelastic epilepsy in the Wisconsin series was .3% (16 of 5000 consecutive cases of epilepsy).

If gelastic seizures are rare, ictal weeping is even less common, although two of the cases of Gascon and Lombroso (1971) had a combination of laughter and crying during their seizures. Offen, Davidoff, Troost, and Richey (1976) described a 60-year-old man with neurosyphilis who had both laughing and crying spells. During an attack consisting of sobbing and lacrimation, the EEG demonstrated rhythmic slow-wave activity over the right cerebral hemisphere. The authors suggested the term "dacrystic" (Greek, $dakryon$ = tear) for epileptic weeping, which they controlled with antiepileptic drugs.

Sethi and Rao (1976) reported an exceptional case in whom epileptic laughter, crying, and running coexisted. They dubbed epileptic weeping as "quiritarian" (Latin, $quiritare$ = to cry) epilepsy. Following the removal of an astrocytoma of the left temporal lobe and the use of antiepileptic drugs, their patient became asymptomatic.

Epileptic laughter and weeping are concurrent at times, and there is a common anatomical basis via lesions of the hypothalamus or temporal lobe. Personal series are too limited to draw conclusions concerning possible lateralizing features with temporal lobe lesions, but analysis of a pooled series could yield interesting data reflecting emotive specialization of the cerebral hemispheres.

PSYCHOSIS

CLASSIFICATION

There have been attempts to link epilepsy with psychosis since at least the nineteenth century. At the Marseilles Colloquium in 1956, participants pooled their knowledge in this area (Dongier, 1960). They classified psychotic episodes associated with epilepsy as (1) ictal or paraictal "which might be considered to be merely prolonged seizures or postictal confusional states" or (2) interictal "nonseizure states" considered "true psychotic or psychoneurotic phenomena." After gathering descriptions of 536 psychotic episodes from 516 patients, the participants concluded that centrencephalic epileptics are prone to relatively brief psychotic episodes, usually confusional states, associated with continuous discharges or diffuse slow-wave activity on EEG. By contrast, psychomotor epileptics were prone to psychotic episodes lasting days to weeks, and their EEGs were not appreciably different from previous interictal records. Flor-Henry (1972) concurred in the proposed classification.

Based on the consensus from Marseilles, psychotic episodes may be classified in relationship to the ictus (Table 1). Differentiation among ictal, postictal, and interictal psychoses offers a useful approach to management of the epileptic psychoses. Several authorities (Fenton, 1978; Hara, Hoshi, Takase, & Saito, 1980) are in general agreement on this point.

ICTAL AND POSTICTAL PSYCHOSES

The ictal and postictal psychoses usually present as acute confusional states. Wells (1975) described acute psychotic episodes in two older women, each of whom caused initial diagnostic diffi-

TABLE 1. *Psychosis associated with epilepsy*

Temporal relationship to seizures	Manifestations of psychosis	Duration	EEG	Treatment
Ictal	Confusional	Hours to days	Continuous discharges	Antiepileptic drugs
Postictal	Confusional	Hours to days	Diffuse slow waves	Reassess antiepileptic drug regimen
Interictal	Affective or schizophreniform	Weeks to months	Focal spikes, often from temporal lobe(s)	Psychotropic drugs (e.g., antidepressants or haloperidol)

culty. One case had delirium, for which no cause was immediately evident, while the second case presented as psychotic depression. In each case continuous, generalized discharges were seen on EEG, and psychosis cleared with the use of antiepileptic drugs. Wells offered four clinical features which merit consideration of "transient ictal psychosis": (1) abrupt onset of psychosis in a person who was previously psychologically healthy, (2) unexplained delirium, (3) history of similar attacks with sudden onset and offset, and (4) history of associated fainting or falling spells. Goldensohn and Gold (1960) presented five cases with similar EEG abnormalities in whom confusion with slow and incomplete responses to the environment were common features.

Engel, Ludwig, and Fetell (1978) described a 19-year-old woman who had recurrent, prolonged behavioral changes associated with both ictal and postictal states. In the ictal phase, their patient had fluctuations between slight clouding of consciousness and near unresponsiveness. EEG during this time was consistent with partial complex status epilepticus, revealing fast and sharp waves alternating with slow waves in a bilateral temporo-occipital distribution. During the postictal phase, the patient was alert, but she had profound retrograde and anterograde amnesia which cleared over several weeks. EEG at that point demonstrated the expected diffuse slow-wave activity in addition to bilaterally independent temporal lobe spikes. Antiepileptic drug withdrawal may contribute to postictal confusional states (Sironi, Franzini, Ravagnati, & Marossero, 1979).

INTERICTAL PSYCHOSIS

Interictal psychosis associated with epilepsy has provoked the most interest and the greatest controversy. Some related studies may have limited application to the general population of epileptics because they have been restricted to special groups such as neurosurgical or psychiatric series. Correlations between psychosis and specific seizure types have most often led to a greater than expected association with complex partial (temporal lobe, psychomotor) epilepsy. Investigations in this area have addressed possible relationships between prevalence and type of psychiatric disorder and laterality of EEG abnormalities, underlying pathology of the brain, social and educational influences, and effects of antiepileptic drugs.

The possible association of "schizophrenia-like psychosis" and temporal lobe epilepsy has been widely considered. Slater and Beard (1963) argued against mere chance association between schizophrenia and epilepsy, noting that the predicted prevalence from chance association alone "to become either schizophrenic epileptics or epileptic schizophrenics" would be only 40 in one million. The authors contended that their own series greatly exceeded that prevalence. They also noted that if there were a common basis for conventional schizophrenia and schizophrenia-like psychosis of epilepsy, the premorbid personality for the latter should also be schizoid, but the premorbid personality in epileptic cases was normal. Slater and Beard (1963) found a mean latency of 14 years between the onset of epilepsy and the onset of psychosis. They found a positive correlation between the ages at onset of epilepsy and psychosis. They were not able to confirm a direct relationship between psychosis and the degree of seizure control and saw no evidence of the "forced normalization" of EEG during psychotic episodes as described by Landolt.

The onset of schizophrenia-like psychosis as depicted by Slater and Beard is usually insidious with variable initial features such as apathy, depression, delusions, and auditory hallucinations. Schizophrenia-like psychosis differs from the usual schizophrenic state in that affect usually remains warm in the former, and paranoid delusions—often with religious connotations—are more common than in schizophrenia. Prognosis is improved if the tempo of onset is acute or subacute. Typical features of the psychosis include mystic delusional experiences, feelings of special powers, delusions of persecution, hallucinations, thought disorder, and affective change. There was a disproportionately high incidence of temporal lobe epilepsy in their series.

Perez and Trimble (1980) used a standardized psychiatric interview protocol to compare patients with process schizophrenia and psychotic epileptics. Patients with both temporal lobe epilepsy and generalized epilepsy were studied. The authors found that schizophrenia is significantly associated with temporal lobe epilepsy, but other types of psychosis were associated as well. In Falconer's temporal lobectomy series (1973) there was an association between the appearance of a schizophrenia-like state and hamartoma in the resected temporal lobe. Temporal lobectomy in psychotic patients improved seizure control, but there was only slight improvement of psychosis after surgery. In a review of patients selected from the same surgical series, Taylor (1975) reaffirmed the relationship between "alien tissue" and psychosis. He also found that left-handed patients and women were more susceptible to psychosis.

A review of young adults with temporal lobe epilepsy (Pritchard, Lombroso, & McIntyre, 1980) showed a 36% incidence of psychological complications. Left temporal lobe epileptics and males were more susceptible, but not to a significant degree. Psychological complications were more likely to occur when seizure onset was in the second hemidecade of life (Figure 1). Seizures nearly always antedated the onset of psychological complications, but there was no direct correlation between the age at seizure onset

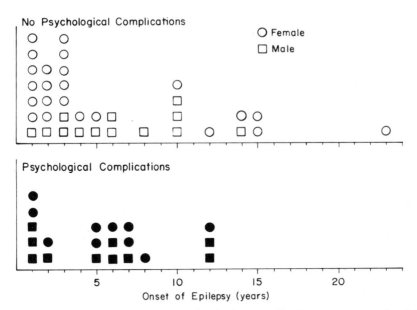

FIGURE 1. *Occurrence of psychological complications compared with the age at onset of temporal lobe epilepsy. From "Psychological Complications of Temporal Lobe Epilepsy" by P. B. Pritchard, C. T. Lombroso, and M. McIntyre,* Neurology, *1980, 30, 227–232. Copyright 1980 by* Neurology. *Reprinted by permission.*

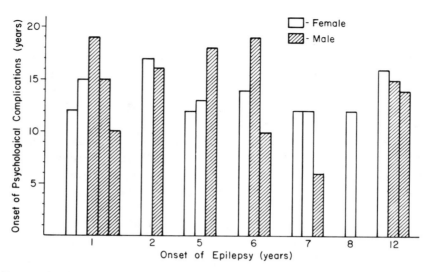

FIGURE 2. *Age at onset of temporal lobe epilepsy versus age at appearance of psychological complications. From "Psychological Complications of Temporal Lobe Epilepsy" by P. B. Pritchard, C. T. Lombroso, and M. McIntyre,* Neurology, *1980, 30, 227–232. Copyright 1980 by Neurology. Reprinted by permission.*

and the onset of psychological abnormality (Figure 2). Psychological complications usually appeared in adolescence, and the incidence of psychosis was 11%.

In a long-term, prospective study of temporal lobe epilepsy, Lindsay, Ounsted, and Richards (1979c) found an incidence of psychosis of 10.3%. In their initial analysis of 1964, 26% of the group was hyperkinetic, and 36% had catastrophic rage attacks. Both of these entities were poor prognostic indicators for eventual social outcome.

Lindsay *et al.* offered the optimistic outlook that, as adults, the majority of their patients are now free of psychiatric disorder. A comparison between temporal lobe epilepsy and generalized epilepsy (Shukla, Srivastava, Katiyar, Joshi, & Mohan, 1979) from India confirmed a high incidence of childhood emotional disorders associated with temporal lobe epilepsy, and they found an incidence of schizophrenia of 17% in temporal lobe epileptics. In a related study Shukla and Katiyar (1980) addressed laterality of temporal lobe discharge foci, but they detected no significant association with normality, psychosis, or behavior disorder. Sherwin (1981) found a significant increase of schizophrenic-like psychosis in epileptics with left temporal lobe lesions from Crandall's surgical series, confirming the results from the Maudsley Hospital. Jensen and Larsen (1979a, 1979b) were not able to confirm any clear relationship between laterality of the abnormal temporal lobe and likelihood of psychosis. EEG recordings using sphenoidal electrodes in another series (Kristensen & Sindrup, 1978) showed a positive correlation between psychosis and mesiobasal location of the temporal lobe spike discharge focus.

The overall incidence of psychiatric complications of temporal lobe epilepsy was 44% in a large outpatient series (Currie, Heathfield, Henson, & Scott, 1971). The most common manifestations were anxiety or depression, and the incidence of schizophrenia was only 2%.

Stevens (1966) disputed the proposed susceptibility of temporal lobe epileptics to interictal psychosis, having determined a similar incidence of psychiatric disorder in both psychomotor and grand mal epileptics. Stevens maintained that there is an increased risk of psychiatric disorder for all types of epilepsy. One should note that her sole criterion of psychiatric disorder was history of admission to a residential psychiatric hospital, so that psychiatric problems may have been underdetected. A comparison of psychomotor and nonpsychomotor epileptics from the National Institutes of Health (Mignone, Donnelly, & Sadowsky, 1970) also discovered a high incidence of psychopathy without any significant difference between the groups. However, the majority of their patients were studied retrospectively, and the psychiatric histories were not fully recorded in retrospective cases. In addition, both groups of patients were in rather poor seizure control; the majority were having more than 50 seizures per week.

Flor-Henry (1969) studied 100 psychotic patients with temporal lobe epilepsy. He found a relationship between right temporal lobe EEG foci and affective disorders, such as manic–depressive psychosis. Discharge foci in the left cerebral hemisphere were more often associated with schizophrenia. An effort was made to study the determinants of affective symptoms in epileptics (Roy, 1979); 23 patients with temporal lobe epilepsy were compared with 19 patients with other types of epilepsy, type not specified. Using several inventories for depression and anxiety, Roy found an increased likelihood of affective symptoms with temporal lobe epilepsy, but his figures were not statistically significant. Several surveys (Hawton, Fagg, & Marsack, 1980; Editorial, 1980) have described a several-fold increased risk of suicide in epileptics, in relation to which David Taylor has coined the term "ictal defenestration syndrome." Actually, the most common modality employed in suicide attempts is medication (often antiepileptic drugs) overdose (Hawton *et al.*, 1980).

However the type and location of underlying brain pathology may influence the pathogenesis of psychosis in the epileptic, the management of epilepsy and simultaneous psychosis presents a therapeutic challenge. The emergence of interictal psychosis in a given epileptic patient bears no predictable relationship to the degree of seizure control at a particular time. Pharmacologic intervention must be directed separately toward seizure control and psychiatric manifestations (Geschwind, Shader, Bear, North, Levin, & Chetham, 1980). Although there is some theoretical objection to phenothiazines because of the tendency to lower seizure threshold, the actual impact is usually unimportant (Scott, 1978).

MEDICOLEGAL IMPLICATIONS

If there are behavioral complications of epilepsy, one must consider the possibility that some behavior associated with or affected by the epileptic process might offend the established mores of society or traverse the bounds of legality. The interpretation of such behavior as it relates to the epileptic has medical, social, and legal implications.

Most of the literature in this area relates to aggressive or assaultive behavior. Ounsted (1969) described catastrophic rage attacks interictally in 36% of his series of children with epilepsy.

He found an increased invidence of rage attacks with seizure onset in the first year of life and with posttraumatic and postinfectious seizure etiology. There was no clear relationship of rage attacks to seizure frequency or gender of the patient. Ounsted did not further describe whether aggression per se was involved. Taylor (1969) found an incidence of aggressive behavior in about one-third of his patients with temporal lobe epilepsy. In contrast to Ounsted, Taylor noted improved behavior with better seizure control. Of the patients classified as psychopathic, there was overrepresentation of males, lower social classes, early-life onset of seizures, and left-hemispheric lesions. Taylor saw no proven instance of ictal aggression.

Rodin (1973) photographed seizures in 150 patients, also noting no evidence of ictal aggression. Although one patient demonstrated "incipient aggression" with an angry facial expression and a clenched fist after an attempt was made to restrict him during the seizure, there was no goal-directed assault. Williams (1969) reviewed EEGs carried out in a large number of subjects in custody for "crimes of aggression," over half of which included major acts of violence. Most of his patients were young men. He found that abnormal EEGs were five times as likely in the group with habitual aggression as opposed to the group who had committed isolated acts of violent crime, but were not habitually aggressive. Most EEG abnormalities in the former group were bilateral, generally involving temporal or frontal areas of the brain.

Rodin (1973) also mentioned that there were no cases of disrobing or exhibitionism in his series, although one patient unbuttoned his shirt. Overt exhibitionism has been associated with temporal lobe seizures (Hooshmand & Brawley, 1969), but the authors contrasted the behavior of their patients with the usual exhibitionist. In a recent review of aggressive behavior in epilepsy in which intensive monitoring of seizures was done (Delgado-Escueta, Mattson, King, Goldensohn, Spiegel, Madsen, Crandall, Dreifuss, & Porter, 1981), a single man was reported to have sexually accosted women by history, but the videotaped seizures did not demonstrate this behavior. In a report of "sexual seizures" (Currier *et al.*, 1971) the behavior observed in three cases was deemed not appropriate or purposeful, "more like pseudo-intercourse," and the authors opined it unlikely that rape could be attributed to ictal behavior of a temporal lobe seizure.

Cope and Donovan (1979) reported the case of a 36-year-old man who had a previous history consistent with focal seizures. The man was arrested after he found himself holding a knife after he had stabbed a total stranger, apparently occurring immediately after one of his typical seizures. Although he held a previous criminal record, his previous crimes had been nonviolent. Clinical investigation showed a fibrillary astrocytoma in the left frontal lobe. There were no ictal EEG or videotape recordings. Gunn (1978) reported a case in which an epileptic man murdered his wife and claimed amnesia for the attack. Although the diagnosis of epilepsy was well established, there was again no ictal EEG recording or videotape. The man in question pleaded diminished responsibility because of diffuse brain damage, and the jury accepted his plea. A recent case of violent automatism as a part of a complex partial seizure (Ashford, Schulz, & Walsh, 1980) was well documented, but the violent behavior in this case was nondirected and could not be considered socially aggressive.

Pincus (1980) in a recent review article emphasized the relative rarity of personal violence. Pincus suggested that the current definition of epileptic seizures may not be sufficiently broad to allow full consideration of violence as an ictal manifestation. He also noted that no control study has been done with antiepileptic drugs to see if violent behavior can be altered, as in a criminal population. In an earlier study (Pincus, Lewis, Shanok, & Glaser, 1979) a survey of juvenile delinquents who were incarcerated showed objective evidence of "seizure tendency" in over one-third of violent subjects and in none of the nonviolent subjects. There was a similar discrepancy in the neurological exam, with abnormal examination in 96% of violent subjects. Beresford (1980) pointed out that even if the evidence for ictal violence has not been established, reports of interictal aggressive behavior associated with some epileptic populations could be considered in defense against criminal charges under the legal concept of diminished responsibility.

Stevens and Hermann (1981) criticized previous attempts to relate aggressive behavior to temporal lobe epilepsy because of lack of proper controls and other shortcomings. They urged examination of more specific variables and suggested that there is better evidence for a contribution to psychotic behavior in the epileptic from basal EEG discharges and evidence of diffuse anatomical and physiological dysfunction.

An international panel (Delgado-Escueta *et al.*, 1981) studied 19 patients believed to have aggressive ictal behavior, selected from a population of 5400 epileptics. Seven patients showed recorded evidence of directed violence, but there was no example of personal violence likely to elicit serious bodily harm. There was evidence of directed violent behavior, however. Even so, the typical features of ictal violence were short duration (30 seconds or less), amnesia for the act, and confusion afterwards. The panel suggested further study of violence prone populations. Pincus (1981) concurred with the plan to study violent criminals, but he suggested that the panel's definition of ictal violence may have been too limited and that some potential participants in the study could have been inappropriately excluded.

ACKNOWLEDGMENT

The author acknowledges with gratitude the assistance of Judy B. Knox, who helped immensely in obtaining reference materials and typing the manuscript.

REFERENCES

Ashford, J. W., Schulz, S. C., & Walsh, G. O. Violent automatism in a complex partial seizure: Report of a case. *Archives of Neurology*, 1980, *37*, 120–122.

Bear, D. M. Temporal lobe epilepsy—A syndrome of sensory–limbic hyperconnection. *Cortex*, 1979, *15*, 357–384. (a)

Bear, D. M. Interictal behavior in temporal lobe epilepsy: Possible anatomic and physiologic bases. *Journal of Psychiatric Research*, 1979, *16*, 283–294. (b)

Bear, D. M., & Fedio, P. Quantitative analysis of interictal behavior in temporal lobe epilepsy. *Archives of Neurology*, 1977, *34*, 454–467.

Beresford, H. R. Can violence be a manifestation of epilepsy? *Neurology*, 1980, *30*, 1339–1340.

Chen, R. C., & Forster, F. M. Cursive epilepsy and gelastic epilepsy. *Neurology*, 1973, *23*, 1019–1029.

Cherlow, D. G., & Serafetidines, E. A. Speech and memory assessment in psychomotor epileptics. *Cortex*, 1976, *12*, 21–26.

Cogen, P. H., Antunes, J. L., & Correll, J. W. Reproductive function in temporal lobe epilepsy: The effect of temporal lobectomy. *Surgical Neurology*, 1979, *12*, 243–246.

Cope, R. V., & Donovan, W. M. A case of insane automatism? *British Journal of Psychiatry*, 1979, *135*, 574–575.

Currie, S., Heathfield, K. W. G., Henson, R. A., & Scott, D. F. Clinical course and prognosis of temporal lobe epilepsy: A survey of 666 patients. *Brain*, 1971, *94*, 173–190.

Currier, R. D., Little, S. C., Suess, J. F., & Andy, O. J. Sexual seizures. *Archives of Neurology*, 1971, *25*, 260–264.

Daly, D. D. Ictal clinical manifestations of complex partial seizures. In J. K. Penry & D. D. Daly (Eds.), *Complex partial seizures and their treatment*. New York: Raven, 1975.

Daly, D. D., & Mulder, D. W. Gelastic epilepsy. *Neurology*, 1957, *7*, 189–192.

Dansky, L. V., Andermann, E., & Andermann, F. Marriage and fertility in epileptic patients. *Epilepsia*, 1980, *21*, 261–271.

Delgado-Escueta, A. V., Mattson, R. H., King, L., Goldensohn, E. S., Spiegel, H., Madsen, J., Crandall, P., Dreifuss, F., & Porter, R. J. The nature of aggression during epileptic seizures. *New England Journal of Medicine*, 1981, *305*, 711–716.

Dikmen, S., & Reitan, R. M. Neuropsychological performance in post-traumatic epilepsy. *Epilepsia*, 1978, *19*, 177–183.

Dodrill, C. B. A neuropsychological battery for epilepsy. *Epilepsia*, 1978, *19*, 611–623.

Dodrill, C. B. Rapid evaluation of intelligence in adults with epilepsy. *Epilepsia*, 1980, *21*, 359–367.

Dodrill, C. B., Batzel, L. W., Queisser, H. R., & Temkin, N. R. An objective method for the assessment of psychological and social problems among epileptics. *Epilepsia*, 1980, *21*, 123–135.

Dodrill, C. B., & Troupin, A. S. Psychotropic effects of carbamazepine in epilepsy: A double-blind comparison with phenytoin. *Neurology*, 1977, *27*, 1023–1028.

Dodrill, C. B., & Wilkus, R. J. Neuropsychological correlates of anti-convulsants and epileptiform discharges in adult epileptics. *Contemporary Clinical Neurophysiology*, 1978, *34*, 259–267. (a)

Dodrill, C. B., & Wilkus, R. J. Neuropsychological correlates of the electroencephalogram in epileptics: III. Generalized nonepileptiform abnormalities. *Epilepsia*, 1978, *19*, 453–462. (b)

Dongier, S. Statistical study of clinical and electroencephalographic manifestations of 536 psychotic episodes occurring in 516 epileptics between clinical seizures. *Epilepsia*, 1960, *1*, 117–142.

Editorial. Suicide and epilepsy. *British Medical Journal*, 1980, *281*, 530.

Engel, J., Ludwig, B., & Fetell, M. Prolonged partial complex status epilepticus: EEG and behavioral observations. *Neurology*, 1978, *28*, 863–869.

Falconer, M. A. Reversibility by temporal-lobe resection of the behavioral abnormalities of temporal-lobe epilepsy. *New England Journal of Medicine*, 1973, *289*, 451–455.

Fenton, G. W. Epilepsy and psychosis. *Journal of the Irish Medical Association*, 1978, *71*, 315–324.

Flor-Henry, P. Psychosis and temporal lobe epilepsy: A controlled investigation. *Epilepsia*, 1969, *10*, 363–395.

Flor-Henry, P. Ictal and interictal psychiatric manifestations in epilepsy: Specific or non-specific? *Epilepsia*, 1972, *13*, 773–783.

Franks, S., Jacobs, H. S., Martin, N., & Nabarro, J. D. N. Hyperprolactinemia and impotence. *Clinical Endocrinology*, 1978, *8*, 277–287.

Falconer, M. A. Reversibility by temporal-lobe resection of the behavioral abnormalities of temporal-lobe epilepsy. *New England Journal of Medicine*, 1973, *289*, 451–455.

Gascon, G. G., & Lombroso, C. T. Epileptic (gelastic) laughter. *Epilepsia*, 1971, *12*, 63–76.

Gastaut, H., & Colomb, H. Étude du comportement sexuel chez les épileptiques psychomoteurs. *Annales Médico-Psychologiques (Paris)* 1954, *112*, 659–696.

Geschwind, N., Shader, R. I., Bear, D., North, B., Levin, K., & Chetham, D. Behavioral changes with temporal lobe epilepsy: Assessment and treatment. *Journal of Clinical Psychiatry*, 1980, *41*, 89–95.

Goldensohn, E. S., & Gold, A. P. Prolonged behavioral disturbances as ictal phenomena. *Neurology*, 1960, *10*, 1–9.

Gunn, J. Epileptic homicide: A case report. *British Journal of Psychiatry*, 1978, *132*, 510–513.

Hara, T., Hoshi, A., Takase, M., & Saito, S. Factors related to psychiatric episodes in epileptics. *Folia Psychiatrica et Neurologica Japonica*, 1980, *34*, 329–330.

Hawton, K., Fagg, J., & Marsack, P. Association between epilepsy and attempted suicide. *Journal of Neurology, Neurosurgery and Psychiatry*, 1980, *43*, 168–170.

Hermann, B. P., & Chhabria, S. Interictal psychopathology in patients with ictal fear: Examples of sensory–limbic hyperconnection? *Archives of Neurology*, 1980, *37*, 667–668.

Hermann, B. P., Dikmen, S., Schwartz, M. S., & Karnes, W. E. Interictal psychopathology in patients with ictal fear: A quantitative investigation. *Neurology*, 1982, *32*, 7–11.

Hermann, B. P., Schwartz, M. S., Karnes, W. E., & Vahdat, P. Psychopathology in epilepsy: Relationship of seizure type to age at onset. *Epilepsia*, 1980, *21*, 15–23.

Hermann, B. P., Schwartz, M. S., Whitman, S., & Karnes, W. E. Aggression and epilepsy: Seizure-type comparisons and high-risk variables. *Epilepsia*, 1980, *22*, 691–698.

Hodgman, C. H., McAnarney, E. R., Myers, G. J., Iker, H., McKinney, R., Parmelee, D., Schuster, B., & Tutihasi, M. Emotional complications of adolescent grand mal epilepsy. *Journal of Pediatrics*, 1979, *95*, 309–312.

Hooshmand, H., & Brawley, B. W. Temporal lobe seizures and exhibitionism. *Neurology*, 1969, *19*, 1119–1124.

Jensen, I., & Larsen, J. K. Mental aspects of temporal lobe epilepsy: Follow-up of 74 patients after resection of a temporal lobe. *Journal of Neurology, Neurosurgery and Psychiatry*, 1979, *42*, 256–265. (a)

Jensen, I., & Larsen, J. K. Psychoses in drug-resistant temporal lobe epilepsy. *Journal of Neurology, Neurosurgery and Psychiatry*, 1979, *42*, 948–954. (b)

Kristensen, O., & Sindrup, E. H. Psychomotor epilepsy and psychosis: II. Electroencephalographic findings (sphenoidal electrode recordings). *Acta Neurologica Scandinavica*, 1978, *57*, 370–379.

Lindsay, J., Ounsted, C., & Richards, P. Long-term outcome in children with temporal lobe seizures: I. Social outcome and childhood factors. *Developmental Medicine and Child Neurology*, 1979, *21*, 285–298. (a)

Lindsay, J., Ounsted, C., & Richards, P. Long-term outcome in children with temporal lobe seizures: II. Marriage, parenthood, and sexual indifference. *Developmental Medicine and Child Neurology*, 1979, *21*, 433–440. (b)

Lindsay, J., Ounsted, C., & Richards, P. Long-term outcome in children with temporal lobe seizures: III. Psychiatric aspects in childhood and adult life. *Developmental Medicine and Child Neurology*, 1979, *21*, 630–636. (c)

Loiseau, P., Cohadon, F., & Cohadon, S. Gelastic epilepsy: A review and report of five cases. *Epilepsia*, 1971, *12*, 313–323.

MacLeod, C. M., Dekaban, A. S., & Hunt, E. Memory impairment in epileptic patients: Selective effects of phenobarbital concentration. *Science*, 1978, *202*, 1102–1104.

McIntyre, M., Pritchard, P. B., & Lombroso, C. T. Left and right temporal lobe epileptics: A controlled investigation of some psychological differences. *Epilepsia*, 1976, *17*, 377–386.

Matthews, C. G., & Klove, H. MMPI performances in major motor, psychomotor, and mixed seizure classifications of known and unknown etiology. *Epilepsia*, 1968, *9*, 43–53.

Mignone, R. J., Donnelly, E. F., & Sadowsky, D. Psychological and neurological comparisons of psychomotor and non-psychomotor epileptic patients. *Epilepsia*, 1970, *11*, 345–359.

Milner, B. Interhemispheric differences in the localization of psychological processes in man. *British Medical Bulletin*, 1971, *27*, 272–277.

Milner, B. Hemispheric specialization: Scope and limits. In F. O. Schmitt & F. G. Warder (Eds.), *The neurosciences: Third study program*. Cambridge, Mass.: MIT Press, 1974.

Offen, M. L., Davidoff, R. A., Troost, B. T., & Richey, E. T. Dacrystic epilepsy. *Journal of Neurology, Neurosurgery and Psychiatry*, 1976, *39*, 829–834.

Ounsted, C. Aggression and epilepsy: Rage in children with temporal lobe epilepsy. *Journal of Psychosomatic Research*, 1969, *13*, 237–242.

Perez, M. M., & Trimble, M. R. Epileptic psychosis: Diagnostic comparison with process schizophrenia. *British Journal of Psychiatry*, 1980, *137*, 245–249.

Pincus, J. H. Can violence be a manifestation of epilepsy? *Neurology*, 1980, *30*, 304–307.

Pincus, J. Violence and epilepsy. *New England Journal of Medicine*, 1981, *305*, 696–698.

Pincus, J., Lewis, D. O., Shanok, S. S., & Glaser, G. H. Psychomotor symptoms in violent delinquents. *Journal of Psychiatric Research*, 1979, *16*, 1–6.

Pritchard, P. B. Hyposexuality: A complication of complex partial epilepsy. *Transactions of the American Neurological Association*, 1980, *105*, 193–195.

Pritchard, P. B., Lombroso, C. T., & McIntyre, M. Psychological complications of temporal lobe epilepsy. *Neurology*, 1980, *30*, 227–232.

Pritchard, P. B., Wannamaker, B. B., Sagel, J., & deVillier, C. Postictal hyperprolactinemia in complex partial epilepsy. *Annals of Neurology*, 1981, *10*, 81–82.

Reynolds, E. H. Anticonvulsants and mental symptoms. *Acta Neurologica Scandinavica*, 1981, *62*, 46–52.

Rodin, E. A. Psychomotor epilepsy and aggressive behavior. *Archives of General Psychiatry*, 1973, *28*, 210–213.

Roy, A. Some determinants of affective symptoms in epileptics. *Canadian Journal of Psychiatry*, 1979, *24*, 554–556.

Saunders, M., & Rawson, M. Sexuality in male epileptics. *Journal of Neurological Sciences*, 1970, *10*, 577–583.

Sethi, P. K., & Rao, T. S. Gelastic, quiritarian, and cursive epilepsy. *Journal of Neurology, Neurosurgery and Psychiatry*, 1976, *39*, 823–828.

Scott, D. F. Psychiatric aspects of epilepsy. *British Journal of Psychiatry*, 1978, *132*, 417–430.

Sherwin, I. Psychosis associated with epilepsy: Significance of the laterality of the epileptogenic lesion. *Journal of Neurology, Neurosurgery and Psychiatry*, 1981, *44*, 83–85.

Shukla, G. D., & Katiyar, B. C. Psychiatric disorders in temporal lobe epilepsy: The laterality effect. *British Journal of Psychiatry*, 1980, *137*, 181–182.

Shukla, G. D., Srivastava, O. N., Katiyar, B. C., Joshi, V., & Mohan, P. K. Psychiatric manifestations: A controlled study. *British Journal of Psychiatry*, 1979, *135*, 411–417.

Sironi, V. A., Franzini, A., Ravagnati, L., & Marossero, F. Interictal acute psychoses in temporal lobe epilepsy during withdrawal of anticonvulsant therapy. *Journal of Neurology, Neurosurgery and Psychiatry*, 1979, *42*, 724–730.

Slater, E., & Beard, A. W. The schizophrenia-like psychoses of epilepsy: Psychiatric aspects. *British Journal of Psychiatry*, 1963, *109*, 95–112.

Stevens, J. R. Psychiatric implications of psychomotor epilepsy. *Archives of General Psychiatry*, 1966, *14*, 461–471.

Stevens, J. R., & Hermann, B. P. Temporal lobe epilepsy, psychopathology, and violence: The state of the evidence. *Neurology*, 1981, *31*, 1127–1132.

Stores, G. School-children with epilepsy at risk for learning and behavior problems. *Developmental Medicine and Child Neurology*, 1978, *20*, 502–508.

Taylor, D. C. Sexual behavior and temporal lobe epilepsy. *Archives of Neurology*, 1969, *21*, 510–516. (a)

Taylor, D. C. Aggression and epilepsy. *Journal of Psychosomatic Research*, 1969, *13*, 229–236. (b)

Taylor, D. C. Appetitive inadequacy in the sex behavior of temporal lobe epileptics. *Journal of Neurovisceral Relations*, 1971, *Suppl. X*, 486–490.

Taylor, D. C. Factors influencing the occurrence of schizophrenia-like psychosis in patients with temporal lobe epilepsy. *Psychological Medicine*, 1975, *5*, 249–254.

Timiras, P. S., & Hill, H. F. Antiepileptic drugs, hormones, and epilepsy. In G. H. Glaser, J. K. Penry, & D. Woodbury (Eds.), *Antiepileptic drugs: Mechanisms of action*. New York: Raven, 1980.

Tizard, B. The personality of epileptics: A discussion of the evidence. *Psychological Bulletin*, 1962, *59*, 196–210.

Toone, B. K., Wheeler, M., & Fenwick, P. B. C. Sex hormone changes in male epileptics. *Clinical Endocrinology*, 1980, *12*, 391–395.

Walker, A. E. The libidinous temporal lobe. *Schweizer Archiv für Neurologie, Neurochirurgie und Psychiatrie (Zurich)*, 1972, *111*, 473–484.

Waxman, S. G., & Geschwind, N. The interictal behavior syndrome of temporal lobe epilepsy. *Archives of General Psychiatry*, 1975, *32*, 1580–1586.

Wells, C. E. Transient ictal psychosis. *Archives of General Psychiatry*, 1975, *32*, 1201–1203.

Williams, D. Neural factors related to habitual aggression. *Brain*, 1969, *92*, 503–520.

Wolf, S., & Forsythe, A. Behavior disturbance, phenobarbital, and febrile seizures. *Pediatrics*, 1978, *61*, 728–731.

Zern, D., Kenney, H. J., & Kvaraceus, W. C. The relationship of cognitive style to overt behavior in a group of emotionally disturbed adolescents. *Exceptional Child*, 1974, *14*, 194–195.

Ziegler, R. G. Psychologic vulnerability in epileptic patients. *Psychosomatics*, 1979, *20*, 145–148.

NEUROPSYCHOLOGICAL STUDIES IN PATIENTS WITH PSYCHIATRIC DISORDERS

Pierre Flor-Henry

NEUROPSYCHOLOGICAL TESTING

NEUROPSYCHOLOGICAL BATTERIES

The American school of neuropsychology has grown from the work of Halstead. In 1935 he began developing tests that would identify patients who, in spite of sometime massive frontal lobe lesions, were surprisingly normal on conventional neurological examination and whose psychometric intelligence remained intact on formal examination. By 1947 he had constructed a test battery consisting of seven tests that successfully discriminated patients with frontal lesions from those with nonfrontal lesions (Halstead, 1947). The tests were: Category, Critical Flicker Frequency, Tactual Performance, Seashore Rhythm, Speech Sounds Perception, Finger Oscillation, and Time Sense Tests. Subsequently Reitan—who was Halstead's first graduate student—enlarged the battery to include the Wechsler Intelligence Scale, an Aphasia and Sensory Perceptual Battery, the Trail-Making Test, and Dynamometric Hand Strength. The Halstead–Reitan Battery no longer includes Critical Flicker Frequency and Time Sense (as these two tests discriminate poorly between brain-damaged and control populations; Reitan, 1955a).

Reitan (1966) illustrated how the clinical neuropsychological profile analysis of the Halstead–Reitan Battery and of the Wechsler

Pierre Flor-Henry. Admission Services, Alberta Hospital, Edmonton, and Department of Psychiatry, University of Alberta, Edmonton, Alberta, Canada.

Scales can lead to remarkably accurate predictions with respect to the lateralization, localization, and even neuropathological nature of independently verified cerebral lesions. The first validation of the Halstead–Reitan Battery by investigators independent of the Chicago and Indiana Schools was that of Vega and Parsons (1967) who found that the battery correctly classified brain-damaged populations from controls with 73% accuracy. Earlier, Reitan (1964) correctly identified 57 of 64 patients with *focal* cerebral lesions (or 89%) and 46 of 48 patients with diffuse brain damage (or 95.8%). The hit-rate for right-hemisphere lesions was 68.75% and for the left hemisphere 62.5%. The neuropathological identification was of the order of 90% for diffuse central nervous system diseases and varied between 50 and 90% for other specific neurological disorders. These very impressive results have since been confirmed by a number of studies (see Filskov & Goldstein, 1974, and Boll, 1981, for detailed reviews). For example, Filskov and Goldstein (1974) find in the screening of neurological patients that the neuropsychological battery is accurate in identifying cerebral dysfunction 100% of the time; brain scan 40%; EEG 60%; angiography 85%; and pneumoencephalography 80%; with skull X-rays showing a hit-rate of only 16%. Similarly impressive results were achieved by Schreiber, Goldman, Kleinman, Goldfader, and Snow (1976) in the investigation of 78 neurological patients. Of the 62 patients who proved to have neurological disease, together with the 16 subjects who turned out to be neurologically normal, the Halstead–Reitan Battery was 97% accurate in predicting no brain damage, unilateral left, unilateral right, diffuse, bilateral left > right, or bilateral right > left cerebral dysfunction. A comparable correct prediction rate was made in 85% of cases by Wheeler (1964) applying linear discriminant functions to seven dichotomized measures taken from the Halstead–Reitan Battery and including Wechsler Scale variables and age in 224 subjects, 92 of whom were found to be neurologically and neuropsychologically normal.

On repeat examination 20 weeks apart, it has been demonstrated that the test–retest reliability of the Halstead–Reitan Battery is very high in normal subjects, brain-damaged populations, and chronic schizophrenics (Matarazzo, Wiens, Matarazzo, & Goldstein, 1974; Matarazzo, Matarazzo, Wiens, Gallo, & Klonoff, 1976).

Golden, in Nebraska, has standardized the administration and developed objective scoring methods for the Luria Neuropsychological Investigation. The battery, consisting of 282 items, has been found to discriminate between brain-damaged and control populations with 93% accuracy (Hammeke, Golden, & Purisch, 1978); to achieve a 98% hit-rate in the identification of unilateral left, unilateral right, and diffuse brain-injured subjects (Osmon, Golden, Purisch, Hammeke, & Blume, 1979) and also to generate patterns of deficits related to localized cerebral dysfunction (Lewis, Golden, Moses, Osmon, Purisch, & Hammeke, 1979).

INTELLIGENCE TESTING: VERBAL/PERFORMANCE DIFFERENCES AND LESION LATERALITY

Reitan (1955b) demonstrated that the verbal and performance scales of the Wechsler–Bellevue (Form I), under certain circumstances, function as a sensitive neuropsychological instrument in the detection of unilateral right or left cerebral lesions. Thirteen of the 14 patients with left-sided lesions had a verbal IQ lower than performance (12 IQ point decrement average), while 15 of the 17 patients with right-brain disease had a performance IQ deficit of 11 points, compared with the verbal score. The 31 patients with bilateral diffuse cerebral disease were evenly distributed with respect to verbal/performance IQ discrepancies. The single subtest most impaired in the left-brain-damaged group was Digit Span, and in the right-brain-damaged group was Digit Symbol. These findings, despite nonconfirmation by Smith (1966), have been abundantly verified in large series of unilateral temporal lobe epileptics subjected to anterior temporal lobectomy, in both Montreal and London. In this special population a verbal/performance Wechsler Adult Intelligence Scale (WAIS) IQ discrepancy of the order of 7–10 points correctly identifies the laterality of the epilepsy, confirmed both electroencephalographically and by surgical exploration (Milner, 1954; Blakemore & Falconer, 1967). Parsons, Vega, and Burn (1969) examined 142 patients (in two experiments) with unilateral brain damage, right and left, and bilateral cerebral disease, using the Vocabulary and Block Design subtests of the WAIS. These two subtests were chosen because they have the highest loadings on the verbal and perceptual organization factors and also the highest correlation with verbal and performance IQ. There were 44 subjects with left, 41 with right, and 57 with bilateral damage. Fifty controls were also included. The Halstead–Reitan Battery had been given to all subjects and showed that the severity of cerebral dysfunction was similar in the left- and right-brain-damaged groups. A significant impairment in Vocabulary scores, relative to Block Design, was found in the unilateral left-lesional group and the converse in the right-sided series. It was also found that if all the subtests of the verbal and performance scale were used, the effects were attenuated: The left-lesion group had significantly lower verbal IQ than the right, but the right-lesion group did not significantly differ from the left on performance IQ.

Woods (1980) has shown that the age at which the lesions are acquired has an influence on the verbal/performance patterns. Before the age of 1, lesions of either the right or the left hemisphere lower both scales; after the age of 1, only the right-brain lesions produce a lateralized decrement of performance IQ which is significant, later lesions of the left hemisphere being associated (like the early lesions) with a reduction of both verbal and performance scores. Nevertheless, Woods calculated the verbal and performance IQ from seven published papers cumulating 178 left- and 204 right-hemisphere lesions of adult onset, and found an average IQ in the left series of verbal = 87.1, performance = 91.4, and in the right series of verbal = 97.2, performance = 85.4. Taylor (1976), in the detailed analysis of verbal and performance IQ before and after temporal lobectomies carried out in the treatment of unilateral epilepsy, has a sample consisting of very-early-onset cerebral disorganization—alien tissue tumors, which arise during embryogenesis; mesial temporal sclerosis, which is postnatal; and an acquired adult lesion—the temporal resection itself. He showed that through complex interactions, the age of the individual at lesion onset, the neuropathological nature and laterality of the lesion, as well as the sex and handedness of the patient all influenced the direction and size of consequent psychometric abilities. If the size of the difference between verbal IQ and performance IQ is not taken into account and the entire population is analyzed, then in the preoperative material, left-temporal epilepsy was associated with reduced verbal and right with reduced performance IQ at a very significant level ($p < .001$). An analysis of variance, however, showed the verbal/performance difference was significant for the right- but not the left-lesion group, a finding highly consistent with that of Woods. At the same time the left-lesion group differed significantly from the right-lesion group on verbal (lower) but not on performance scores. Of importance to the question of psychopathological implications was Taylor's observation that higher intelligence was correlated with neurosis and right temporal lesions, while psychopathy was associated with lower IQ, the male sex, and left temporal lesions. Lansdell and Urback (1965) observed that the Wechsler Scale lateralization after temporal lobectomy was found only in males. In spite of the obvious complexity of the multiplicity of interacting factors, it seems reasonable to conclude that the direction and amount of discrepancy in the verbal/performance scores of the WAIS (and especially some critical subtests) are lateralizing neuropsychological indices.

The evidence reviewed establishes that the systematic application of standardized and validated neuropsychological test batteries is perhaps the most sensitive technique for establishing the presence of cerebral dysfunction, its lateralization and its localization.

NEUROPSYCHOLOGICAL STUDIES IN PSYCHOPATHOLOGICAL POPULATIONS

SCHIZOPHRENIA VERSUS BRAIN DAMAGE

Since 1969 the Halstead–Reitan Battery has been applied to the study of psychopathological populations, notably to schizophrenia. Heaton, Baade, and Johnson (1978) have reviewed 94 studies that were published between 1960 and 1975 and which compare the test scores of adult psychiatric patients with brain-damaged groups or against established norms. It should be noted that only six of the published studies in this period utilized the full Halstead–Reitan Battery, and only four incorporated the Wechsler Scales. The majority of studies employed only one or two tests—often the Trail-Making Test, Bender–Gestalt Test, or Memory for Designs. Excluding chronic schizophrenia, the test(s) discriminated with a median hit-rate of 75% between all the psychiatric categories and the brain-damaged groups. In the case of chronic schizophrenia the hit-rate of 54% was essentially at chance level. Heaton and Crowley (1981), in a similar review of studies published between 1975 and 1978 (24 studies), find a median hit-rate of 56% for chronic schizophrenia and 76% for other psychiatric categories. Heaton and Crowley emphasize the methodological defects present in most of the investigations they considered. For example, all but seven studies in their first review had three or more of the following inadequacies: The psychiatric populations were not operationally defined; it was not specified how subjects were selected and if they were clinically representative; the neurological bases for the diagnosis of organicity in the brain-damaged groups were not given; the formal exclusion of brain disease in the psychiatric groups was not done; chronicity not controlled for; and no age or education correction was undertaken. A more difficult methodological point is raised by Heaton and Crowley (1981). Some of the studies match their groups for full-scale WAIS IQ, a measure which itself is sensitive to cerebral dysfunction, and then compare the groups on neuropsychological variables, thereby obscuring the sensitivity of the latter. To the extent that on the whole there are, in normal subjects, few correlations between WAIS and neuropsychological variables, the argument is legitimate. However, Wiens and Matarazzo (1977) found that there was a positive correlation between the Digit Span subtest and the Seashore Rhythm, as well as a negative correlation between this WAIS subtest and the Trail-Making B, whereas the Block Design subtest showed a negative correlation with the Category Test, Tactual Performance Test, and Halstead Impairment Index. Further, the WAIS performance IQ correlated negatively with Tactual Performance, nonpreferred hand and both hands. Thus, there is a tendency for certain aspects of psychometric intelligence to correlate with neuropsychological variables which reflect the integrity of dominant and nondominant hemispheric functions, and therefore not controlling for total IQ will also produce an interference in group comparisons. There is probably no satisfactory solution to this dilemma. Wiens and Matarazzo (1977) also showed that, in normal subjects, there was no correlation between personality (Minnesota Multiphasic Personality Inventory; MMPI) and neuropsychological scores on the Halstead–Reitan Battery, so that the critical question becomes the point at which severity of emotional dysfunction is translated into specific patterns of neuropsychological impairment.

The standardized Luria Neuropsychological Battery achieved the separation of schizophrenics from brain-damaged subjects with 88% accuracy. The latter consisted predominantly of cases of cerebral trauma, tumors, cerebrovascular disease, and dementia. Thirty-eight of the 50 schizophrenics had paranoid schizophrenia (or 76%), and the average length of hospitalization was a little over 1 year, with average onset at 32 years and average chronicity of the order of 10 years. Thus, the relative absence of the early onset, deteriorating, nonparanoid forms of schizophrenia may be partly responsible for the high discrimination obtained in this study[1] (Purisch, Golden, & Hammeke, 1978). Of interest, is the fact that of the 14 indices, only four—rhythm, impressive speech, memory (including verbal), and intelligence (essentially verbal)—did not discriminate between the schizophrenic and the brain-damaged patients. The implication is that the denominator common to schizophrenia and brain damage is a shared disorganization of dominant (temporal) hemispheric systems.

SCHIZOPHRENIA AND LATERALIZED BRAIN DYSFUNCTION

DeWolfe, Barrell, Becker, and Spaner (1971) compared schizophrenics against a control group of patients with bilateral brain damage, and found a specific deficit pattern for comprehension in both the young and older groups with chronic schizophrenia. The older group also showed a specific impairment in Picture Completion and a significant relative sparing for Block Design. In this pattern analysis each subject's mean on all subtests are subtracted from each of his or her subtest scores, thus the pattern of deficit across subtests is independent of group mean levels of perfor-

---

1. Heaton, Vogt, Hoehn, Lewis, Crowley, and Stallings (1979) in the comparison of 25 schizophrenics, 25 controls, 25 acute, and 25 chronic brain-damaged groups report that schizophrenics who are clinically more paranoid are significantly less impaired neuropsychologically (Halstead–Reitan). Further, there was a significant and positive correlation between the degree of EEG abnormality present and the degree of neuropsychological impairment.

mance. The authors conclude that "the hypothesis that the pattern of intellectual deficit in chronic schizophrenia varies from the pattern for nonlateralized brain damage" is supported. It is clear that the emerging pattern in this case is of predominantly dominant hemispheric dysfunction. During one of their studies on the evolution of neuropsychological and psychometric variables over an 8-year period in chronic schizophrenia, Klonoff, Fibiger, and Hutton (1970) found a significant decrement of verbal over performance IQ (101.6 vs. 107.8, respectively) on the Wechsler–Bellevue I, although the WAIS gave a nonsignificant difference in the opposite direction. In a multivariate analysis of WAIS–MMPI relationships in brain-damaged patients, process schizophrenics, acute schizophrenics, neurotics, and alcoholics, Holland and Watson (1980) reported on the unique features of each group by contrasting its mean with the unweighted mean of the total sample. The brain-damaged group was the most impaired, the neurotic the least, and the reactive schizophrenics did not differ from the total sample, but the process schizophrenics were characterized by their low scores on comprehension and arithmetic. The sensitivity of the comprehension subtest in schizophrenia is also reflected in the findings of Bigelow, Donnelly, Torrey, and Lee (1979) who note that this item is stable through time on test–retest at weekly intervals in both normals and stabilized chronic schizophrenics, but that in schizophrenics who are unmedicated at admission and who are treated with neuroleptics, comprehension improves significantly. Fredericks and Finkel (1978) present a related observation. Testing across drug (chlorpromazine) and placebo in 44 recently hospitalized male schizophrenics, the only Halstead–Reitan subtest that significantly declined during placebo condition was Speech Perception. In the neuropsychological studies of schizophrenia undertaken at the Alberta Hospital in Edmonton, we found (Flor-Henry, 1976) that mean performance IQ was similar in schizophrenia and affective psychoses (mania and depression combined), being 87 and 89, respectively. There was a trend approaching significance, suggesting a lower verbal IQ in schizophrenia ($p < .07$) compared with affective syndromes (93 vs. 98, respectively). An analysis of the subtests revealed that the schizophrenics were significantly impaired on two subtests with dominant-hemisphere loading—Vocabulary ($p < .05$) and

Digit Span ($p < .04$)—when compared with the affectives. Similar results were found by Gruzelier and Hammond (1976) whose 19 adult chronic schizophrenics showed a significant reduction on Similarities, Vocabulary, and Comprehension relative to Block Design and Object Assembly. What is more, Gruzelier, Mednick, and Schulsinger (1979), in the analysis of 70 boys and 70 girls between the ages of 10 and 13 at risk for schizophrenia because of having one parent with the illness, showed that the children at risk had a significantly lower verbal IQ than matched control children: verbal = 99.1, performance = 108.4, full-scale = 103.8 in the experimental group; verbal = 107.1, performance = 111.1, full-scale = 109.8 in the controls ($p < .05$). This reduction of the verbal scale was because of impaired Vocabulary and Similarities. In the comparison of the WAIS characteristics of 52 manic–depressives and 17 schizophrenics, Abrams, Redfield, and Taylor (1981) found in the full-scale IQ the progression of 84.5, 94.6, and 99.7 as the diagnostic groups went from schizophrenia, through mania, to depression. The schizophrenic total IQ was significantly lower than in the other two psychoses. This was because of impaired Comprehension, Similarities, and Vocabulary in schizophrenia (subtests significantly different at the $p < .01$ probability level).

In a study with the cognitive laterality battery, Shenkman, Gordon, and Heifetz (1980) investigated 15 patients with "acute schizophrenia"—5 of whom, however, could have been classified as manic–depressives. All 15 showed signs of impaired left-hemisphere functions which were most pronounced in simple schizophrenia and least in the possibly affective depressive patient.

Consequently, the evidence derived from psychometric patterns in schizophrenia, on balance, strongly implicates the cerebral regions of the dominant hemisphere which underlie verbal/linguistic systems.

Schwartz, Marchok, and Flynn (1977) and Schwartz, Marchok, Kreinick, and Flynn (1979) developed the Quality Extinction Test. This is a test of tactile extinction in which two sets of common material such as velvet and wire mesh are presented simultaneously to both hands, whole and half–half items. Brain-lesion correlations show that parietal lesions, on this particular test, evoke a contralateral deficit, right parietal lesions producing significantly more extinctions than left parietal lesions. Further, left frontal lesions alone produce ipsilateral extinction. Scarone, Garavaglia, and Cazzullo (1981), on these bases, compared 30 schizophrenics with 30 controls matched for age, sex, and handedness. The schizophrenics' extinctions were on the left side 97% of the time, on the right side 0% of the time. The Short Aphasia Screening Test given to the same subjects revealed dominant dysfunction in 63% of the schizophrenics, 17% of whom also had nondominant dysfunction. Even though there is a nonsignificant tendency in normals for left-sided extinction to be more common than right-sided extinction, the comparisons here are significantly different from each other and implicate dominant frontotemporal dysfunction in chronic schizophrenia.

AGGRESSIVE PSYCHOPATHY AND LATERALIZED BRAIN DYSFUNCTION

Wechsler (1958) was the first to observe the systematic elevation of performance IQ over verbal IQ in psychopathy. We were able to confirm this association (Flor-Henry & Yeudall, 1973) in the comparisons of verbal, performance, and full-scale IQ in 35 depressed patients, 28 aggresive criminal psychopaths, and 7 aggressive criminals who suffered from clinical depression. Although the full-scale IQ was identical in both groups, the verbal and performance IQ of the psychopathic and depressed patients systematically varied in opposite directions: verbal lower than performance in psychopathy, performance lower than verbal in depression. The lateralized dysfunction suggested by those subjects' performance on IQ testing was verified by the results of neuropsychological testing using the Halstead–Reitan Battery (generating 25 neuropsychological indicators). There was a significant correlation between diagnosis and laterality of dysfunction ($p <$ .001). The small group of depressed criminals exhibited nondominant hemispheric dysfunction. In large-scale subsequent verifications, Yeudall (1977) and Yeudall and Fromm-Auch (1979) found that in 145 aggressive psychopaths (homicide, rape, physical assault) satisfying Cleckley's criteria for primary psychopathy, 90% had abnormal neuropsychological profiles. The battery used was an expanded Halstead–Reitan totaling 32 neuropsychological tests. In 72% of the cases the pattern of cerebral dysfunction was bilateral frontal, left > right, and left temporal. A reduced verbal, compared with performance IQ was again found, with a particular vulnerability of the Comprehension subtest. Wardell and Yeudall (1980) found that subcultural psychopaths had the largest verbal/ performance discrepancy in a large sample ($n = 188$), characterized by psychopathy and schizophrenia MMPI elevations and an excess of sinistrality of 14%. Ninety-nine delinquent adolescents, two-thirds of whom were males, showed predominantly nondominant hemispheric signs: As a group they were not physically violent and had depressive symptoms (Yeudall, Fromm-Auch, & Davies, 1982). A series of 188 alcoholics, principally males, were divided into those with personality disorder ($n = 100$) and those with depressive features. In two-thirds of cases the former had predominantly dominant, the latter nondominant cerebral dysfunction (Yeudall & Fromm-Auch, 1979).

Affective Disorders and Lateralized Brain Dysfunction: Affective Disorders versus Schizophrenia

Taylor, Abrams, and Gaztanaga (1975), investigated 11 schziophrenic and 24 manic–depressive patients, consecutive patients who satisfied their strict research criteria culled from 247 admissions over a 7-month period. These were subjected to the Reitan modification of the Halstead–Wepman Aphasia Screening Test (which incorporates a few measures of nondominant cerebral functions) and the Trail-Making Test. The schizophrenics had significantly more abnormal responses on the aphasia battery, in which they also made more errors than the affectives. On the Trail-Making Test the schizophrenics were also more impaired than the affectives, but this did not reach significance. Taylor, Greenspan, and Abrams (1979) reported on 22 schizophrenics, 105 affectives (83 manics and 22 depressives), and 99 age-matched normal controls, similarly selected over a 22-month period from a cohort of 465 admissions. They were tested with the Aphasia Screening Test alone. The earlier results were confirmed: The schizophrenics made significantly more total errors than the affectives and significantly more dominant temporal and dominant parietal errors. Compared with the controls, both the schizophrenics and affectives (a majority of manics) had more errors relating to the left and to the right hemispheres. Taylor *et al.* (1979) showed the laterality by diagnosis interaction was independent of age, sex, past or present drug administration, or severity of illness by a hierarchical multiple regression analysis (with the Aphasia Screening Test as the dependent variable): Of the six independent variables, only the research diagnosis was found to have a positive correlation with the AST errors. Taylor, Redfield, and Abrams (1981) next evaluated 52 affective disorders (43 manics and 9 depressives), 17 schizophrenics (who, although not selected for chronicity, were all patients with a chronic course), and 8 chronic brain syndromes. These were studied with Smith's Neuropsychological Test Battery: the Wechsler Scale (WAIS), Peabody Picture Vocabulary Test, Sentence Repetition Test, Purdue Pegboard, Single and Double Simultaneous Stimulation Test, Hooper Visual Organization Test, and Raven's Progressive Matrices. The schizophrenics were found to have bilateral cerebral dysfunction, whereas the affectives had dysfunction primarily of the nondominant hemisphere. The schizophrenics were significantly more impaired than the affectives for dominant hemispheric functions, although nondominant dysfunction was similar in both. A discriminant function analysis (entering the variables which discriminated between the groups: WAIS Information, Comprehension, Object Assembly, and Hooper Visual Organization) applied to a jackknifed classification matrix correctly classified the schizophrenics and the affectives with 84% accuracy. At the same time, but quite independently of Taylor and his collaborators, we were investigating the neuropsychological characteristics of the endogenous psychoses in Edmonton (Flor-Henry, Yeudall, Stefanyk, & Howarth, 1975; Flor-Henry 1976; Flor-Henry & Yeudall, 1979). Our psychotic series consisted of 54 schizophrenics and 60 affective psychotics who satisfied Feighner's criteria (Feighner, Robins, Guze, Woodruff, Winokur, & Muñoz, 1972). However, our definition of schizophrenia was essentially the same as the restricted definition of Taylor because, in addition, we included in the manic-depressive group most "acute" or "atypical" schizophrenias, that is, acute, thought-disordered, hallucinatory syndromes with symptoms of the first rank, if they were periodic in course, if they had exhibited previous episodes of clear depression or mania, or if they had a clear affective component at the diagnostic interview. We labeled this subgroup "schizoaffective." The neuropsychological test battery was a modified and amplified Halstead–Reitan, eliminating the Category Test, and adding Oral Word Fluency, Graham–Kendal Memory for Designs, Raven's Colored Progressive Matrices, the Organic Integrity Test, Purdue Pegboard, and Williams Clinical Memory Scales. The WAIS was also administered. The neuropsychological profile analysis revealed a mirror-like effect: 45 of 53 schizophrenics showed asymmetric fronto-temporal dysfunction, left > right, and 45 of 49 affectives showed the opposite pattern, frontotemporal, right > left. (The sinistrals were excluded from this analysis.) A statistical analysis of the 75 patients who had completed all the tests (schizophrenics, $n = 35$; affectives, $n = 40$) showed that the schizophrenics were significantly more impaired than the affectives on neuropsychological variables with dominant-hemisphere loading: Speech Sounds, Oral Word Fluency, Aphasia Screening Test, Tactual Form Board for the preferred hand as well as on some bilateral frontal indicators (Trail-Making A and B), and some more posterior signs bilaterally (Finger Localization). A specific dominant parietal index, ideomotor apraxia, was present only in schizophrenics. On a variety of nondominant hemisphere indices—Memory for Designs, Constructional Apraxia, Tactual Formboard (globally), and Purdue Pegboard—both schizophrenic and affective psychoses were comparably impaired. A multiple stepwise discriminant function analysis yielded 85% correct classification for schizophrenia and 94% correct classification for the manic–depressive syndrome. In order of diminishing discriminatory power the first five variables were: Speech Sound Perception, Oral Word Fluency, Purdue Pegboard Assemblies, Aphasia Screening Test, and Finger Oscillation for the preferred hand. Four of these relate to dominant hemispheric functions. Thus, the discrimination hinges on extracting from the total group of psychosis those subjects with maximal dysfunction of the dominant frontal and temporal regions, thereby isolating the schizophrenias (Flor-Henry, 1976). Like Taylor and his collaborators we found no significant differences when we compared the neuropsychological parameters of mania and depression. However, when we carried out an analysis of covariance (holding age and full-scale IQ constant) between depression, mania, schizophrenia, and controls (Flor-Henry & Yeudall, 1979), a continuum of increasing cerebral disorganization emerged: depression with minimal dysfunction of the nondominant hemisphere, mania with more extensive dysfunction of the nondominant hemisphere together with some degree of dominant frontotemporal dysfunction, and schizophrenia with maximal dysfunction, both of the dominant and nondominant hemisphere. With respect to the intensity of neuropsychological impairment, the schizophreniform subgroup of schizophrenia (schizophrenia with secondary affective features—distinguished from "schizoaffective" states as previously defined) fell between mania and schizophrenia. Mania differed from schizophrenia in showing significantly less impairment on five variables: Tactual Formboard (preferred hand), Seashore Rhythm, Verbal Learning (trials), Oral Word Fluency, and Memory for Design, all indices of dominant frontotemporal dysfunction, except for the last. A curious finding occurred in the analysis of Dynamometric Hand Strength. Like the controls, depressed, manic, and schizophrenic subjects in this overwhelmingly dextral population (8 patients were sinistral) had a stronger right-hand grip. However, the difference between the strength of the right and left hand was 2.7 kg in normals, 3.6 kg in depressed, 5.9 kg in manics, and 6 kg in schizophrenics. The three psychoses were, at the same time, bilaterally weaker than the controls and this weakness was most pronounced (bilaterally) in depressed and manics and for the left hand of schizophrenics. This suggests that simultaneous with the nondominant, nondominant plus dominant, and maximal degree of bilateral disorganization which underlies depression, mania, and schizophrenia, respectively, there is a progressive severe disruption of right frontal systems in the endogenous psychoses. This effect was neither age-dependent nor sex-dependent, and was statistically significant. It is clear that the findings of Taylor *et al.* in the United States and the author's in Canada are remarkably convergent. In the preliminary analysis of an ongoing replication study, totaling 11 patients with depression, 16 with mania, and 11 with schizophrenia, now tested on a larger neuropsychological test battery, all the findings of the first psychosis series are essentially confirmed. Furthermore, there is evidence that these lateralized dimensions of psychopathology are quite general.

A novel, automated "cognitive laterality battery" has been designed by Kushnir, Gordon, and Heifetz (1980). It consists of a portable 35-mm slide–audiocassette and Super-8 movie system with an internal screen for answers written on special sheets. The subtests, totaling nine, have been standardized against schoolchildren and adults. The four tests attributed to right-hemisphere functions are visual localization, orientation, form completion, and touching cubes—all tests of visual perceptual accuracy. The five tests of left-hemisphere integrity are serial sound recognition, serial numbers, word production, visual sequencing, and search for details. On this battery 9 out of 11 depressed patients had impairment of right-hemisphere functions, compared with left, while 4 manic patients had impairment of relative left-hemisphere abilities. One manic, retested later when depressed, shifted to relative right-hemisphere impairment.[2]

NEUROPSYCHOLOGICAL DYSFUNCTION ASSOCIATED WITH THE OBSESSIVE–COMPULSIVE SYNDROME AND HYSTERIA

In a study of 11 consecutive patients with primary obsessive–compulsive syndrome who were compared on 28 neuropsychological variables with 11 controls matched for age, years of educa-

---

2. I have discussed elsewhere (Flor-Henry, 1978; Flor-Henry & Koles, 1980) the reasons why it is probable that the symptomatology of mania—essentially verbal–motor disinhibition, euphoric irritability, and hypersexuality—reflects an abnormal activation of dominant frontotemporal systems brought about by a more fundamental disorganization of the nondominant hemisphere, disrupting transcallosal neural inhibition emanating from the right and, normally, stabilizing the left hemisphere. The characteristic hypersexuality of mania is the result of the activation of the neural systems subtending the orgasmic response in the right hemisphere, of which the opposite pole is the hyposexuality of depression (Flor-Henry, 1980). The single case described here is therefore theoretically important. That mania fundamentally hinges on right-hemisphere perturbations is further supported by the fact that all the cases of secondary mania published to date are found with lesions of the nondominant hemisphere (Cohen & Niska, 1980). Consistent with this hypothesis are the observations of Kolb and Taylor (1981) on the effects of unilateral right and left frontal excisions: impoverishment of spontaneous speech with left frontal lesions, excessive talking after right frontal lesions. Positron emission tomography (PET) studies of bipolar affective psychoses in their excited phases have revealed huge unilateral hypermetabolism of deoxyglucose in the right hemisphere (Farkas, 1980, 1981).

tion, and full-scale WAIS IQ, we found that the obsessionals were characterized by a bilateral frontal and dominant frontotemporal pattern of cerebral dysfunction (Flor-Henry et al., 1979). The obsessionals were the most significantly impaired for Wepman–Jones Aphasia Screening Test and Purdue Pegboard, both hands ($p < .005$). They were also significantly impaired on the Category Test, Seashore Rhythm, Symbol Gestalt, Tactual Performance, and Purdue Pegboard, right and left hands ($p < .05$). A moderate degree of bilateral hemispheric dysfunction, left > right, is also present, and the grouped data suggested an anterior gradient of dysfunction. There was a surprisingly high incidence of sinistrality —27%. This pattern of cerebral dysfunction in the obsessional syndrome, of maximal intensity in the dominant frontal regions, was confirmed in a larger sample of 19 patients, studied in collaboration with Fromm-Auch and Schopflocher (Flor-Henry, 1981). The pattern of neuropsychological dysfunction, determined from 32 neuropsychological tests, was anterior > posterior in 92% of the cases and left > right in 85% of instances. Compared with 19 matched normal controls, the obsessionals were significantly impaired in their scores for Wepman–Jones, Category, written Word Fluency, as well as Tactual Performance and Purdue Pegboard. They were particularly impaired on Wisconsin Card Sorting. A cluster analysis, entering the neuropsychological scores of the 19 obsessionals, indicated that the syndrome is heterogeneous with the formation of four distinct clusters along an axis of suggested increasing neuropsychological deficit. Very similar findings were reported by Rappoport (1981) in obsessional children. There was a striking preponderance of boys, some 50% of which were sinistral and the majority of the group, both dextral and sinistral, failed to show the expected right-ear superiority in the detection of verbal signals under dichotic conditions. Further, their pattern of neuropsychological deficits, relatively normal on the Rey–Ostereith figure, but impaired on Maze Tests, again implicated frontal and dominant hemispheric systems.

In a recent publication (Flor-Henry, Fromm-Auch, Tapper, & Schopflocher, 1981) we reported the results of a study of the stable syndrome of hysteria, investigated with a neuropsychological test battery which, including the WAIS, generated 58 neuropsychological variables. Globally, compared with controls matched for age, sex, handedness, and full-scale WAIS IQ, hysteria was characterized by bilateral frontal impairment (right = left) and predominantly nondominant hemispheric dysfunction. A G-analysis provided a complete separation between the hysteria and the controls. However, a D-index analysis showed that the hysteria group was more impaired than the normals and depressives because of greater dysfunction of the dominant hemisphere, while schizophrenia showed greater dysfunction of the nondominant hemisphere (the depressives and schizophrenics were similarly matched and tested). Further, a cluster analysis of the 40 subjects produced three clusters: normal controls, depressives, and a schizophrenia–hysteria group. These findings were interpreted as suggesting that dominant hemisphere dysfunction is fundamentally related to the syndrome of hysteria, and that the dysfunction of the nondominant hemisphere is brought about by associated features: the female excess, the emotional instability and dysphoric mood, the presence of asymmetrical pain, and conversion symptomatology.

LATERALIZED NEUROLOGICAL DISEASE AND PSYCHOPATHOLOGY

Louks, Calsyn, and Lindsay (1976) selected 20 patients with deficits lateralized to the left hemisphere and 34 with deficits lateralized to the right hemisphere from a pool of 94 veterans who had been referred for psychological examination from both medical and psychiatric sources and who had been given the Halstead–Reitan battery (slightly abbreviated). Fifteen patients with lateralized left and 15 with lateralized right cerebral dysfunction were then matched for overall severity of dysfunction, age, and education (all were males). The "Neurotic–Psychotic Index" (L+Pa+Sc −Hy−Pt) was calculated from the MMPI of these 30 subjects with a cutoff of 45 for the dichotomization into neurotic or psychotic categories. There was a significant association between right-hemisphere deficits and "neurotic" and left-hemisphere deficits and "psychotic" distributions. (For further discussion of affective changes associated with neurological disease see Heilman *et al.*, Chapter 2, this volume.)

NEURORADIOLOGICAL STUDIES
IN SCHIZOPHRENIA AND THEIR RELATIONSHIP
TO NEUROPSYCHOLOGICAL TESTS

The objection is raised by some neuropsychologists that since neuropsychological status fails to distinguish between a "functional" disorder and a "nonfunctional" disorder, that is, between chronic schizophrenia and brain damage, it is therefore improper to apply tests valid for neurological populations to functional groups and to interpret the results within this framework. This argument, as discussed elsewhere (Flor-Henry & Yeudall, 1979), is not persuasive. There is a very large body of evidence which has accumulated in the last 50 years, derived from pneumoencephalographic studies of chronic schizophrenia, that has proved that this syndrome is a brain damage "organic" syndrome with cortical atrophy and ventricular dilatation in 80% of instances for the deteriorating forms. It is a curious fact that these investigations, all convergent in their conclusions and emanating from many countries—Norway, Germany, and Japan, to name but a few—were all but ignored until in the last few years when computer tomography (CT) studies of schizophrenia in England, the United States, and Japan confirmed and amplified them.

Donnelly, Weinberger, Waldman, and Wyatt (1980) studied 15 *young* chronic schizophrenics (average age of 27.5 years) with mean duration of hospitalization of 4.8 years with the Halstead–Reitan Battery and the WAIS and correctly predicted, on the basis of neuropsychological and WAIS impairment, the presence of cerebral atrophy with 80% accuracy. There were only three misclassifications in this investigation in which 50% of the patients exhibited cerebral atrophy. Interestingly, the Block Design subtest of the WAIS was the most sensitive item associated with the presence of structural cerebral abnormalities in schizophrenia. Applying the Luria–Nebraska Battery, Golden, Moses, Zelazowski, Graber, Zatz, Horvath, and Berger (1980) confirmed these findings. These authors demonstrated in a sample of 42 young chronic schizophrenics (average age of 32.3 years) a significant correlation between impairment on test scores and ventricular brain ratio: Increasing ventricular dilatation was significantly correlated with impaired neuropsychological performance for 8 of the 14 scales of the battery.

SOMATIC THERAPIES
AND NEUROPSYCHOLOGICAL TESTING

PSYCHOPHARMACOLOGICAL AGENTS

Heaton and Crowley (1981), in their review of the "effects of
psychiatric disorders and their somatic treatments on neuropsychological test results," cover more than 18 studies which have
appeared in the last 20 years on the effects of neuroleptic tranquilizers in both normal and schizophrenic subjects, as well as 6 studies
on the effects of tricyclic antidepressants on neuropsychological
variables. With respect to neuroleptics, the conclusion is that in
normal subjects sedative neuroleptics with anticholinergic action
impair performance on a variety of motor and cognitive tests, while
piperazine phenothiazines and haloperidol have little effect. In
schizophrenics, on the other hand, neuroleptics do not produce any
further impairment on neuropsychological functions, but, if anything, may improve neuropsychological scores. In normals, the
tricyclic antidepressants have no effect on neuropsychological
scores, and in depressives, either have no effect or lead to an
improvement in neuropsychological functions. Spohn, Lacoursiere,
Thompson, and Coyne (1977) evaluated the effects of phenothiazines on attentional–perceptual, psychophysiological, and cognitive measures in chronic schizophrenia. Attentional measures
included reaction time, continuous performance, and selective
attention tests, while cognitive aspects were measured by Proverbs
Tests, Conceptual Breadth Tests, and a shortened version of the
Wechsler Scales. Phenothiazines improved attentional and psychophysiological but not cognitive variables, which were unchanged.
Of interest was the observation that a factor analysis on the correlation matrix derived from 17 performance and cognitive measures
obtained from 44 drug-free patients, after a 6-week washout period,
and before allocation to placebo or neuroleptic, produced five
orthogonal factors, only two of which were test-specific, thus
suggesting that the performance of schizophrenics on these tests
was not the result of "primarily generalized dysfunction but rather
appeared to be organized in terms of several underlying dimensions of dysfunctional behavior." Howard, Hogan, and Wright
(1975) examined the relationship between type and amount of
psychotropic medication on the Halstead–Reitan Battery scores.
The patients consisted of 43 schizophrenics and 25 affective psy-

choses together with 80 neurotic depressions. The general finding was that psychotropic drugs did not seem to have a differential effect on neuropsychological test performance. About half of the neurotic depressions were treated with tranquilizers and half with tricyclic antidepressants: The higher drug levels were significantly correlated with indices of nondominant hemisphere dysfunction, namely, left-sided auditory suppression, lowered performance IQ, Block Design, and Object Assembly, as well as Dynamometric Hand Strength for the left hand. Further, there was an interaction between astereognosis for the left hand and mean tricyclic antidepressant dosage. Since later studies have shown that, in depression, tricyclics improve neuropsychological scores, the conclusion is that the more severe neurotic depressions (which require more medication) have more severe, preexisting dysfunction of the nondominant hemisphere.

The treatment of major depressive illness in 11 children with tricyclic antidepressants (Staton, Wilson, & Brumback, 1981) monitored before treatment and after recovery, 3 to 6 months later, with extensive neuropsychological tests and the WAIS reveals a significant improvement in frontal and right-hemispheric functions. On the WAIS there was an improvement in both the verbal and performance scales with a trend (nonsignificant) for a relatively greater improvement in the performance scale. In this context Staton *et al.* cite the studies of Ossofsky (1974), who found recovery on this type of antidepressant in a large sample of depressed children. Staton and his collaborators describe two very dramatic illustrations of imipramine–right-hemisphere interactions in depression. These are of two boys with melancholia, left hemiparesis, and left Babinski who, after treatment, recovered not only from depression but also from their left-sided neurological signs. The generality of the right-hemisphere vulnerability (with its performance IQ psychometric correlate) in affective disorders of endogenous type is suggested by the report of Decina, Kestenbaum, Farber, Gargan, Krone, and Fieve (1981). These authors studied 30 children, aged 7 to 14, who were at risk for affective psychosis because of having at least one parent with bipolar illness, and found a significant impairment of WISC-R performance IQ when the at-risk children were compared with matched controls who had no family history for manic–depressive psychosis. Goldstein, Filskov, Weaver, and

Ives (1977) similarly find, on giving the Halstead–Reitan Battery to 20 cases of endogenous depressive psychoses, results "indicative of right cerebral hemisphere impairment."

ELECTROCONVULSIVE THERAPY

Studies which have compared neuropsychological scores of depressed patients before and after electroconvulsive therapy (ECT) (bilateral, unilateral left, and unilateral right) have the same implication. It is now established that the most effective therapy for certain forms of depression is the electrical induction of seizures and that, in dextral subjects, bilateral ECT is as effective as unilateral nondominant ECT—indeed there is increasing evidence that unilateral nondominant ECT is probably superior to bilateral ECT in its therapeutic efficacy (see Flor-Henry, 1979, for review and discussion). Fromm-Auch (1982) has reviewed in detail all studies published after 1965 which have compared the effect on neuropsychological scores of either bilateral ECT versus unilateral ECT, or unilateral left versus unilateral right ECT in depression. A total of 21 studies providing quantitative memory measurements were collected. In all instances unilateral left ECT was followed by an impairment in verbal functions. Bilateral and unilateral left ECT inconsistently lead to an improvement in visuospatial, nondominant hemispheric functions. The vast majority of studies using unilateral nondominant ECT were associated with improvement or complete normalization of neuropsychological indices of nonverbal memory indices after a minimum of five seizure inductions. Some findings in the older literature are surprisingly consistent. For example, Small, Small, Milstein, and Moore (1972) find that unilateral right ECT produces a significant improvement in contralateral left-hand finger oscillation, while no corresponding effect appears after unilateral left ECT.

The more recent experience of Small, Milstein, and Small (1981) is also consistent with these general trends. The authors compared a large previously studied sample of bilateral ECT patients with 28 patients given unilateral right ECT, using Halstead–Reitan and Wechsler scores obtained after the fifth treatment and after 2 to 3 weeks, and found a comparable clinical improvement in the two populations. However, the cognitive measures followed different curves: In the bilateral group, they are U-shaped through time, worsening around the fifth period and then gradually returning to baseline, whereas in the unilateral right ECT group there is a gradual and continuous improvement for most neuropsychological scores. Of the Wechsler subtests, only Object Assembly, a visuospatial subtest, is significantly improved at 3 weeks, compared with the pre-ECT value.

CONCLUSIONS

In conclusion, the evidence reviewed shows that neuropsychological parameters are extremely sensitive indices of altered cerebral functions, with considerable lateralizing and localizing power when sufficient neuropsychological indicators are evaluated in relation to each other. It is important to keep in mind that although localized or lateralized, structural brain disease evokes specific patterns of neuropsychological dysfunction, the presence of that dysfunction in psychopathological syndromes does not necessarily imply structural cerebral changes—although this may be the case in certain instances. Like the EEG, neuropsychological alterations may reflect the topography of systematic functional cerebral states. In its application to the study of psychopathology, particularly schizophrenia and the manic–depressive syndrome, the findings of independent investigations are remarkably concordant. Neuropsychological approaches are of extreme value to psychopathological studies, for they represent a technique, independent of the psychic symptoms, which is sufficiently sensitive to provide, for the first time, external criterion to the clinical syndromes of psychiatry. Thus, classification, and probably prognosis and therapeutic responses, can be externally evaluated and validated.

REFERENCES

Abrams, R., Redfield, J., & Taylor, M. A. Cognitive dysfunction in schizophrenia, affective disorder and organic brain disease. *British Journal of Psychiatry*, 1981, *139*, 190–194.

Bigelow, L. B., Donnelly, E. F., Torrey, E. F., & Lee, C. A. Assessment of clinical status of schizophrenic patients by the WAIS comprehension subtest. *Journal of Clinical Psychiatry*, 1979, *22*, 258–261.

Blakemore, C. B., & Falconer, M. A. Long term effects of anterior temporal lobectomy in certain cognitive functions. *Journal of Neurology, Neurosurgery and Psychiatry*, 1967, *30*, 346–367.

Boll, T. J. The Halstead–Reitan neuropsychology battery. In S. B. Filskov & T. J. Boll (Eds.), *Handbook of clinical neuropsychology*. New York: Wiley, 1981.

Cohen, M. R., & Niska, R. W. Localized right cerebral hemisphere dysfunction and recurrent mania. *American Journal of Psychiatry*, 1980, *137*, 847–848.

Decina, P., Kestenbaum, C. J., Farber, S. L., Gargan, M. A., Krone, L., & Fieve, R. R. *Children at risk for affective disorders.* Paper presented at the 134th annual meeting of the American Psychiatric Association, New Orleans, 1981.

DeWolfe, A. S., Barrell, R. P., Becker, B. C., & Spaner, F. E. Intellectual deficit in chronic schizophrenia and brain damage. *Journal of Consulting and Clinical Psychology*, 1971, *36*, 197–204.

Donnelly, E. F., Weinberger, D. R., Waldman, I. N., & Wyatt, R. J. Cognitive impairment associated with morphological brain abnormalities on computed tomography in chronic schizophrenic patients. *Journal of Nervous and Mental Disease*, 1980, *168*, 305–308.

Farkas, T. Presentation at the annual meeting of the Society of Biological Psychiatry, Boston, 1980, and personal communication, 1981.

Feighner, J. P., Robins, E., Guze, S. B., Woodruff, R. A., Winokur, G., & Muñoz, R. Diagnostic criteria for use in psychiatric research. *Archives of General Psychiatry*, 1972, *26*, 57–63.

Filskov, S. B., & Goldstein, S. G. Diagnostic validity of the Halstead–Reitan neuropsychological battery. *Journal of Consulting and Clinical Psychology*, 1974, *42*, 382–388.

Flor-Henry, P. Lateralized temporal–limbic dysfunction and psychopathology. *Annals of the New York Academy of Sciences*, 1976, *280*, 777–797.

Flor-Henry, P. The endogenous psychoses: A reflection of lateralized dysfunction of the anterior limbic system. In K. E. Livingston & O. Hornykiewicz (Eds.), *Limbic mechanisms*. New York: Plenum, 1978.

Flor-Henry, P. On certain aspects of the localization of the cerebral systems regulating and determining emotion. *Biological Psychiatry*, 1979, *14*, 677–698.

Flor-Henry, P. Cerebral aspects of the orgasmic response: Normal and deviational. In R. Forleo & W. Pasini (Eds.), *Medical sexology*. Amsterdam: Elsevier/North-Holland, 1980.

Flor-Henry, P. *EEG and neuropsychological studies of the obsessive-compulsive syndrome.* Paper presented at Symposium on Treatment of Obsessive–Compulsive Disorders, 3rd World Congress of Biological Psychiatry, Stockholm, 1981.

Flor-Henry, P., Fromm-Auch, D., Tapper, M., & Schopflocher, D. A neuropsychological study of the stable syndrome of hysteria. *Biological Psychiatry*, 1981, *16*, 601–626.

Flor-Henry, P., & Koles, Z. J. EEG studies in depression, mania and normals: Evidence for partial shifts of laterality in the affective psychoses. *Advanced Biological Psychiatry*, 1980, *4*, 21–43.

Flor-Henry, P., & Yeudall, L. Lateralized cerebral dysfunction in depression and in aggressive criminal psychopathy: Further observations. *International Research Communications System*, 1973, (*73*-7), 5-0-4.

Flor-Henry, P., & Yeudall, L. T. Neuropsychological investigation of schizophrenia and manic–depressive psychoses. In J. Gruzelier & P. Flor-Henry (Eds.), *Hemisphere asymmetries of function in psychopathology*. Amsterdam: Elsevier/North-Holland, 1979.

Flor-Henry, P., Yeudall, L. T., Koles, Z. J., & Howarth, B. G. Neuropsychological and power spectral EEG investigations of the obsessive–compulsive syndrome. *Biological Psychiatry*, 1979, *14*, 119–130.

Flor-Henry P., Yeudall, L. T., Stefanyk, W., & Howarth, B. The neuropsychological correlates of the functional psychoses. *IRCS Medical Science: Neurology, Neurosurgery, and Psychiatry, Clinical Psychology*, 1975, *3*, 34.

Fredericks, R. S., & Finkel, P. Schizophrenic performance on the Halstead–Reitan battery. *Journal of Clinical Psychology*, 1978, *34*, 26–30.

Fromm-Auch, D. Selective memory impairment with ECT. *British Journal of Psychiatry*, 1982, *141*.

Golden, C. J., Moses, J. A., Zelazowski, R., Graber, B., Zatz, L. M., Horvath, T. B., & Berger, P. A. Cerebral ventricular size and neuropsychological impairment in young chronic schizophrenics. *Archives of General Psychiatry*, 1980, *37*, 619–623.

Goldstein, S. G., Filskov, S. B., Weaver, L. A., & Ives, J. O. Neuropsychological effects of electroconvulsive therapy. *Journal of Clinical Psychology*, 1977, *33*, 798–806.

Gruzelier, J., & Hammond, N. Schizophrenia: A dominant hemisphere temporal–limbic disorder? *Research Communications in Psychology, Psychiatry, and Behavior*, 1976, *1*, 33–72.

Gruzelier, J., Mednick, S., & Schulsinger, F. Lateralised impairments in the WISC profiles of children at genetic risk for psychopathology. In J. Gruzelier & P. Flor-Henry (Eds.), *Hemisphere asymmetries of function in psychopathology*. Amsterdam: Elsevier/North-Holland, 1979.

Halstead, W. C. *Brain and intelligence: A quantitative study of the frontal lobes*. Chicago: University of Chicago Press, 1947.

Hammeke, T. A., Golden, C. J., & Purisch, A. D. A standardized, short, and comprehensive neuropsychological test battery based on the

Luria neuropsychological evaluation. *International Journal of Neuroscience*, 1978, *8*, 135–141.

Heaton, R. K., Baade, L. E., & Johnson, K. L. Neuropsychological test results associated with psychiatric disorders in adults. *Psychological Bulletin*, 1978, *85*, 141–162.

Heaton, R. K., & Crowley, T. J. Effects of psychiatric disorders and their somatic treatments on neuropsychological test results. In S. B. Filskov & T. J. Boll (Eds.), *Handbook of clinical neuropsychology*. New York: Wiley, 1981.

Heaton, R. K., Vogt, A. T., Hoehn, M. M., Lewis, J. A., Crowley, T. J., & Stallings, M. A. Neuropsychological impairment with schizophrenia vs. acute and chronic cerebral lesions. *Journal of Clinical Psychology*, 1979, *35*, 46–53.

Holland, T. R., & Watson, C. G. Multivariate analysis of WAIS–MMPI relationships among brain-damaged, schizophrenic, neurotic, and alcoholic patients. *Journal of Clinical Psychology*, 1980, *36*, 352–359.

Howard, M. L., Hogan, T. P., & Wright, M. W. The effects of drugs on psychiatric patients' performance on the Halstead–Reitan neuropsychological test battery. *Journal of Nervous and Mental Disease*, 1975, *161*, 166–171.

Klonoff, H., Fibiger, C. H., & Hutton, G. H. Neuropsychological patterns in chronic schizophrenia. *Journal of Nervous and Mental Disease*, 1970, *150*, 291–300.

Kolb, B., & Taylor, L. Affective behavior in patients with localized cortical excisions: Role of lesion site and side. *Science*, 1981, *214*, 89–91.

Kushnir, M., Gordon, H., & Heifetz, A. *Cognitive asymmetries in bipolar and unipolar depressed patients*. Paper presented at the 8th annual meeting of the International Neuropsychological Society, San Francisco, February 1980.

Lansdell, H., & Urback, N. Sex differences in personality measures related to size and side of temporal lobe ablations. *Proceedings of the American Psychological Association*, 1965, 113–114.

Lewis, G. P., Golden, C. J., Moses, J. A., Osmon, D. C., Purisch, A. D., & Hammeke, T. A. Localization of cerebral dysfunction with a standardized version of Luria's neuropsychological battery. *Journal of Consulting and Clinical Psychology*, 1979, *47*, 1003–1019.

Louks, J., Calsyn, D., & Lindsay, F. Personality dysfunction and lateralized deficits in cerebral functions as measured by the MMPI and Reitan–Halstead battery. *Perceptual and Motor Skills*, 1976, *43*, 655–659.

Matarazzo, J. D., Matarazzo, R. G., Wiens, A. N., Gallo, A. E., & Klonoff, H. Retest reliability of the Halstead Impairment Index in a normal, a schizophrenic, and two samples of organic patients. *Journal of Clinical Psychology*, 1976, *32*, 338–349.

Matarazzo, J. D., Wiens, A. N., Matarazzo, R. G., & Goldstein, S. G.

Psychometric and clinical test–retest reliability of the Halstead Impairment Index in a sample of healthy, young, normal men. *Journal of Nervous and Mental Disease*, 1974, *158*, 37–49.

Milner, B. Intellectual functions of the temporal lobes. *Psychological Bulletin*, 1954, *51*, 42–62.

Osmon, D. C., Golden, C. J., Purisch, A. D., Hammeke, T. A., & Blume, H. G. The use of a standardized battery of Luria's tests in the diagnosis of lateralized cerebral dysfunction. *International Journal of Neuroscience*, 1979, *9*, 1–9.

Ossofsky, H. J. Endogenous depression in infancy and childhood. *Comprehensive Psychiatry*, 1974, *15*, 19–25.

Parsons, O. A., Vega, A., & Burn, J. Different psychological effects of lateralized brain damage. *Journal of Consulting and Clinical Psychology*, 1969, *33*, 551–557.

Purisch, A. D., Golden, C. J., & Hammeke, T. A. Discrimination of schizophrenic and brain-injured patients by a standardized version of Luria's neuropsychological tests. *Journal of Consulting and Clinical Psychology*, 1978, *46*, 1266–1273.

Rappoport, J. *Obsessive–compulsive disorders in children.* Paper presented at Symposium on Treatment of Obsessive–Compulsive Disorders, 3rd World Congress of Biological Psychiatry, Stockholm, 1981.

Reitan, R. M. Investigation of the validity of Halstead's measures of biological intelligence. *Archives of Neurology and Psychiatry*, 1955, *73*, 28–35. (a)

Reitan, R. M. Certain differential effects of left and right cerebral lesions in human adults. *Journal of Comparative and Physiological Psychology*, 1955, *48*, 474–477. (b)

Reitan, R. M. Psychological deficits resulting from cerebral lesions in man. In J. M. Warren & K. A. Akert (Eds.), *The frontal granular cortex and behavior.* New York: McGraw-Hill, 1964.

Reitan, R. M. Problems and prospects in studying the psychological correlates of brain lesions. *Cortex*, 1966, *2*, 127–154.

Scarone, S., Garavaglia, P. F., & Cazzullo, C. L. Further evidence of dominant hemisphere dysfunction in chronic schizophrenia. *British Journal of Psychiatry*, 1981, *138*, 354–355.

Schreiber, D. J., Goldman, H., Kleinman, K. M., Goldfader, P. R., & Snow, M. Y. The relationship between independent neuropsychological and neurological detection and localization of cerebral impairment. *Journal of Nervous and Mental Disease*, 1976, *162*, 360–365.

Schwartz, A. S., Marchok, P. L., & Flynn, R. E. A sensitive test for tactile extinction: Results in patients with parietal and frontal lobe disease. *Journal of Neurology, Neurosurgery and Psychiatry*, 1977, *40*, 228–233.

Schwartz, A. S., Marchok, P. L., Kreinick, C. J., & Flynn, R. E. The asymmetric lateralization of tactile extinction in patients with unilateral cerebral dysfunction. *Brain*, 1979, *102*, 669–684.

Shenkman, A., Gordon, H., & Heifetz, A. *Cognitive asymmetries in acute schizophrenics.* Paper presented at the 8th annual meeting of the International Neuropsychological Society, San Francisco, February 1980.

Small, I. F., Milstein, V., & Small, J. G. Relationship between clinical and cognitive change with bilateral and unilateral ECT. *Biological Psychiatry*, 1981, *16*, 793–794.

Small, I. F., Small, J. G., Milstein, V., & Moore, J. E. Neuropsychological observations with psychosis and somatic treatment. *Journal of Nervous and Mental Disease*, 1972, *155*, 6–13.

Smith, A. Verbal and nonverbal test performances of patients with "acute" lateralized brain lesions (tumors). *Journal of Nervous and Mental Disease*, 1966, *141*, 517–523.

Spohn, H. E., Lacoursiere, R. B., Thompson, K., & Coyne, L. Phenothiazine effects on psychological and psychophysiological dysfunction in chronic schizophrenics. *Archives of General Psychiatry*, 1977, *34*, 633–644.

Staton, R. D., Wilson, H., & Brumback, R. A. Cognitive improvement associated with tricyclic antidepressant treatment of childhood major depressive illness. *Perceptual and Motor Skills*, 1981, *53*, 219–234.

Taylor, D. C. Developmental stratagems organizing intellectual skills: Evidence from studies of temporal lobectomy for epilepsy. In R. M. Knights & D. J. Bakker (Eds.), *The neuropsychology of learning disorders: Theoretical approaches.* Baltimore: University Park Press, 1976.

Taylor, M. A., Abrams, R., & Gaztanaga, P. Manic–depressive illness and schizophrenia: A partial validation of research diagnostic criteria utilizing neuropsychological testing. *Comprehensive Psychiatry*, 1975, *16*, 91–96.

Taylor, M. A., Greenspan, B., & Abrams, R. Lateralized neuropsychological dysfunction in affective disorder and schizophrenia. *American Journal of Psychiatry*, 1979, *136*, 1031–1034.

Taylor, M. A., Redfield, J., & Abrams, R. Neuropsychological dysfunction in schizophrenia and affective disease. *Biological Psychiatry*, 1981, *16*, 467–478.

Vega, A., & Parsons, O. A. Cross-validation of the Halstead–Reitan tests for brain damage. *Journal of Consulting Psychology*, 1967, *31*, 619–625.

Wardell, D., & Yeudall, L. T. A multidimensional approach to criminal disorders: The assessment of impulsivity and its relation to crime. *Advances in Behavioral Research and Therapy*, 1980, 2, 159–177.

Wechsler, D. *The measurement and appraisal of adult intelligence* (4th ed.). Baltimore: Williams & Wilkins, 1958.

Wheeler, L. Complex behavioral indices weighted by linear discriminant functions for the prediction of cerebral damage. *Perceptual and Motor Skills,* 1964, *19,* 907–923.

Wiens, A. N., & Matarazzo, J. D. WAIS and MMPI correlates of the Halstead–Reitan neuropsychology battery in normal male subjects. *Journal of Nervous and Mental Disease,* 1977, *164,* 112–121.

Woods, B. T. The restricted effects of right-hemisphere lesions after age one: Wechsler test data. *Neuropsychologia,* 1980, *18,* 65–70.

Yeudall, L. T. Neuropsychological assessment of forensic disorders. *Canada's Mental Health,* 1977, 7–15.

Yeudall, L. T., & Fromm-Auch, D. Neuropsychological impairments in various psychopathological populations. In J. Gruzelier & P. Flor-Henry (Eds.), *Hemisphere asymmetries of function in psychopathology.* Amsterdam: Elsevier/North-Holland, 1979.

Yeudall, L. T., Fromm-Auch, D., & Davies, P. Neuropsychological impairment in persistent delinquency. *Journal of Nervous and Mental Disease,* 1982, *170,* 257–265.

AUTHOR INDEX

SUBJECT INDEX